G000109632

# The
# Office

# BOOK OF
# LISTS

# The Office

# BOOK OF LISTS

**Chip Carter**

THE OFFICIAL GUIDE
to Quotes, Pranks,
Characters,
and
Memorable
Moments from
DUNDER MIFFLIN

RUNNING PRESS

PHILADELPHIA

The Office © 2022 Universal Television LLC. All Rights Reserved.
Cover copyright © 2022 by Hachette Book Group, Inc.

Hachette Book Group supports the right to free expression and the value of copyright. The purpose of copyright is to encourage writers and artists to produce the creative works that enrich our culture.

The scanning, uploading, and distribution of this book without permission is a theft of the author's intellectual property. If you would like permission to use material from the book (other than for review purposes), please contact permissions@hbgusa.com. Thank you for your support of the author's rights.

Running Press
Hachette Book Group
1290 Avenue of the Americas, New York, NY 10104
www.runningpress.com
@Running_Press

Printed in China

First Edition: March 2022

Published by Running Press, an imprint of Perseus Books, LLC, a subsidiary of Hachette Book Group, Inc. The Running Press name and logo is a trademark of the Hachette Book Group.

The Hachette Speakers Bureau provides a wide range of authors for speaking events. To find out more, go to www.hachettespeakersbureau.com or call (866) 376-6591.

The publisher is not responsible for websites (or their content) that are not owned by the publisher.

The following images are copyright © by Getty Images Plus collection. Cover: Michael Burrell (binder), stuartbur (index cards); endpages: Pornprasit; interior throughout: kyoshino (binder spine); Page ii: wdstock; Pages 2-3: Hey Darlin; Page 15: JerryB7; Page 19: thumb (paper); Page 43: trigga (paper); Page 46: TokenPhoto; Page 58: ScottKrycia; Page 69: baiajaku; Page 99: slobo; Page 104: Bozena_Fulawka; Page 105: wojtal78 (refrigerator), Juanmonino (marijuana); Page 106: Sergey Peterman; Page 109: etienne voss; Page 113: Heinsbergsphoto; Page 117: muratseyit; Page 148: Floriana; Page 158: svrid79; Page 161: photodanila (bow), adisa (gloves); Page 163: zoom-zoom; Page 165: Symkin; Page 190: Floortje; Page 221: mayakova; Page 226: katiko-dp; Pages 228-229: Alex Potemkin; Page 237, clockwise from top left: Hey Darlin/DigitalVision Vectors, Illustrator, Maksim Shchur; Page 240: undefined; page 246: spxChrome, belterz.

Page 91 blackberry photo by Chaq MH/shutterstock.

Print book cover and interior design by Susan Van Horn

Library of Congress Control Number: 2021944227

ISBNs: 978-0-7624-7864-4 (hardcover), 978-0-7624-7865-1 (ebook)

RRD-S

10  9  8  7  6  5  4  3  2  1

**DUNDER MIFFLIN, INC.**
PAPER COMPANY

TO SUSAN ASKEW AND FRAN ZANKOWSKI,
my siblings in the Pangea Philosophical
Bowling League—may we never split.

# CONTENTS

# INTRODUCTION

Whether it was Michael Scott's inappropriate behavior, Jim Halpert's highly detailed pranks, Dwight Schrute's memeable sayings, or the cringeworthy Dundie Awards doled out to the staff of the Scranton branch of Dunder Mifflin, *The Office* kept fans laughing for nine hilarious seasons and continues to do so to this day.

But pranks and one-liners alone don't turn a TV show into a cultural phenomenon. Anyone who has ever worked in an office can relate to a Dwight, a Phyllis, or an Angela—but hopefully not to a Creed! At the heart of the show, it's the characters who made the stories relatable and highlighted the silliness we see in today's modern cubicle culture. Let's face it: Not many people love their office job, but if you had Michael Scott for a boss? Now *that* might be a job worth waking up for.

Just as the documentary crew filming the staff at Dunder Mifflin found, it was the relationships between the colorful and quirky cast of employees that took center stage, often evolving into friendships, hostilities, rivalries, and even romances.

Michael finally found love with the perfect woman for him, though it took him from Scranton. Jim and Pam's sweet friendship turned into a thriving relationship and later marriage.

Kelly and Ryan remained dramatic and messy. Michael and Dwight had the most enviable of office bromances. Andy never got the girl, but he did get back together with Cornell. Dwight and Angela snuck around and bounced back and forth, only to end up standing in graves at their traditional Schrute wedding.

Episode after episode, fans cheered and gossiped about their favorites scenes and characters at their own office watercoolers. Somewhere along the way, this scrappy Scranton crew became our family. And while the show ended in 2013, it is perhaps more popular now than ever before and remains one of the most beloved comedies of all time.

Included within these pages are more than one hundred lists that break down your favorite episodes, scenes, characters, and themes to celebrate every corner of *The Office* universe. Our hope is that you'll recall favorite moments from the series and discover new and compelling facts and trivia about story lines and cherished characters. Ultimately, we hope you're reminded why you fell in love with *The Office* in the first place and why it remains iconic. We think Pam may have said it best in the finale: "There's a lot of beauty in ordinary things."

LAKE
HURON

LAKE
ONTARIO

**DUNDER MIFFLIN** INC.
PAPER COMPANY
**ROCHESTER**

**DUNDER MIFFLIN** INC.
PAPER COMPANY
**BUFFALO**

LAKE
ERIE

PENNSYLVANIA

**DUNDER MIFFLIN** INC.
PAPER COMPANY
**AKRON**

OHIO

# Chapter One:
# Orientation

## DUNDER MIFFLIN BRANCHES

Robert Dunder started his company in 1949 as an industrial supplier of metal brackets for construction. He met Robert Mifflin at a rotary club or at a tour of Dartmouth—there are conflicting details—and they began to sell paper. Mifflin killed himself in 1972. By the early 2000s, paper suppliers in general were suffering and Dunder Mifflin was no exception. The company at one point had a corporate office and twelve branches. At the time the Scranton branch documentary began filming, several branches had already been shut down and more still were in jeopardy.

- Scranton, Pennsylvania
- Albany, New York
- Buffalo, New York
- Yonkers, New York
- Binghamton, New York
- Utica, New York
- Rochester, New York

- Syracuse, New York
- Camden, New Jersey
- Nashua, New Hampshire
- Pittsfield, Massachusetts
- Stamford, Connecticut
- Akron, Ohio

the office book of lists

# CORPORATE STAFF

**Alan Brand:** CEO of Dunder Mifflin until the Sabre buyout. Alan and the board decide they can't justify both a Scranton branch and a Stamford branch. *(Pilot)*

**Jan Levinson-Gould:** Vice president of sales and Michael Scott's boss. *(Pilot)*

**Randall:** Former CFO who was laid off for sleeping with his secretary. *(Sexual Harassment)*

**David Wallace:** CFO who replaces Randall. *(Valentine's Day)* After he buys the company from Sabre, he becomes CEO. *(Free Family Portrait Studio)*

**Sherri:** Jan's assistant for a time. Eventually she is replaced by a new young assistant named Hunter. Michael feels threatened by Hunter and calls him James van der Beek. *(Halloween / The Negotiation)*

**Ryan Howard:** After beginning as a temp, Ryan's business savvy and business school degree help him leapfrog to become Michael's boss, replacing Jan as VP of sales. However, he commits fraud, is arrested, and then comes back as a temporary employee again. *(The Job)*

**Charles Miner:** VP for the Northeast region after Ryan is arrested. He is let go during the Sabre buyout. *(New Boss)*

**Brenda:** Goes on the retreat cruise to learn from Michael but ends up writing notes about his inappropriate behavior. *(Booze Cruise)*

**Grace:** Receptionist at the Corporate office. *(The Job)*

**Brent:** Tells Jim how intense the fantasy football was at Corporate. *(The Job)*

**Kendall:** HR representative. During Jim's interview, David Wallace mentions that this irritating HR guy is the only person Jim probably won't like. *(The Job / Business Ethics)*

**Robert Dunder:** Michael asks founder Robert Dunder to come to his age discrimination meeting. *(Dunder Mifflin Infinity)*

**Thomas Dean:** Ryan uses Thomas's office for some of the documentary filming, even after Thomas tells him to do it in his own office or the hall. *(Launch Party)*

**Diane Kelly:** The company's chief legal counsel. *(The Deposition)*

**Stephanie:** David Wallace's secretary. *(New Boss)*

## SABRE STAFF

**Gabe Lewis:** Coordinating director of merging regions. *(Sabre)*

**Jolene Bennett:** CEO, breast cancer survivor, close personal friend of Nancy Pelosi, and dog owner to multiple dogs. She has slept with three of the same guys Truman Capote did. *(The Manager and the Salesman)*

**Nellie Bertram:** President of special projects. *(Tallahassee)*

**Robert California:** Joins Sabre as regional manager of Scranton but convinces Jo to give him her job as CEO. *(The List)*

## STAMFORD STAFF

**Josh Porter:** Regional manager. *(Pilot)*

**Jim Halpert:** Assistant regional manager when he transfers from Scranton. *(Gay Witch Hunt)*

**Karen Filippelli:** Salesperson. *(Gay Witch Hunt)*

**Hannah Smoterich-Barr:** Hannah makes others at the office uncomfortable by pumping her breastmilk at her desk. She is transferred to Scranton, but quits while Michael is on vacation after filing some complaints about being a working mother. *(Back from Vacation)*

**Tony Gardner:** After Michael forces the overweight Tony to get up on the conference table on the first day, Tony quits, claiming he doesn't like Michael's management style. *(The Merger)*

**Martin Nash:** An ex-con who Josh hires to get the federal Work Opportunity Tax Credit. He was convicted for insider trading. Martin quits after Michael locks all the staff in the conference room when he gets the impression they all think prison is better than the office. *(The Convict)*

## UTICA STAFF

**Ben Nugent:** Utica's top salesperson. *(Branch Wars)*

**Rolando:** Receptionist. *(Branch Wars)*

the office book of lists

# SCRANTON OFFICE STAFF

There are four departments and management in the Scranton branch. Human Resources technically reports to Corporate, but has an HR rep stationed in each branch office. In Scranton, during the years the documentary is filmed, the main personnel in each department are as follows.

## Management/ Administration

**Michael Scott, regional manager:** Michael is kindhearted but totally inappropriate, and often delusional. He is the regional manager for a number of years before leaving to marry Holly Flax. He is succeeded by several regional managers, including Andy Bernard and Dwight Schrute.

**Pam Beesly, receptionist, office manager, and sales representative:** A frustrated artist engaged to Roy in the warehouse, Pam has trouble speaking up for herself and navigating into a career in art and design. Eventually she and Roy break up and she marries Jim and paints murals for various buildings.

DUNDER MIFFLIN INC.
PAPER COMPANY

MICHAEL SCOTT
REGIONAL MANAGER

**Erin Hannon, receptionist:** Erin's real name is Kelly, but to avoid confusion with Kelly Kapoor, she goes by her middle name, Erin. Usually happy, if not the brightest, Erin takes over as receptionist after Pam quits to work for The Michael Scott Paper Company.

## Sales

**Dwight K. Schrute, sales representative:** Beet farmer, top salesman, and *Battlestar Galactica* fan, Dwight will do whatever it takes to become manager of the Scranton branch. It takes about nine years.

**Jim Halpert, sales representative:** At first Jim is a slacker who fills his days goofing off and playing elaborate pranks on Dwight. As his friendship with Pam eventually grows into a relationship, a marriage, and a family, he begins to apply himself to support his family and helps start a sports marketing company in Philadelphia.

**Stanley Hudson, sales representative:** One of the best salespeople at Dunder Mifflin, Stanley longs for only one thing—retirement. And pretzels. And women other than his wife. And crossword puzzles.

**Phyllis Lapin-Vance, sales representative:** A longtime salesperson for the company, Phyllis is the same age as Michael and went to school with him, a fact Michael often seems to forget. Phyllis wears White Diamonds by Elizabeth Taylor and once gave a baby up for adoption. She marries Bob Vance of Vance Refrigeration.

**Ryan Howard:** See page 5.

**Andy Bernard, sales representative:** The worst salesman in the office, Andy somehow becomes regional manager, then throws it all away to try his hand at acting. He also fails at that, eventually ending up at his alma mater in the admissions office.

**Todd Packer, traveling salesman:** The Scranton branch's traveling salesman, Packer isn't often seen, but when he is, no one seems to like him much except Michael. He eventually gets fired.

## Accounting

**Angela Martin, head of accounting:** Angela has strict ideas about behavior and morality. She also takes her duties as head of party planning quite seriously.

**Oscar Martinez, accountant:** Oscar sees himself as the voice of reason in the Accounting department and the office. Oscar is at first a closeted gay man, but he eventually comes out. He may have had an affair with Matt the warehouse worker before getting involved with Angela's husband, Senator Robert Lipton. He also had a long-term relationship at one time with Gil.

**Kevin Malone, accountant:** Kevin is a good-natured accountant who claims to have scored over 100 on an IQ test. He likes sports and gambling and has been in several bands as the drummer and singer.

PRINCESS LADY B

Sprinkles ♥ RIP

Diane

B
A
N
D
I
T
2

Garbage

E
M
B
E
R

MR ASH

Milky Way

PETALS Crinklepuss

LUMPY Tinkie
PHILIP

**DID YOU KNOW?** Angela has owned a lot of cats, including Sprinkles, who gets sick and whom Dwight eventually kills *(Fun Run)*; Garbage, who Dwight gifts to Angela as an apology for killing Sprinkles *(Dunder Mifflin Infinity)*; Ash, the dominant male of Sprinkles's litter *(Traveling Salesman)*; Bandit, whom Angela brings to work the day Dwight starts a fire *(Stress Relief)*; Princess Lady, a hypoallergenic third-generation show cat, whose father was in *Meet the Parents* and whom Angela buys after selling Andy's engagement ring for $7,000 on eBay *(Lecture Circuit)*; Mr. Ash, who humps Princess Lady on the nanny cam *(Lecture Circuit)*; Petals *(Lecture Circuit)*; Ember; Milky Way; Diane; Lumpy; Comstock, who has long hair and denim pants *(New Guys)*; Tinkie; Crinklepuss; Bandit 2; and Pawlick Baggins and Lady Aragorn and their ten kittens *(Paper Airplane)*.

## Quality Control / Customer and Supplier Relations

**Kelly Kapoor, customer service representative:** Kelly's middle name is Rajanighanda, which Kevin thinks is a boy's name. She loves drama and singing and tries to brand herself as the Business Bitch, the Diet Bitch, the Shopping Bitch, and the Etiquette Bitch.

**Meredith Palmer, supplier relations representative:** Never one to shy away from being loud and proud about her sexual promiscuity, Meredith is often sexually and socially inappropriate or hungover.

**Creed Bratton, quality assurance representative:** Almost anything known about Creed could be and probably is a lie. The most senior person in the office, he has a shady past, a shady present, and most likely a shady future. He is eighty-two years old at the time of the fun run.

## HR

**Toby Flenderson, Corporate HR representative:** Toby can never quite figure out why Michael hates him so much. If he won the lotto, he would start a podcast called *The Flenderson Files*. He is writing a series of mystery novels featuring Chad Flenderman. One features Chad's archnemesis, Dr. Lucifer Wu, and one is based on a murdered TV star.

## Security

**Hank:** Hank, the security guard, doesn't actually work for Dunder Mifflin but works for the building. He plays guitar and manages Dwight's Caffeine Corner.

## SCRANTON WAREHOUSE STAFF

**Darryl Philbin, warehouse foreman:** The no-nonsense head of the warehouse, Darryl eventually gets promoted upstairs. By the time the documentary crew finishes filming, Darryl has left Dunder Mifflin to join Jim's sports marketing company, Athlead.

**Lonny:** An outspoken member of the warehouse crew, Lonny is in favor of forming a union.

**Roy Anderson:** Roy was engaged to Pam for three years and kept stalling on setting a wedding date.

**Madge**: Madge is the first one to make a sale when drivers begin selling paper on their routes.

**Glenn**: Darryl selects Glenn to take over the warehouse, but he does not do a good job.

**Michael:** Warehouse Michael gives Michael Scott a ride home for an hour in traffic, and yet Michael Scott can't remember his name.

**Hide:** Hide was the number-one heart surgeon in Japan. After he made a mistake during a Yakuza boss's operation, he fled to America. Later he reveals that he failed the heart operation on purpose. Hide loses all his winnings from the lottery when he invests his money in energy drinks for Asian homosexuals. One flavor is coconut penis.

**Val:** Gabe and Darryl have a crush on this new warehouse worker, who later becomes the foreman.

**Frank:** Frank defaces Pam's mural because he doesn't like her art.

## SCRANTON FORMER STAFF

While the Scranton branch boasts some longtime employees like Michael, Stanley, Dwight, Phyllis, Jim, Pam, and Creed, it also lost a number of people over the years. Some Michael remembers and some he does not.

**A young Guatemalan guy:** He once worked in the office and asked Michael to be godfather to his child. It was his first job and Michael had to let him go because he "sucked." *(Pilot)*

**Catherine:** Michael claims he could have had sex with Catherine, who used to work there. *(Sexual Harassment)*

**Tom:** Tom worked in Accounting and put a note in the suggestion box saying that the company needed better outreach for employees fighting depression. He later killed himself. *(Performance Review)*

**Devon:** Forced to fire one person to cut costs, Michael initially attempts to fire Creed, who then convinces him to fire Devon instead on Halloween. *(Halloween)*

**Ed Truck:** Ed was Michael's predecessor as manager, and Michael says he was a jerk. *(The Carpet)* Ed is decapitated in a car accident. *(Grief Counseling)*

**Miles:** Dwight wonders if Miles, who left to form his own company, used to sit at his desk. It was actually Todd Packer. *(The Carpet)*

**Gary Trundle:** Gary worked in the warehouse and made a deal to have sex with Meredith on their last day. *(Branch Closing)*

**Roy:** Roy is fired when he attacks Jim, after learning Pam kissed him. *(The Negotiation)*

**Michael Scott:** Upset that Charles canceled his fifteenth anniversary party and that he has to drive to

the office book of lists

New York to get David Wallace to talk to him, Michael quits, even though David relents and says he can have the party. *(New Boss)* Charles has security guard Hank escort Michael out of the building before his two weeks are up when he finds the Dunder Mifflin order form that has been altered to be the Michael Scott Paper Company form. *(Two Weeks)*

**Karen Filippelli:** When the Stamford and Scranton branches merge, Karen transfers to the Scranton office for a short time. *(The Merger)* After Karen and Jim end their relationship, she then transfers to the Utica branch and becomes regional manager.

**Ryan Howard:** Ryan relocates to New York after being offered a job to work for Corporate, taking over Jan Levinson's vacated position. *(The Job)* He eventually joins the Michael Scott Paper Company when he's released from his Corporate job for misleading shareholders.

**Pam Beesly:** Pam decides to go with Michael to start a new company, the Michael Scott Paper Company, but she wants to be a salesperson, not a receptionist. *(Two Weeks)*

**Henry Rostock:** Henry was the boss for nine years and four months. *(The Manager and the Salesman)*

## NEW HIRES

Every office needs some new blood, and over the years the Scranton branch has hired a number of new people. Few have lasted, perhaps due to the tight bond the Scranton colleagues have . . . or perhaps because it takes a special type of person to work with Dwight, Andy, and Michael.

**Holly Flax:** Holly is transferred to Scranton and becomes the new HR person when Toby moves to Costa Rica. *(Goodbye, Toby)*

**Ronni:** Ronni is hired as a replacement receptionist when Pam goes to art school. *(Weight Loss)*

**Erin Hannon:** Charles hires Erin to become the new receptionist when Pam and Michael leave to form a new company. *(Michael Scott Paper Company)*

**Nate:** Dwight picks up Nate as a day laborer, and he became the new maintenance worker for the building. He ends up working in the warehouse. *(Sex Ed)*

**Danny Cordray:** Michael hires Danny to be a traveling salesman, forgetting they already have Todd Packer doing that. *(The Sting)*

**Jordan Garfield:** When Deangelo is regional manager he hires a new executive assistant, Jordan, whose previous job was at Anthropologie. *(The Inner Circle)*

**Cathy Simms:** Andy hires Cathy to temporarily replace Pam while she is on maternity leave. *(Doomsday)*

**Pete and Clark:** They are hired and called the "New Jim" and "Dwight Jr." *(New Guys)*

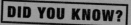

**DID YOU KNOW?**

When Andy is regional manager, he hires new warehouse workers, including Bruce Kenwood, Oscar's most-defined trainer at Planet Fitness; Nate *(Doomsday)*; and Val Johnson.

**DID YOU KNOW?** Dwight interviews several people for the junior salesman position, including Rolf Ahl, his best friend; Trevor, a failed hitman; Melvina, his former babysitter and lover; Mose, his cousin; Gabor, who went to the same fake X-Men-type school Dwight did and claims to have night hearing; Zeke, his cousin; Nate, his assistant / maintenance worker; Hide, a former warehouse worker who lost his lotto winnings; Troy, a former colleague of Ryan's; Wolf, a friend of Dwight's from paintball; Sensei, his karate sensei; and Clark, who gets the job. *(Junior Salesman)*

## BACKGROUND CHECKS

While many of the employees at Dunder Mifflin have been there for quite some time, for most of the staff, Dunder Mifflin is not their first job. While only Toby has access to everyone's files, some of the staff are not shy about letting others know what is on their résumé.

**Andrew (Andy) Baines Bernard** went to Cornell, was drunk the whole time, and sang in an a capella group called Here Comes Treble. *(Gay Witch Hunt)* Andy took Intro to Philosophy twice. *(Business Ethics)* As a freshman, Andy wrote an op-ed column called "Bernard's Regards" at the *Cornell Daily Sun*. *(Costume Contest)* Andy wrote a companion piece to *The Vagina Monologues* when he took a "crapload" of women's studies courses at Cornell. He called it *The Penis Apologies*. *(The Inner Circle)* While in Stamford, he lived with a dominatrix mistress named Lila, and she taught him more than any college professor at Cornell. *(Women's Appreciation)* Andy worked at Bear Stearns, Lehman

the office book of lists

Brothers, and AIG and did a summer at Enron. *(Scott's Tots)* Andy was originally named Walter Jr. and bore this name until he was six and his brother was born; his parents felt his brother better exemplified the name. *(The Delivery)* Andy claims he was a cute baby and could have modeled. He hated golf lessons as a kid and hung out with the sailing club instead. *(Job Fair)* Andy is petrified of his nipples chafing. *(Fun Run)* A passionate musician and performer, Andy played a bat boy in *Damn Yankees*. *(The Chump)*

**Pam Beesly** went to Valley View High School. *(Job Fair)* She gets accepted to Pratt Institute's School of Design. *(Goodbye, Toby)* She played volleyball in junior high. And in high school. And a little in college. And went to volleyball camp most summers. *(Company Picnic)*

**Toby Flenderson** went to Bishop O'Hara. He went to seminary for a year, then dropped out to follow his girlfriend to Scranton. *(Casual Friday)* Toby has a degree in social work from Temple University. *(Counseling)* He took a course at the Weintraub Memory Academy and remembers that he sat next to a woman named Beverly Brook, who had a Greek salad for lunch. *(New Guys)*

**Michael Scott** once applied to be "bottle capper" at a factory. *(The Convention)*

**Josh Porter** from Stamford lived on a kibbutz where he grew oranges and joined the Coast Guard. *(The Convention)*

## DID YOU KNOW?

Andy has three rules for getting ahead:
1) name repetition
2) personality mirroring
3) never breaking off a handshake.

NAME **ANDY BERNARD**

No.

CONFIDENTIAL

## DID YOU KNOW?

The members of Here Comes Treble included Carl 1, Carl 2, Broccoli Rob, Spare Rib, Doobie, Lunch Box, Boner Champ (that's Andy), Sandwich, Pubey Lewis and the News, Hopscotch, Jingle Jangle *(Weight Loss)*, and JC, who was called Blorville because he looked like a Black Orville Redenbacher. *(Nepotism)*

**Holly Flax** is from Des Moines and was a hall monitor in middle school. *(Business Ethics)*

**Angela Martin**, during her pageant days, was Miss Tiny Mid-Atlantic Bride when she was ten. *(Frame Toby)*

**Kelly Kapoor** was in Berks County Youth Center from April 1995 to December 1996 for stealing her ex-boyfriend's father's boat. *(Lecture Circuit)*

**Charles Miner** previously worked at Saticoy Steel. *(New Boss)*

**Erin Hannon** is an orphan who spent much of her life in foster homes. When stressed, Erin hides behind her hair, since in her foster home, her hair was her room. Her last job before joining Dunder Mifflin as the receptionist was at a Taco Bell Express. *(Secretary's Day)*

**Dwight K. Schrute** went to a school he thought was like Charles Xavier's School for Gifted Youngsters in the *X-Men* comics. It was a con; however, it took him several years to figure that out. *(Junior Salesman)*

**Pete** wanted to be a gym teacher and worked on a PE degree in college. *(Moving On)*

## PROMOTIONS, DEMOTIONS, AND CAREER PATHS

Part of corporate life is about the politics of moving up the ladder. At Dunder Mifflin, the ladder often seems to go up, down, sideways, and counterclockwise. Still, some people manage to navigate to where they want to be, to where they should be, or out of work entirely.

- Michael promotes Dwight from assistant to the regional manager to assistant regional manager after their fight but wants to keep it secret. *(The Fight)*

- Michael makes Dwight the official security supervisor of the branch, and Hank the security guard names him honorary volunteer corporal in charge of assisting all activities' security. *(Drug Testing)*

- Ryan takes Jim's place and becomes a junior sales associate when Jim transfers to Stamford. *(Gay Witch Hunt)*

- Jim gets a promotion to assistant regional manager when he moves to Stamford. *(Gay Witch Hunt)*

- Oscar was going to quit after Michael outed him as gay, but Jan bribes him to stay by offering him a three-month paid vacation and a company car. *(Gay Witch Hunt)*

- Bob Vance tells Phyllis he will hire her as a senior adviser and she will be paid in cash and not have to come into the office. *(Branch Closing)*

the office book of lists

- Closing Scranton and merging its staff with Stamford has largely been dependent on Josh running what would be Dunder Mifflin Northeast. However, he leverages his new position to quit and take a senior management position at Staples. *(Branch Closing)*

- When Dwight quits Dunder Mifflin, he goes to work at Staples as a sales associate, while continuing his employment search. *(The Return)*

- When Dwight becomes regional manager for one day, he plans to demote Jim. Dwight's ideal number two would be Jack Bauer. However, he is unavailable, fictional, and overqualified. Instead, Dwight promotes Andy to his number two and Pam to secret assistant to the regional manager. *(The Job)*

- After Ryan is arrested and loses his job at Corporate, he returns as the replacement receptionist while Pam is at art school. *(Weight Loss)*

- Kevin takes over as receptionist temporarily when Pam goes to work for the Michael Scott Paper Company. *(Dream Team)*

- Jo likes Darryl's idea about shipping paper and printers separately and moves Darryl from the warehouse to the office. *(St. Patrick's Day)*

- When Pam realizes she doesn't have the "sales gene," she manages to bluff Gabe into thinking she has been the office administrator for three months and effectively creates the job. *(Counseling)*

- Jan becomes director of office purchasing for a hospital, raises her daughter, and releases an album of Doris Day covers on her own label. *(Sex Ed)*

- Once Pam becomes office administrator, she jokes that she is "full-on corrupt" when she snags a new computer for Andy in exchange for "finding" Darryl some extra sick days. *(Todd Packer)*

- After Robert California is offered the regional manager job, he quits on the first day, drives to Florida, convinces Jo to give him her job as CEO, and then promotes Andy to regional manager of Scranton. *(The List)*

- Dwight is promoted to special projects manager and takes a team to Tallahassee for three weeks to develop and launch a chain of Sabre retail stores. *(Special Project)*

- After the successful launch of the Sabre store, Nellie plans to name Dwight vice president. *(Test the Store)*

- Jim discovers that Robert California plans to tank the Sabre store and that Dwight, as the new VP, will be fired. Jim helps Dwight by getting Nellie to name Todd Packer VP of Sabre Retail. Packer then gets fired. *(Last Day in Florida)*

- On her first day claiming to be regional manager, Nellie gives out raises and says that by using the Tinkerbell effect, they will be real. *(Get the Girl)*

- Clark briefly goes to work as Jan's assistant at the Scranton White Pages, takes a trip with her as her lover, and then comes back to Dunder Mifflin, ending up as a junior salesman. *(The Whale)*

- Frank from the warehouse is fired after he almost attacks Pam. *(Vandalism)*

- David makes Dwight regional manager after Andy leaves to pursue his dream of becoming famous. *(Livin' the Dream)*

- Dwight offers Jim the assistant regional manager job. He refuses, calling that a "made-up" job. He will, however, take the title "assistant to the regional manager." *(Livin' the Dream)*

- Jim and Dwight hold auditions for the new position of assistant to the assistant regional manager. Ultimately, Dwight is the only one qualified for this position. *(A.A.R.M.)*

|  | PROS | CONS |
|---|---|---|
| JIM | • Smart<br>• Cool<br>• Good-looking | • Not a hard worker |
| DWIGHT | • Has the best sales record in the office<br>• Loves the work | • He is, however, an idiot |
| STANLEY | • Because of all the good Black people have done for America | |
| ANDY | • Classy<br>• Really gets me<br>• Went to Cornell<br>• I trust him | • I don't really trust him |

*(Beach Day)*

When Michael thinks he is taking Jan's job at Corporate, he lists pros and cons for several candidates for his job. Michael ends up naming Dwight to succeed him as regional manager when Michael thinks he has gotten the job at Corporate. Dwight's reign lasts for one day.
*(The Job)*

## REVOLVING REGIONAL MANAGERS

No position seems to be more coveted than regional manager of the Dunder Mifflin Scranton branch. It seems like an easy job, unless someone like Jan, Ryan, or Jo is above you, insisting work get done and goals get met. Otherwise, the regional manager has time to watch movies, take a three-month sabbatical, or wait in line for pretzels.

- At the start of the documentary's filming, Michael Scott, who has been with Dunder Mifflin for twelve years, has been regional manager for his last four years in Scranton. *(Pilot)*

Michael lists all the things that happened to his bosses. He says that:

- Ed Truck got decapitated
- Charles Miner got fired
- David Wallace got fired
- and Jan Levinson went crazy.

*(Viewing Party)*

- When Michael quits to form his own company, the Michael Scott Paper Company, Charles interviews people for his job. Isaac Silby is the first one. *(Two Weeks)*

- Jim Halpert becomes co-manager with Michael for a time. *(The Meeting)*

- Jo Bennett decides that either Jim or Michael should return to sales. Jim volunteers, wanting the no-cap commissions. Then Michael decides he wants it, so Jim becomes regional manager for four and a half hours, until Michael realizes he wants to be manager again. *(The Manager and the Salesman)*

- Deangelo Vickers takes over after Michael moves to Colorado. Deangelo loves the American Southwest, has a peanut allergy, and is just as

# MICHAEL SCOTT
## PAPER COMPANY INC.

Serving Scranton's Paper Needs Since 2009

the office book of lists

comfortable at a ball game as at the opera. He tries to keep his daily caloric intake under 1,200. He claims to be a juggler. *(Training Day)* However, after he tries to prove he can dunk and a basketball hoop falls on him, Deangelo suffers brain damage and falls into a coma. *(The Inner Circle)*

- Jo asks Jim if he wants to be temporary acting manager. She then calls Dwight Schrute, who accepts. *(Dwight K. Schrute, (Acting) Manager)*

- When Dwight fires his gun in the office, Jo forms a search committee composed of Jim, Gabe, and Toby and charges them with finding a new manager. Creed Bratton, who has seniority, becomes acting manager. *(Dwight K. Schrute, (Acting) Manager)*

- Darryl, Andy, Kelly, and Dwight all apply for the regional manager job. Since Jo won't interview Dwight, he dresses as a fully bandaged burn victim named Jacques Souvenir. *(Search Committee)* The committee chooses an outside candidate, Robert California, as regional manager. On his first day, Robert travels to Florida and convinces Jo to give him her job as CEO of Sabre. *(The List)*

- Andy Bernard is named regional manager after Robert California becomes Sabre's CEO. *(The List)*

- While Andy is in Florida convincing Erin to come back to Dunder Mifflin, Nellie Bertram takes his office and effectively becomes manager. *(Get the Girl)*

- Andy refuses to be demoted to salesman when Nellie takes over, and Robert fires him. *(Angry Andy)* After Andy lands Binghamton's largest client, he tries to blackmail Robert into rehiring him, but it doesn't work. Instead, Andy convinces David Wallace to buy Dunder Mifflin *(Turf War)*, becomes manager again, and allows Nellie to remain on as special projects manager. *(Free Family Portrait Studio)*

**DID YOU KNOW?**

Darryl becomes Andy's "consigliere," which is what Andy calls the assistant regional manager position.
*(Roy's Wedding)*

- After David Wallace fires Andy for being too distracted with his new acting career, Dwight's karate sensei tells David impressive things about Dwight that lead David to consider making Dwight regional manager. When Jim backs up the sensei's assessment, David finally makes Dwight the regional manager of the Scranton branch. *(Livin' the Dream)*

WORLD'S
BEST

WORLD'S
BEST BOSS

# Chapter Two:
# Core (In)Compe-
# tencies

# MICHAEL'S CHARACTERS

While Michael Scott is a character unto himself, he loves to create and play different characters. He attributes this to the time he was a kid at a school assembly and a giant owl gave an impassioned speech about giving hoots and not polluting. Around the office, Michael becomes dozens of characters.

- Michael pretends to be Dr. Bergerstein, Packer's proctologist, when he calls Packer. *(Basketball)*

- Michael plays a fortune-teller character based on Johnny Carson's Carnac the Magnificent character. *(The Dundies)*

- Ping is the offensive Asian stereotype character Michael plays. *(The Dundies)*

- Agent Michael Scarn is Michael's James Bond–like character. Michael eventually films a whole movie about Scarn, starring the office staff, called *Threat Level Midnight*. *(The Client)* He also calls himself Agent Michael Scoon once in improv class. *(Email Surveillance)*

- Michael also claims to be Michael Scarn, a local business owner, to find out about Prince Family Paper's prices. This Scarn owns a law firm. *(Prince Family Paper)*

- Prison Mike was convicted for theft, robbery, and kidnapping the president's son and holding him for ransom. He says the worst thing about prison was the dementors flying around. *(The Convict)*

- Michael the Magic isn't able to escape from a straitjacket and chains when Jim hides the key with his foot. *(Cocktails)*

- Michael says Toby has been cruising for a bruising for twelve years, and Michael declares he is now Toby's cruise director, Captain Bruisin'. *(Goodbye, Toby)*

- When rapping with Holly, Michael's name is MC Mike Scott. *(Weight Loss)*

- Michael Klump comes in to the office to talk about body image, wearing a semi-inflated sumo suit. *(Weight Loss)*

- Michael always wanted to be in the witness protection program and picks out a name and occupation—Lord Rupert Everton, a shipping merchant who raises fancy dogs. *(Money)*

- When Dwight calls David Wallace's secretary, claims to be Michael Scotch, and says that he has kidnapped Wallace's son, Michael as Michael Scotch calls back to say Wallace's son is fine. *(New Boss)*

- Blind Guy McSqueezy is a character Michael workshopped in improv. He fell into a vat of acid eyes first, and his lack of vision got him in all sorts of trouble. *(The Lover)*

the office book of lists

- Michael does an Elvis impersonation. *(Scott's Tots)*

- When Michael realizes he's on a date, he changes into Date Mike, puts on a beret, unbuttons his shirt, and tries to be suave. *(Happy Hour)*

## Hi, I'm

### Date Mike

### NICE TO MEET ME.

- Michael is working on a British character named Reginald Pooftah. *(The Seminar)*

- Michael's Greek character who acts as a plant in Andy's small business seminar is Mikonas, who is loosely based on another Greek character he did, Spiros. Michael later calls Holly "his partner, Necropolis." *(The Seminar)*

- Michael's millionaire character who farts popcorn is named Orville Tootenbacher. *(The Search)*

- Michael dresses up as Jo Bennett, Angela, Jim, and Phyllis in the video introduction to his last Dundies. *(Michael's Last Dundies)*

## JIM'S NICKNAMES

Jim is an easygoing guy and collecting nicknames never seems to bother him, though after Andy starts calling him Big Tuna, he wonders if anyone in Stamford even knows his real name.

- Fat Halpert *(The Dundies)*

- Slim Jim *(Office Olympics)*

- Jim-bag *(The Secret)*

- Andy calls Jim Big Tuna for eating a tuna sandwich on his first day at Stamford. *(Gay Witch Hunt)*

- After seeing Jim's hipster *Second Life* avatar, Pam calls it Philly Jim. *(Local Ad)*

- When roleplaying sales with Dwight, Jim names his client Bill Buttlicker. *(Customer Survey)*

- Michael calls Jim James, then Jimothy when he becomes co-manager. *(The Promotion)*

- Dwight calls Pam and Jim Tweedle Dee and Tweedle Dumbass while they are on parental leave. *(St. Patrick's Day)*

- Dwight most often just calls Jim "idiot." *(multiple episodes)*

### DID YOU KNOW?

Andy's nickname for Jim goes through a number of iterations, including Big Haircut, when Jim gets a haircut for his job interview at Corporate *(The Job)*; Wet Tuna, when Jim comes in from the rain after proposing to Pam *(Weight Loss)*; T-Money, when Andy can't decide to address the save-the-date for his wedding to J-Money or T-Money *(Crime Aid)*; Tunes *(Frame Toby)*; Tuna Boss *(The Lover)*; Dr. Tuna, MD *(Scott's Tots)*; Tuna Turner *(The Seminar)*; T-Bag Bone *(The Incentive)*; and Thin-Sliced Tuna *(Livin' the Dream)*.

the office book of lists

# PAM'S NICKNAMES

Although Michael's antics and inappropriate behavior in the office often make Pam cringe or worse, she and Michael gradually become good friends and are able to turn to each other for advice or support. Michael has lots of endearing nicknames for Pam and often mashes up her name with questionable cultural references.

- Pam-Pam: Inspired by Bamm-Bamm Rubble from *The Flintstones*. *(Pilot)*

- Pamelama Ding Dong: From a 1950s song. *(Health Care)*

- Pam Pam, Thank You, Ma'am: Inspired by "wham, bam, thank you, ma'am." *(Basketball)*

- Pamera: Spoken with an offensive Asian accent. *(Office Olympics)*

- Spamster: From "Spam" plus "hamster." *(The Carpet)*

- I Am Pam: Spoken in Jeff Spicoli's voice. *(The Carpet)*

- Christmas Pam; Side of Candied Pam; Pam Chops with Mint: Inspired by Christmas themes. *(A Benihana Christmas)*

- Pam-casso: Inspired by Pablo Picasso. *(Business School)*

- Pamcake: Jim gives Pam this name when she is leaving for art school and not part of the weight loss competition. *(Weight Loss)*

- Paaam-o-laaaa: Inspired by Ricola commercials. *(Crime Aid)*

- Pamtown Lady, Sing This Song: Inspired by "Camptown Races." *(Frame Toby)*

- The Bart Simpson of Scranton: Pam tells Jim that this is what she's known as at the office. *(Nepotism)*

# DWIGHT'S NICKNAMES

Always Dwight K. Schrute in his own mind, Dwight isn't one for calling others (or himself) by nicknames, although he does call Jim "idiot" on many occasions. There are, however, many nicknames that others call Dwight.

- Michael mocks Dwight as Elwyn Dragonslayer, after Dwight corrects him on a *Lord of the Rings* character's name. *(Basketball)*

- Dwight identifies himself using the code name Possum when he speaks to Angela on their walkie-talkies. *(A Benihana Christmas)*

- The Benihana waitress calls Dwight the Giant Baby. *(A Benihana Christmas)*

- If he were a serial killer, Dwight would call himself the Overkill Killer. *(Survivor Man)*

- Andy assumes Dwight is short for D-Money, and that's what he writes on the save-the-date envelope for Dwight and Angela's wedding. *(Crime Aid)*

- Andy calls Dwight his bro-migo at the company picnic. *(Company Picnic)*

- Dwight blames having lice the first day of school for why classmates called him Freak, Four Eyes, Sci-Fi Nerd, and Girl Puncher. *(Lice)*

- Dwight's girlfriend Esther calls him Schru-berry Blue. *(Livin' the Dream)*

the office book of lists

# ANDY'S NICKNAMES

Andy was born Walter Bernard Jr., but after the birth of his younger brother, his parents changed his name to Andy because they felt his younger brother better embodied the name. Andy had numerous nicknames in college, and by the time he starts working for Dunder Mifflin Scranton, the name that has stuck is 'Nard Dog, including its many iterations.

- When Michael reviews Andy's file, he calls Andy Saint Bernard. *(Branch Closing)*

- After Andy completes anger management training, he tries to go by Drew and brings cookies to the office. *(Safety Training)*

- Mr. Bernard Johnson, MD (*Product Recall—deleted scene*)

- Hubble / El Guapo (*Diwali—deleted scene*)

- Kevin nicknamed Andy the Penguin for wearing a Penguin-brand shirt. *(The Merger)*

- Dwight calls Andy Moon Face. *(Women's Appreciation)*

- Michael calls Andy the 'Nard Dog. *(Local Ad)*

- When he brings his baby picture to the office, Andy calls himself 'Nard Puppy. *(Baby Shower)*

- In college, Andy's nickname was Puke. Since he aced all his courses, with straight Bs, his friends also called him Ace and Buzz. *(Moroccan Christmas)*

- Michael's nephew, Luke, calls Andy 'Nard Man. *(Nepotism)*

- Andy says they used to call him King Tut because he's so good at keeping things under wraps. Actually, it was King Butt because he had a king-sized butt. *(Jury Duty)*

- Andy says he had the nickname Boner Champ as part of his a capella group, Here Comes Treble. *(Here Comes Treble)*

- Dwight calls Andy Burning Man when he comes back from his boat trip. *(Couples Discount)*

- Dwight calls Andy Turd Dog when he loses the Scranton White Pages account. *(Couples Discount)*

## OTHER NICKNAMES

From Michael's efforts to make the office more fun to Andy's continual creation of different iterations of people's names, almost everyone gets called something they don't want to be called over the years.

- Michael calls Darryl Mr. Rogers, which morphed from Darryl Philbin to Regis Philbin to Regis to Rege to Roger to Mr. Rogers. *(Basketball)*

- Michael calls Katy Pam 6.0. When introducing Katy around, Michael calls Oscar Oscar the Grouch. *(Hot Girl)*

- Michael calls Todd Packer Pac-Man. *(Basketball)*

- When giving out ice cream, Michael calls Stanley Stanley the Manly. *(Health Care)*

- Todd Packer calls Michael Michael Snot. *(Sexual Harassment)*

- Ryan never wanted to be known as a "something guy," like Stanley is known as the "Crossword Puzzles Guy." He ends up being Fire Guy after accidentally starting a fire in the kitchen. *(The Fire)*

- Stanley gets the "bo banley banana fana fo fanley" treatment from Michael. *(Booze Cruise)*

- A concussed Dwight calls Pam Pan. *(The Injury)*

- Michael calls Packer Packster and Wacky Pack. *(The Carpet)*

- Dwight calls Carol Code Name Re/Max and Jan Lan Jevinson when he acts as Michael's wingman on Casino Night. *(Casino Night)*

- Dwight's pet name for Angela is Monkey. *(The Coup)*

- Phyllis is known (at least to Bob Vance) as Mrs. Bob Vance, First Lady of Vance Refrigeration. *(The Coup)*

- When Jim returns to the Scranton branch, he pretends not to know some of the staff, and Pam points out Meredith as Janet Fenstermaker. *(The Merger)*

- Michael calls Carol Christmas Carol. *(A Benihana Christmas)*

- Andy calls Michael a PhD doctor of sales. *(Traveling Salesman)*

### DID YOU KNOW?

When deciding on a nickname for Nellie, Darryl tells the office staff that the warehouse has code names for them. Andy is Jelly Roll, Michael is Dennis the Menace, and Ryan is Douche Bag. Pam suggests Monday for Nellie (because no one likes Mondays) and Ryan suggests Pam. *(Welcome Party)*

the office book of lists

- Michael calls Stanley Superfly when picking his dream team of salespeople. *(Traveling Salesman)*

- Andy calls Ryan Big Turkey in a nod to his Big Tuna nickname for Jim. *(The Return)*

- Andy calls Michael Notorious B.I.G. Boss, but Michael doesn't like it. *(The Return)*

- Michael says Phyllis's nickname in high school was Easy Rider. *(Phyllis' Wedding)*

- Michael calls Madge from the warehouse Pudge and Patch, but not as nicknames; he seems to simply not know her name. *(Safety Training)*

- Michael and Kelly both call Lonnie a sea monster, as he is so large. *(Safety Training)*

- Dwight calls Phyllis Phallus while working on the Emergency Anti-Flashing Task Force. *(Women's Appreciation)*

- Kevin wants to call Pam and Jim PB&J for Pam Beesly and Jim. *(Fun Run)*

- Michael calls Stanley Stankley when he is fundraising for the fun run. *(Fun Run)*

- Kevin calls Ryan little old man-boy and bearded man-boy. *(Dunder Mifflin Infinity)*

- Kevin says that in high school his nickname was Kool-Aid Man. *(Local Ad)*

- Michael calls Karen Fillipellers when he calls to tell her not to poach Stanley. *(Branch Wars)*

- While Michael is at the job fair, Creed calls Angela Pumpkin. *(Job Fair)*

- Michael asks Holly if she is real or a Hollygram. *(Goodbye, Toby)*

- After secretly having sex, Dwight calls Angela Half-Pint. *(Weight Loss)*

- When Michael raps with Holly, her nickname is DJ Jazzy Flex. *(Weight Loss)*

- Michael calls Ronni Rice-A-Ronni. *(Weight Loss)*

- Kevin calls Ryan Fired Guy after he loses his job at Corporate. *(Weight Loss)*

- The save-the-date Kevin receives from Andy is addressed to K-Money. *(Crime Aid)*

- When discussing Ryan's job loss and reemployment, Kevin calls Ryan Hired Guy. *(Business Ethics)*

- Michael calls Holly Holly-lujah and Holly calls him Mike-raculous when they are trying to discuss the whole Meredith thing. *(Business Ethics)*

- In a Canadian bar, Andy calls two people he suspects are gay Dandy Dale and Foppy McGee before trying to hook Oscar up with them. *(Business Trip)*

- Pam calls Michael Hot Tie Guy when she tries to flatter him into choosing a new copy machine. *(The Surplus)*

- Kevin suggests they call Meredith Fire Girl after her hair catches fire, but then asks if it's too soon. *(Moroccan Christmas)*

- Not remembering his name at first, Michael calls Tony from Stamford Jabba the Hutt, Pizza the Hut, and Pepperoni Tony. *(Lecture Circuit)*

- Michael calls Ryan the Rye Guy and Rye Bread when they recruit him for the Michael Scott Paper Company. *(Dream Team)*

- On their honeymoon, Pam and Jim meet a couple named Frank and Benny whom they call Frank and Beans. *(The Lover)*

### DID YOU KNOW?

Meredith claims she's never been called a narc, but she *has* been called Floozy, Alkie, Einstein (sarcastically), Vomit Mop, Floor Meat, and Flesh Hoover.
*(Couples Discount)*

- Michael calls Pam's mother, Helene, Pickle. *(The Lover)*

- Andy calls Pam's unborn child Little Soybean. *(Koi Pond)*

- Kids in high school called Michael Ponytail because he got his ponytail stuck in a power drill. *(Koi Pond)*

- Andy calls his boss Michael the Machine Scott. *(Shareholder Meeting)*

- To keep their identities in Dwight's plan secret, Dwight is Dragon and Ryan is Bobcat. *(The Manager and the Salesman)*

- Jo Bennett calls Michael Puddin'. *(St. Patrick's Day)*

- Creed thinks Darryl's name is Darnell. *(The Cover-Up)*

- Michael's nephew, Luke, calls himself the Coffee Monkey. *(Nepotism)*

- Luke calls Darryl Daryl Hannah and Phyllis Venus. *(Nepotism)*

- Packer calls Gabe Gabe-wad. *(Costume Contest)*

- Oscar is known as Actually, because he always inserts himself into conversations to correct grammar or add facts. *(China)*

- Dwight calls Erin Space Orphan and Holly Princess Nincompoop. *(The Search)*

- Erin says Michael answers to Michael, Michael G. Scott, Michael J. Fox, Mr. Fox, and the Incredible Mr. Fox. *(The Search)*

### DID YOU KNOW?

Michael and Todd Packer have a few choice nicknames for Jan, most of which they call her behind her back, including Hillary Rodham Clinton and Jan Godzillary *(Pilot)*, Jamaican Jan, Sun Princess, and the Ice Queen *(Back from Vacation)*. At their dinner party, Michael and Jan keep shouting an increasingly hostile "Babe" at each other, making everyone uncomfortable. *(Dinner Party)*

- When fake signing up for a cell phone plan, Holly uses Fanny Smellmore as her name. *(The Search)*

- When both women are pregnant at the same time, Angela calls herself Little Pregs and Pam Big Pregs. *(The List)*

- Andy calls Oscar C-SPAN, abbreviated from "cocker spaniel"—"spaniel" due to his Spanish bloodline and "cocker" because . . . *(The Incentive)*

- Andy calls Dwight D-dub Dog and D-Bone and wants Erin to call everyone things like P-Dog (Pam) and E-Dog (Erin). *(The Incentive)*

- Val calls the people working upstairs popsicles because they have sticks up their butt. Nate thought it was because they were so rich they could eat popsicles all the time. *(Christmas Wishes)*

- Andy is called Iceman in Outward Bound and calls Pete Plop and Clark Fart. *(New Guys)*

- When Jim and Dwight pretend to be family to get family-owned businesses to use them as their paper provider, they go by Handsome and Stinky Paper Brothers for Hire. *(Suit Warehouse)*

- Andy calls Clark Clarker Posey a.k.a. Clarkwork Orange and Zero Clark Thirty. *(Moving On)*

- Andy calls David David Walrus. *(Livin' the Dream)*

- Dwight refers to Jim, Pam, and himself as the Three Amigos. *(Finale)*

Big Turkey
Douche Bag
Little Old Man-boy
Bearded Man-boy
Rye guy
Fire guy
Rye bread
Bobcat

# MICHAEL'S QUOTES

Michael Scott has a way with words. He uses them often, and often they aren't used correctly.

- "No, I'm not going to tell them about the downsizing. If a patient has cancer, you don't tell them." *(Pilot)*

- "Abraham Lincoln once said that 'if you're a racist, I will attack you with the North,' and these are the principles I carry with me in the workplace." *(Diversity Day)*

- "I live by one rule: No office romances, no way. Very messy, inappropriate . . . no. But I live by another rule: Just do it . . . Nike." *(Hot Girl)*

- "I'm an early bird and I'm a night owl, so I'm wise and I have worms." *(Office Olympics)*

- "Stupid Corporate wet blankets. Like booze ever killed anybody." *(Christmas Party)*

- **"Well, happy birthday, Jesus. Sorry your party's so lame."** *(Christmas Party)*

- After he burns his foot and has only bubble wrap to protect his injury, Michael tells Jim to "please stop popping my cast." *(The Injury)*

- Angry at the staff, Michael says he would have previously given a kidney to anyone there, but now, "Uh, no. I only give my organs to my real friends. Get yourself a monkey kidney." *(The Carpet)*

- "Pam! I'm public speaking. Stop public interrupting me!" *(Dwight's Speech)*

- "Two queens on Casino Night. I am going to drop a deuce on everybody." *(Casino Night)*

- **Upon seeing Jim at the convention, Michael says, "It's like firemen. You don't leave your brother behind, even if you find out that there is a better fire in Connecticut."** *(The Convention)*

- Michael says to Jim, "I love inside jokes. I'd love to be part of one someday." *(The Convention)*

- "Wikipedia is the best thing ever. Anyone in the world can write anything they want about any subject. So you know you are getting the best possible information." *(The Negotiation)*

- "Those warehouse guys think that we are all flabby, middle management Nerf balls. Well, I'm going to show them that we have Nerfs of steel." *(Safety Training)*

- "I'm not superstitious, but I am a little stitious." *(Fun Run)*

the office book of lists

34

- "Do I need to be liked? Absolutely not. I like to be liked. I enjoy being liked. I have to be liked. But it's not like a compulsive need to be liked. Like my need to be praised." *(Fun Run)*

- "You don't know me—you've just seen my penis." *(Fun Run)*

- Frustrated, wet, and angry that old clients won't do business with them anymore, Michael goes back to a former client he gave a gift basket to and demands the now-opened basket back, yelling, "Where are the turtles?!" *(Dunder Mifflin Infinity)*

- "I am running away from my responsibilities. And it feels good." *(Money)*

- "Yeah, I'm trying to lure these kids into my booth, but kids are very aware about being lured these days. Thank you, *Dateline*." *(Job Fair)*

- "You cheated on me? When I specifically asked you not to?" *(Goodbye, Toby)*

- When David Wallace asks Michael why his branch is outperforming all the others, his response is "My philosophy is basically this. And this is something that I live by. And I always have. And I always will. Don't ever, for any reason, do anything to anyone for any reason ever, no matter what, no matter where, or who you are with, or, or where you are going, or, or where you've been. Ever. For any reason. Whatsoever." *(The Duel)*

- "Sometimes I'll start a sentence and I don't even know where it's going. I just hope I find it along the way."

   *(The Duel)*

- "Nobody should have to go to work thinking, 'Oh this is the place that I might die today.' That's what a hospital is for. An office is for not dying. An office is a place to live life to the fullest. To the max. To . . . an office is a place where dreams come true."

   *(Stress Relief)*

- "They always say that it's a mistake to hire your friends. And they are right. So, I hired my best friends. And this is what I get?!" *(The Michael Scott Paper Company)*

- "This is a dream that I've had . . . since lunch . . . and I'm not giving it up now." *(The Michael Scott Paper Company)*

- "You all took a life here today. You did. The life of the party." *(Café Disco)*

- "I'm not usually the butt of the joke. I'm usually the face of the joke." *(Koi Pond)*

# SCOTT'S TOTS

- "I have made some empty promises in my life, but hands down, that was the most generous."

   *(Scott's Tots)*

- "I'm not a millionaire. I thought I would be by the time I was thirty, but I wasn't even close. Then I thought maybe by forty, but by forty I had less money than I did when I was thirty."

   *(Scott's Tots)*

- "Make friends first, make sales second, make love third. In no particular order." *(New Leads)*

- "I am Beyoncé, always." *(The Chump)*

- "If I had a gun with two bullets and I was in a room with Hitler, bin Laden, and Toby, I would shoot Toby twice." *(The Chump)*

- "Hey, Goldenface! Go puck yourself!" *(Threat Level Midnight)*

- "The people that you work with are, when you get down to it, your very best friends." *(Michael's Last Dundies)*

- "Whether you're scared of dying, or dying alone, or dying drunk in a ditch, don't be. It's going to be okay." *(Goodbye, Michael)*

- "I feel like all my kids grew up and then they married each other. It's every parent's dream." *(Finale)*

## "THAT'S WHAT SHE SAID"

If there is one punchline Michael Scott loves, it is the extremely sexist "That's what she said." He uses it on other people, but sometimes he just uses it on himself. It works for so many situations, and occasionally other staff members find a good use for it, too. Or at least . . . that's what she said.

- Michael offers Jim some pizza and Jim says, "No, thanks. I'm good." Then Michael says it. *(Sexual Harassment)*

- When Pam says her mother is coming to the office, Michael starts to say it, but he stops himself. *(Sexual Harassment)*

- Jim baits Michael by saying he always leaves him satisfied and smiling. *(Sexual Harassment)*

- Kevin asks why Michael got such a big Christmas tree for the office and then Michael says it. *(Christmas Party)*

- The doctor asks if Michael's burned foot was red and swollen and Dwight says it. *(The Injury)*

- Michael says it when he walks in on Dwight eating grapes, and then has to explain that grapes are seductive. *(Dwight's Speech)*

- When Michael is reviewing complaints and Angela says he already did her, Michael says it. *(Conflict Resolution)*

- After saying he has put the whole "Oscar coming out matter to bed," Michael says, "That's what she said. Or he said." *(Gay Witch Hunt)*

- Michael looks at the camera knowingly and snorts when Jan tells him she can't stay on top of him 24/7 at the convention. *(The Convention)*

- Michael says the pretzels taste so good in his mouth and Stanley says it. *(Initiation)*

**DID YOU KNOW?**

During Michael's deposition, he is asked if he was directly under Ms. Levinson the entire time and he says, "That's what she said." The committee thinks Jan actually said that, and question why his direct superior would say that. When it's finally explained and the court reporter reads off what he said, Michael criticizes her delivery, saying she butchered the joke. He also says it after he says, "Come again." *(The Deposition)*

- Michael says it after the Benihana waitress whispers in his ear. (**A Benihana Christmas**)

- Michael tells Dwight to think long and hard about his future with the company and Dwight says it to him. **(Traveling Salesman)**

- Jan suggests her and Michael "blow off" the CFO's party and Michael says it. **(Cocktails)**

- Jan questions the camera crew about why her relationship with Michael is so hard, then says, "That's what she said," and is horrified by what she's said. **(Cocktails)**

- When Michael tells the hot dog–eating contestants to dip the hot dogs in water so they will slide down their gullets more easily, all the contestants say it. **(Beach Games)**

- When Michael says, "I need two men on this," he says it. **(Product Recall)**

- After telling Angela and Phyllis to make the "Welcome Back, Ryan" banner straighter, Michael says it. He has other lead-ins written down, including "That job looks hard," "You should put your mouth on it," and "You might want to trim it a little." **(Dunder Mifflin Infinity)**

- While Michael tries to give a Power-Point presentation on PowerPoint presentations, he mutters, "Up comes the toolbar," then he says it. **(Money)**

- When Jim tells Michael he doesn't think he'll be here in ten years, Michael says, "That's what I said. That's what she said." **(Survivor Man)**

- When Michael says that he says "that's what she said" to lighten the tension when things get hard, Jim says it. **(Survivor Man)**

- At Michael and Jan's dinner party, when Jan gets angry and says Michael is hardly her first customer, Michael yells it out. **(Dinner Party)**

- When Dwight tells Michael to force his face into the cement as deep as he can, Michael says it. **(Did I Stutter?)**

- Holly explains that it was hard to "rise up" at her old company and Michael starts to say it but stops himself. **(Goodbye, Toby)**

the office book of lists

- Still trying to impress Holly, Michael resists saying it when Dwight tells everyone to take one bite each of éclair and says, "Hold it in your mouth if you can't swallow." Jim looks at Michael and asks, "Really, nothing?" *(Weight Loss)*

- Upset with the toy gavel Phyllis got him for the auction, Michael says, "It squeaks when you bang it. That's what she said." *(Crime Aid)*

- When Michael is driving Holly to Nashua and she says not to make it harder than it needs to be, he whispers it. *(Employee Transfer)*

- Over Jim's tiny Bluetooth, Pam hears Kelly yell at Dwight to get out of her nook, and Pam excitedly says, "That's what she said! That's what she said!" *(Customer Survey)*

- While the staff is on the floor meditating and Stanley's biofeedback machine is beeping, Michael tells Oscar to reach over and "touch his thing" and says, "That's what *he* said. Right guys, 'cause of gay?" *(Stress Relief)*

- When David congratulates Dwight for "his" golden ticket promotion idea after Blue Cross makes Dunder Mifflin its exclusive supplier, David says, "This is huge," and Dwight says, "That's what she said." *(Golden Ticket)*

- After Michael messes up Jim's chance for a promotion, Jim asks Michael if he screwed him. Michael starts to say it and Jim angrily says, "No." *(The Meeting)*

- After Darryl says Michael needs to get back on top, Michael says it. *(New Leads)*

- When Michael tells everyone to get the news clip of him up, he starts to say, "That's what . . ." *(Whistleblower)*

- Angry that the staff thinks Gabe is the boss, Michael argues with Gabe, and Gabe says, "You're making this harder than it has to be." Then Michael says it. *(Viewing Party)*

- When listing what type of playing card everyone is, Michael says to "gimme a hard one" and says, "That's what Oscar said." *(WUPHF.com)*

- David Brent says, "Comedy is where the mind goes to tickle itself," and then follows up with it. *(The Seminar)*

- When Holly tells Michael their long-distance relationship will be hard, but they can make it work, she says it. *(Goodbye, Michael)*

- After Michael says that it will feel so good getting the mic off his chest, he says it. *(Goodbye, Michael)*

- After Michael surprises Dwight by showing up at Dwight's wedding, Dwight exclaims, "Michael! I can't believe you came!" to which Michael replies with a final "That's what she said." *(Finale)*

# MICHAEL'S BUSINESS ADVICE

Like his mug says, Michael Scott is truly "The World's Best Boss"—at least in his own mind. In his sales journals, Michael jots down what he calls "wisdoms," and Ryan once suggested he write a book called *The Fundamentals of Business*. Michael does write a book entirely in his head called *Somehow I Manage*, including some of his "world's best" business advice.

- After Michael throws away the agenda Jan faxed over, he tries to blame it on Pam, and says, "A company runs on efficiency of communication." *(Pilot)*

- Michael says a company's people are more important than cash flow or inventory. *(Pilot)*

- On Ryan's first day, Michael says he's created an atmosphere where he is a friend first and a boss second, and probably an entertainer third. *(Pilot)*

- The most sacred thing Michael thinks he's done is care and provide for his workers, not directly, but by giving them money. And picking a health care plan. *(Health Care)*

- Michael shows Ryan the warehouse and claims he is "managing by walking around." *(Basketball)*

- Michael says decisiveness is one of the keys to success, according to *Small Businessman* magazine. *(Hot Girl)*

According to the Michael Scott School of Business, there are ten rules that Ryan needs to learn. However, Michael shares only a few:

## MICHAEL SCOTT'S "TEN" RULES OF BUSINESS INCLUDE:

**Rule #1:** You need to play to win, but you also have to win to play.

**Rule #2:** Adapt. React. Re-adapt. Act.

**Rule #3:** (Rule #3 got skipped.)

**Rule #4:** "In business, image is everything." —Andre Agassi

**Rule #5:** Safety first, i.e., don't burn the building down.

*(The Fire)*

- Michael figures it makes sense to fire the least popular person, because that has the least effect on morale. *(Halloween)*

- Michael knows there are certain things not to share with his employees—like his salary (as that would depress them), and he won't share with them that he will be reading their emails. *(Email Surveillance)*

- Michael says there's always a natural distance between a boss and the employees—they are intimidated, mostly due to the awareness they are not him. *(Email Surveillance)*

- Michael says if the office were a ship, as its leader, he would be the captain. "But we're in the same boat. Teamwork!" *(Booze Cruise)*

- Michael decides to take a break from being the boss who always teaches people things and to just be "the boss of dancing." *(Booze Cruise)*

- Michael tells Pam her job is being his friend. *(The Injury)*

- Michael says a cluttered desk means a cluttered mind. *(The Secret)*

- Michael knows an office can't function efficiently unless people are at their desks doing their jobs. *(The Secret)*

- Michael swore to himself that if he ever got to walk around the room as manager, people would laugh when they saw him coming and applaud as he walked away. *(The Carpet)*

- Michael puts everyone in a time-out to punish them when no one admits to ruining his carpet. *(The Carpet)*

- Michael says part of his job is knowing how to talk to women. *(Boys and Girls)*

- Michael discusses the five types of conflict in the HR binder "A Mediator's Toolchest." Though he says his "Shaolin Temple style defeats your monkey style," the actual styles are lose/lose; win/lose; compromise; win/win; and win/win/win. *(Conflict Resolution)*

- After he kisses Oscar, Michael is glad that "today spurred social change," as that is part of his job as regional manager. *(Gay Witch Hunt)*

- Michael explains, "Business is like a jungle. And I . . . am like a tiger. And Dwight is like a monkey that stabs the tiger in the back with a stick. Does the tiger fire the monkey? Does the tiger transfer the monkey to another branch? Pun. There is no way of knowing what goes on inside the tiger's head. We don't have the technology." *(The Coup)*

## DID YOU KNOW?

Michael lists the "four" kinds of business to Ryan's class: tourism; food service; railroads; sales; hospitals / manufacturing; and air travel. He also attempts to explain business with candy bars. First you need a building and a supply of something to sell—a Whatchamacallit. You sell those in order to have a PayDay. If you sell enough, you make 100 Grand. Then he asks them if they're satisfied and pulls out a Snickers bar. *(Business School)*

## DID YOU KNOW?

Michael learns some tactics for negotiations on Wikipedia, including these strategies: lean back and whisper to establish a dominant physical position; change the location of the meeting at the last second; take a break; and decline to speak first. *(The Negotiation)*

- When Michael speaks at Ryan's Emerging Enterprises class, he is ready with a great line if they throw their hats in the air: "May your hats fly as high as your dreams." *(Business School)*

- Michael rips pages out of a textbook and tells Ryan's class to replace them with life lessons—then they will have a book worth its weight in gold. *(Business School)*

- Michael explains to Ryan's class that "profit" is a fancy word for money. *(Business School)*

- Michael tells Ryan's class not to overestimate the value of computers, because real business is done on paper. *(Business School)*

- Michael claims that small companies, like Dunder Mifflin, are "David" and will always beat "Goliath," even five Goliaths like Staples, etc. *(Business School)*

### MICHAEL'S "WISDOMS"

- Don't do what I say— say what I do.

- Mistakes are just success that you mess up.

*(Business School)*

- The most inspiring thing Michael has ever said to Dwight is "Don't be an idiot." *(Business School)*

- Michael tells Ryan that business is always personal. It's the most personal thing in the world. *(Business School)*

- Michael says, "Negotiation is an art. Back and forth. Give and take. And today, both Darryl and I took something. Higher salaries. Win-win-win. But, you know, life is about more than just salaries. It's about perks. Like having sex with Jan." *(The Negotiation)*

- During the obscene watermark recall, Michael knows the key to a crisis is dealing with it right away. "Like that aspirin company . . ." *(Product Recall)*

- Michael says, "Mrs. Allen is our most important client, because every client is our most important client." He later adds that the customer is always right. But Mrs. Allen was their customer and she was wrong. But it's not a contradiction because she's not their customer anymore. *(Product Recall)*

- Michael holds a hot dog–eating contest because a good manager has got to be hungry. Hungry for success. *(Beach Games)*

- Michael tells the group on Beach Day that the one thing a great manager needs most of all is courage—and they will prove it by walking across hot coals. *(Beach Games)*

- Michael tells David Wallace during his interview that his weaknesses are that he works too hard, he cares too much, and sometimes he can be too invested in his job. He then says that those are also actually his strengths, too. *(The Job)*

- Michael says people will never be replaced by machines. "In the end, life and business are about human connections. And computers are about trying to murder you in a lake." *(Dunder Mifflin Infinity)*

- Michael thinks Ryan isn't doing a good job as a manager because he suppresses ideas and creativity. *(Local Ad)*

- Michael doesn't want his employees thinking their jobs depend on their performance. *(Business Ethics)*

- Michael doesn't know what David Wallace means by discussing "big picture" stuff. *(The Duel)*

- Michael says that an office is a place where dreams come true. *(Stress Relief)*

- While learning CPR, Michael points out that in sales ABC means "always be closing." *(Stress Relief)*

- Michael says, "A great boss cares more about the happiness of his employees than anything else." *(Blood Drive)*

- Michael tells David Wallace that he thrives under a lack of accountability. *(New Boss)*

- The Michael Scott Paper Company mission statement is "I will not be beat. I never give up. I am on a mission. That is the Michael Scott guarantee." *(Dream Team)*

- Michael tells Pam he does his best work when people don't believe in him. *(Dream Team)*

- During his negotiations with David Wallace to sell his paper company back to Dunder Mifflin, Michael explains, "Business isn't about money to me." *(Broke)*

Michael and Jim make a pros and cons list to decide who should be kept as a salesperson, Ryan or Pam.

| | PROS | CONS |
|---|---|---|
| RYAN | • Went to business school<br>• He's Michael's number-one choice<br>• Michael likes his hair<br>• Environmentally conscious, as his mom drives him to work | • He defrauded the company<br>• He's never made a sale<br>• He stole Jim's iPod |
| PAM | • Michael likes her<br>• She's a fast learner | • She doesn't always follow through, like art school and Roy<br>• When she's tired, she can get a little shrill |

*(Casual Friday)*

- At the shareholder meeting, Michael promises a forty-five-point, forty-five-day plan to get the company back on track and says the company is going completely carbon-neutral.

*(Shareholder Meeting)*

- After he hires his incompetent nephew, Luke, Michael claims mixing family and business is a beautiful thing.

*(Nepotism)*

45

Michael says you have to play the cards you're dealt, then lists some of the staff members and the cards they represent to him:

JIM: Ace

DWIGHT: King up my sleeve

PHYLLIS: Old maid

OSCAR: My queen

TOBY: The instruction card you throw away

PAM: A solid seven

RYAN: A two

MICHAEL: The joker

*(WUPHF.com)*

## MICHAEL'S INAPPROPRIATE BEHAVIOR

At his worst, Michael is inappropriate and offensive. At his best, Michael is inappropriate and offensive. And no matter how many trainings or seminars he goes to, Michael never quite seems to learn his lesson.

✱ During a meeting with Jan, Michael taps her on the knee as he condescendingly says he wouldn't wish downsizing on Josh's men . . . or women, present company excluded. *(Pilot)*

✱ Michael pretends to be a character called Curly Joe Hitler. *(Pilot)*

✱ Michael tells Pam he checks the "jewels" every month. *(Pilot)*

✱ Michael speaks in an overexaggerated Indian accent to Kelly. *(Diversity Day)*

✱ In front of the women, Michael tells the team they are playing like a bunch of girls. *(Basketball)*

✱ Michael likes to forward inappropriate emails—like "Fifty Signs Your Priest Might Be Michael Jackson"—to staff. *(Sexual Harassment)*

✱ Michael thinks the photo of Stanley's daughter by his desk is a "centerfold in a Catholic schoolgirl outfit." *(Sexual Harassment)*

the office book of lists

* Michael is the first one out of the building when the fire alarm goes off, claiming that women are equal in the workplace by law and he'd have a lawsuit on his hands if he let the women out first. *(The Fire)*

* Michael tweaks Ryan's nipples as he calls him Mr. Egghead. *(The Fire)*

* Michael, dressed as Santa, comes into the Party Planning Committee meeting and says, "Ho! Ho! Ho! Pimp!" pointing to each of the women and then to Ryan. *(Christmas Party)*

* When Oscar calls in sick on Spring Cleaning Day, Michael tells him that they could use "some of that famous Hispanic cleaning ethic." *(The Secret)*

* Michael tells Pam her hair is much sexier when it's down. *(The Secret)*

* Michael says he likes Hooters for two reasons—the boobs and the hot wings. *(The Secret)*

* Michael orders a chicken breast at Hooters but tells the waitress to "hold the chicken." *(The Secret)*

* Michael plays with the blow-up doll in the warehouse and then finds out the warehouse staff put a color copy of his face on it. *(Boys and Girls)*

* Michael asks Dwight, "What's the difference between a salesman and a saleswoman? Boobs." *(Boys and Girls)*

* Michael tells Stanley his eighth-grade daughter is a "stone-cold fox." *(Take Your Daughter to Work Day)*

* Michael creates the username "Little Kid Lover" for an online dating service so people will know where his priorities are. *(Take Your Daughter to Work Day)*

* Michael tells Pam that the next time she is in the shower she should give her breasts a self-exam, as "those things are ticking time bags." *(Michael's Birthday)*

* Michael wants actual Boy Scouts to come to Casino Night, but Toby points out that it's a school night, there will be gambling and alcohol in a dangerous warehouse, and Hooters is catering. *(Casino Night)*

* ## Michael says, "No, AIDS is not funny. Believe me, I have tried." *(Casino Night)*

* Michael calls Oscar "faggy" for liking *Shakespeare in Love* more than *Die Hard*. *(Gay Witch Hunt)*

* Michael notes that he wouldn't call actually retarded people "retards," only his friends, when they act retarded. *(Gay Witch Hunt)*

* Michael says, "The company has made it my responsibility today to put an end to one hundred thousand years of being weirded out by gays." *(Gay Witch Hunt)*

- Before Pam's date with Alan, Michael tells Pam to unbutton her top button and let those things breathe. *(The Convention)*

- Michael tells Martin Nash to follow him and he will show him where "all the slaves work." *(The Merger)*

- Michael pretends to be a baby who wants milk in front of Hannah from the Stamford branch. "Because you know where milk comes from!" *(The Convict)*

- Michael sends out a Christmas card with his face Photoshopped over Carol's ex-husband's in a picture from her ski trip two years earlier. *(A Benihana Christmas)*

- Michael tells Pam he was afraid the reason Carol left him was that he didn't want to do the foreign and scary things in bed she wanted. *(A Benihana Christmas)*

- Michael has to mark the arm of the waitress he brings to the Christmas party, because he can't tell her apart from the other waitress. *(A Benihana Christmas)*

- Michael says Karen is very exotic looking and asks if her dad was a GI. *(The Merger)*

- Michael accidentally sends an inappropriate photo of his boss titled "Jamaican Jan Sun Princess" to the warehouse instead of to Todd Packer. *(Back from Vacation)*

- Michael Photoshops a picture to make it look like he and Ryan are on vacation in Egypt. *(Back from Vacation)*

the office book of lists

* Michael says, "With dissatisfied clients, it doesn't matter what you did. All they wanna hear is that you're sorry. They're like women that way. And this client is a woman. So when I say I'm sorry, it will be twice as effective."

*(Product Recall)*

* In the conference room, Michael questions, "Orgasms . . . why can't women have them?" *(Women's Appreciation)*

* Michael tells Phyllis and Karen that if they keep hanging out, they will share the same menstrual cycle. *(The Merger)*

* At the sex shop, Michael can't stop giggling and tries to poke Ryan with a dildo. *(Ben Franklin)*

* Michael claims, "She who denied it, supplied it" on Phyllis's wedding day. *(Phyllis' Wedding)*

* In his apology video about the watermark with cartoon characters having sex, Michael calls it "our embarrassing watermark boner." *(Product Recall)*

* Michael laughs and giggles about Phyllis getting flashed. *(Women's Appreciation)*

* Wanting proof that Toby isn't the flasher, Michael tells Toby to show his penis. *(Women's Appreciation)*

* Michael's safe word with Jan is "foliage." *(Women's Appreciation)*

* If the women in the office get mad, Michael asks them if they're on their period. *(Women's Appreciation)*

* Michael says if Pam wants to show more cleavage she should be able to, and he encourages that. *(Women's Appreciation)*

* Michael thinks Kevin doesn't want to be in the fun run because he's scared people will see his fat legs in shorts. *(Fun Run)*

* Michael tells everyone he thinks Ryan has a gay crush on him. *(Dunder Mifflin Infinity)*

* Michael tells Pam that in order to get hotter, she needs to take her glasses off. *(Did I Stutter?)*

* Michael tells the potential high school intern that Pam is the "office hottie" who will do him. *(Job Fair)*

* When Michael sees Karen on his lecture circuit, he is blown away at how big her baby bump is and keeps mentioning it and questioning if it is Jim's baby. *(Lecture Circuit)*

* As Michael introduces Charles Miner to Accounting, he tells him far too much about the department members' sexual history, but when he gets to Kevin, he says Kevin has no sexual history. *(New Boss)*

* Michael tells Pam that if she's lying, her baby will come out a liar, as babies inherit things through breast milk. *(The Meeting)*

* Michael calls Phyllis dressed as Santa "Tranny Clause." *(Secret Santa)*

* Jim reminds Michael he can't say, "I need this, I need this" as he pins down an employee on his lap. *(Secret Santa)*

* When Ryan says he knows he's tapped Michael financially, Michael says he's tapped him hard. *(WUPHF.com)*

## MICHAEL'S "GOOD IDEAS" FOLDER

Michael Scott is convinced that almost every idea he has is a good one. He once asked Pam if she was, by any chance, writing his daily ideas down in a "Michael Idea" folder. We think that if we were to look into that mythical folder, we'd have a pretty good idea of what we might see.

* Michael has a special filing cabinet for things from Corporate—the waste-basket. *(Pilot)*

* To promote his version of diversity, Michael creates "race cards" that the staff members put to their foreheads. They have to guess which race they are portraying based on how others treat them. *(Diversity Day)*

* Operation: Surprise is Michael's attempt to do something nice for his staff when they get upset about the reduced health care benefits. He investigates a trip to Atlantic City and a tour of a mine shaft before settling on ice cream sandwiches. *(Health Care)*

* When trying to keep the potential downsizing from affecting the staff, Michael implements Operation: Morale Improvement—a birthday party for the next person with a birthday. *(The Alliance)*

* Michael tells Jan he has weekly meetings about the suggestions in the suggestion box. They find suggestions about Y2K preparations and from a deceased employee. *(Performance Review)*

* A guy named Phil recruits Michael to sell prepaid calling cards, and Michael tries to get three more people in the office to sell them. He insists this is not a pyramid scheme. *(Michael's Birthday)*

* Michael gets an email from the son of the deposed king of Nigeria asking for help and Michael sends him money. *(Michael's Birthday)*

* Michael hires fire-eaters for Casino Night in the warehouse. *(Casino Night)*

* Michael basically decorates his condo for free with convention swag. *(The Convention)*

- Michael wants a statue of Ed Truck—with eyes that light up and arms that move—to properly honor a man who gave his life as regional manager. *(Grief Counseling)*

- Michael wants to make a calendar of the "Ladies of Dunder Mifflin." *(Women's Appreciation)*

- Michael suggests adding graphics like a storm cloud or fireworks to the quarterly reports since they're so boring. *(Launch Party)*

- When Michael is having money problems, he asks Kevin for gambling advice on some sure things. *(Money)*

- Michael tells Ryan he is opening a restaurant called Mike's Cereal Shack, and it will have as many varieties of cereal as you can buy in the store. *(Local Ad)*

- When Stanley wants to transfer, Michael decides to go on a "panty raid" to Utica and poach Karen's top salesperson. Dwight and Michael wear ladies' warehouse worker outfits and fake mustaches and try to steal the industrial copier before Karen catches them. *(Branch Wars)*

- Michael puts his face in the drying cement outside the office. *(Did I Stutter?)*

- After his altercation with Stanley, Michael suggests that the sales staff call their loyal clients' assistants, find out their clients' addresses, and then go caroling to their clients' houses in the middle of summer as a summer Christmas sale-abration, called a Summer Sales-A-Lot. *(Did I Stutter?)*

- Michael's grandmother starts sending him birthday checks nine or ten times a year and Michael thinks he should use the money to buy a motorcycle. *(Job Fair)*

- Michael wants something big to help send off Toby at Toby's goodbye party. He wants to feel like he's flying through the air without an ugly weight holding him down—he wants an anti-gravity machine, and Phyllis is tasked with finding him one. *(Goodbye, Toby)*

- Michael asks Oscar to explain a budget surplus to him like he's a five-year-old running a lemonade stand. *(The Surplus)*

- Michael thinks the "golden ticket" promotion from *Willy Wonka* was the greatest idea ever, so he inserts five tickets into "random" paper shipments on the same pallet. Their largest client gets all five and demands 50 percent off their total order. *(Golden Ticket)*

Michael gives Pam a list of places he is and things he is doing for her to use whenever he needs to skirt a phone call. The list includes:

1) Civil rights rally at the Lincoln Memorial
2) Stopping a fight in the parking lot
3) An Obama fashion show
4) Having a colonoscopy
5) Trapped in an oil painting (Pam is saving that one)

*(Golden Ticket)*

## DID YOU KNOW?

Michael tries to prove to David Wallace that he has better ideas than Dwight, like the Toilet Buddy—a net that catches things like change and a wallet from falling into the toilet. It was formerly known as the Toilet Guard. He also has an idea for the Toilet Sponge, which is more absorbent than toilet paper. Dwight responds with ideas for women's urinals and a horse boat—a canoe built around a horse to go from riding to water travel. *(Golden Ticket)*

After Michael tells everyone Stanley is having an affair, Michael tries to spread fake rumors to keep Stanley from finding out. He tells people:

- Michael has an idea for a fancy men's shoe store called Shoe La La. *(Golden Ticket)*

- Michael goes to his nana's investment club to get funding to start his paper company. *(Dream Team)*

1) Kelly is "anorexitec."

2) Erin isn't a good worker.

3) Andy is gay.

4) Creed has asthma.

5) Oscar is the voice of the Taco Bell dog.

6) Toby is a virgin.

7) There is another person inside of Kevin working him with controls.

8) Dwight uses store-bought manure.

9) Someone is a J.Crew model. (Michael meant to say that it was him, but people thought it was Jim.)

10) Pam is pregnant. (This is true, though Jim and Pam haven't told anyone.)

*(Gossip)*

- When the Michael Scott Paper Company doesn't go well on his first day, Michael wonders if he should leave to form a new company. *(The Michael Scott Paper Company)*

- Michael color-codes his sales info—green means "go" so he knows to "go ahead and shut up about it." Orange means "orange you glad you didn't bring it up." Most of his colors actually mean "don't say it." *(Heavy Competition)*

- Michael has an idea for chair pants, so when you sit down you're supported. *(Company Picnic)*

- Jim stops Michael from building Tube City in the office with a lot of plastic hamster tubes and hamsters. *(Murder)*

- Michael comes up with a T-shirt idea called "Goodbyes stink." *(Goodbye, Michael)*

Michael brings a lot of things to put in "happy" and "sad" boxes in case Holly doesn't break up with A.J.:

**HAPPY**
Champagne
Gummi Worms
Tickets to Paula Poundstone
Party hat and noisemaker
Confetti

**SAD**
Sponge (to soak up his tears)
Gummi Bears
Ukuleles (to break)
Two bottles of scotch

*(Ultimatum)*

## MICHAEL'S VOCABULARY

Michael's vocabulary is somewhat legendary in the office. Ryan even gives the camera crew a sound bite designed to let them insert a montage of Michael mispronouncing words and phrases. Still, whether he is "improversationing" something or making sure he isn't the "escape goat," Michael always manages to get his point across.

- Michael mispronounces "incalculable" as "incalculacable." *(Pilot)*

- Michael questions if "open-mindedness" is even a word. *(Diversity Day)*

- Michael tells Stanley that collard greens are "colored greens"—after all, you wouldn't call them "collared people"—that would be offensive. *(Diversity Day)*

- Michael greets Oscar with "buena vista." *(Diversity Day)*

- Michael feels that generosity and togetherness and community all "convalsences" into morale. *(The Alliance)*

- Michael complains to Jan that a cheap health care plan won't be popular around the old "orifice." *(Health Care)*

- Appearing suave, Michael tells Katy he calls Starbucks "the 'Bucks." *(Hot Girl)*

- Michael tells the staff he will probably be "burning the midnight tequila" tonight. *(The Client)*

- Michael wants everyone to get their "constructive compliments" into the suggestion box ASAP. *(Performance Review)*

- Creed corrects Michael on his use of "infer" versus "imply." *(Performance Review)*

- Michael wonders if he needs to be more "approachabler." *(Email Surveillance)*

- Michael wonders where his "evitation" to Jim's barbecue is. *(Email Surveillance)*

- If Dwight agrees to hang out with him, Michael agrees to watch "Battleship Galaxy," or whatever stupid show he wants. *(Email Surveillance)*

- Michael misunderstands Darryl's analogy of the Sales department being like the "sails" of the office ship. Michael thinks Sales is the furnace of the ship, like on the *Titanic*. *(The Injury)*

- Michael says that determining whether the captain or the manager has a higher rank is "nebulose." *(Booze Cruise)*

- Michael claims he is taking medication called "vomicillin." *(Booze Cruise)*

- Michael jokes that he is "collar-blind" about working with white- and blue-collar workers. *(Boys and Girls)*

- Michael calls New York City the "City of Love." *(Valentine's Day)*

- Since Casino Night is for charity, Michael thinks he's a great "philanderer." *(Casino Night)*

- Michael thinks he will donate his Casino Night winnings to "Afghanistanis" with AIDS. *(Casino Night)*

- Michael thinks "faggy" means lame. *(Gay Witch Hunt)*

- Michael wants Dwight to see if Josh has any skeletons in his attic. *(The Convention)*

- Michael spits out the samosas at the Diwali celebration, saying they are disgusting for s'mores. *(Diwali)*

- Michael tells Toby he is holding an "orientation, not a boreientation." *(The Merger)*

- After getting an electric shock, Michael has an "epiphery." *(Ben Franklin)*

- Michael says Bob and Phyllis's celebrity name would be "Phlob" or "Blyllis." *(Phyllis' Wedding)*

- Michael doesn't know how to make a safety presentation on depression sexy and says, "That is the conun . . . the conun . . . the conumbery." *(Safety Training)*

- Michael says it is Jan's "periagative" not to like the message he left on her voicemail in which he breaks up with her. *(Women's Appreciation)*

- Michael thinks that in ten years he will have a remote that works everything in his ear like a "gluetooth." *(The Job)*

- Michael thinks the saying is "Home is where the hardest," until Oscar explains the saying is "Home is where the heart is." *(The Job)*

- Paraphrasing "William Randolph Shakespeare," Michael declares, "Love doth be poison." *(A Benihana Christmas)*

- Michael asks the staff if they are familiar with the Jamaican term "hakuna matata." *(Back from Vacation)*

- Andy tries to convince Michael that "Schruted it" means when you screwed something up in a really irreversible way. *(Traveling Salesman)*

- Michael says the early worm gets the worm. *(Cocktails)*

- Michael tells Jan everyone there is "gruntled." *(The Negotiation)*

- Jan has told Michael not to say "yeppers." *(The Negotiation)*

- Michael reads from the safety manual that a "sedimentary" lifestyle is a particular concern for office workers. *(Safety Training)*

- Michael thinks that the clients angry over the watermark are trying to make him into an "escape goat." *(Product Recall)*

- When Pam changes Meredith's tire, Michael asks if she needs a "crescent Allen" tool. *(Women's Appreciation)*

- Michael misquotes the Bible verse as "Forgiveness is next to godliness." *(Fun Run)*

- Michael thinks getting Sue Grafton in their commercial would be a big "coupe." *(Local Ad)*

- When trying to survive in the "wilderness," Michael cuts his clothes shorter with a knife and worries about cutting his "corroded" artery. *(Survivor Man)*

When Michael is deposed about Jan's firing, he gets a lot of legal terms mixed up:

1) He says the timing of Jan's dismissal is nothing short of "predominant."

2) He tells Ryan he would "abso-fruitly" do anything for the company.

3) He says Jan is completely "rightful" in her actions, since she doesn't consider him to be her boyfriend.

*(The Deposition)*

- Michael calls Jan's "bonfire" candle "James Bondfire." *(Dinner Party)*

- At his dinner party, Michael says the wine has a sorta "oaky afterbirth." *(Dinner Party)*

- Michael tells Andy and Kevin he "shorn't" help them with their parking issue. *(Chair Model)*

- When he congratulates Ryan on Dunder Mifflin Infinity, Michael says that at a time "TDB," all the problems will be in the past. *(Night Out)*

- Michael plans to "euthanize" the office by finding a high school intern. *(Job Fair)*

- Michael downloads some "N3Ps" for a mix CD. *(Goodbye, Toby)*

- Michael thinks Justin the high school student could be a "migraine" worker. *(Job Fair)*

- Both Michael and Holly say, "Ex-squeeze me." *(Weight Loss)*

- Michael jokes with Holly about going to the gym and getting on the "dread-mill." *(Weight Loss)*

- Unhappy with Phyllis's planning for Jan's baby shower, Michael reminds Phyllis that the staff gave her a "golden shower" for her wedding, and he wants to know where *his* golden shower is. *(Baby Shower)*

- Michael tells Holly that Jan is in the "terminal" stages of her pregnancy. *(Baby Shower)*

- When reviewing Jim's customer service scores, Michael reads that Jim is "smudge and arrogance." *(Customer Survey)*

- Michael says that to get Jim and Dwight's service scores up, he needs to manage them with a micro form of management. He asks Jim what that would be called and Jim replies "microgement." *(Customer Survey)*

- Michael tests Pam's chair and says it is "erklenomically" correct. *(The Surplus)*

- Michael calls an improvised conversation an "improversation." *(The Duel)*

- Michael says "Live and let live" is from *James Bond*. *(Prince Family Paper)*

- Michael thinks "hedded" is the past tense of "heed." *(Stress Relief)*

- Jim roasts Michael for using words beyond Jim's vocabulary, like spider-face—as in "Cut off your nose to spider-face." *(Stress Relief)*

- After the roast, Michael sends a text to Dwight saying he is taking a "personnel day." *(Stress Relief)*

- Michael thinks Cupid shoots "sparrows," funny little birds that get the job of love done. *(Blood Drive)*

- Michael's responsibility as manager is to "profiligate" great ideas. *(Golden Ticket)*

- After twelve years at Dunder Mifflin, Michael doesn't know what a pallet is. *(Golden Ticket)*

- Michael calls Charles "hypercritical" for saying no more parties and then bringing in lunch. *(New Boss)*

- When Michael arrives in the conference room to discuss the buyout, he says, "How the turntables . . ." *(Broke)*

- Michael says the new Michael Scott is not to be "truffled" with. *(Casual Friday)*

- After the staff tricks Michael into thinking it's five o'clock, he says they should all go home and he will see them all "tamale." *(Company Picnic)*

- Michael thinks he is a matchmaker and says the office is like "Spaniard fly." *(Gossip)*

- Michael tells Jim to "enliven" him on what his weaknesses are. *(The Promotion)*

- Michael says the staff has a "heart-on" for him and Jim. *(The Promotion)*

- Michael says he will see the staff up in "Viagra Falls" for Jim and Pam's wedding. *(Niagara)*

- Michael censors his story of giving Pam's mother, Helene, a necklace due to "inappropriosity." *(Double Date)*

- Michael, dressed as Jesus, tells David how Jesus heals "leopards." *(Secret Santa)*

- Michael thinks Pam's friend Julie teaches "ESP," not ESL. *(Happy Hour)*

- Michael confuses Guantanamo Bay with Montego Bay. *(Whistleblower)*

- Michael says he won't believe something from one of Andy's "spermed" lovers. *(Whistleblower)*

- Unable to say "herpes" on the phone, Michael spells it "H-I-R-P-E-E-S." *(Sex Ed)*

## MICHAEL'S MOVIES

Michael loves movies and TV shows. In fact, it might be fair to say he spends much of his life believing the tropes of movies and TV shows are happening to him. He also often records ideas for films on a small tape recorder. Michael's taste runs the gamut from *Home Alone* (the saddest movie ever made) to *The Devil Wears Prada*. He takes any opportunity to make presentations into videos or music videos, and ultimately he uses his staff to produce his own action film—*Threat Level Midnight*.

- Unhappy with (and reprimanded by) Mr. Brown's diversity training, Michael makes his own training film, *Diversity Tomorrow*. *(Diversity Day)*

- The office staff discovers that Michael has been working on a screenplay for his action film, *Threat Level Midnight*. *(The Client)*

- Michael's preparation for his financial presentation for Corporate includes a video called *The Faces of Scranton*. Michael adds a slide at the end crediting a production company called Great Scott Films International. *(Valentine's Day)*

- Michael used to be in a kid's show called *Fundle Bundle*. *(Take Your Daughter to Work Day)*

- Michael says the only cure for Monday blues is *Varsity Blues* on Movie Monday. *(The Coup)*

- Pam explains that Movie Mondays started with training videos, then continued with a medical video, half-hour installments of various movies, and one episode of *Entourage* that Michael made them watch six times. *(The Coup)*

the office book of lists

- Michael makes everyone watch *Lazy Scranton* as an orientation video for the Stamford transfers. *(The Merger)*

- Jim remembers his orientation video was *The Scranton Witch Project*. *(The Merger)*

- After Michael accidentally shocks himself, he makes a video about life for his future son, which includes topics like how to jump-start a car and how to take off a woman's bra—Pam won't let him practice on her, so he has to practice on Dwight. *(Ben Franklin)*

- Michael likes Pam to run the camera when he makes apology videos. He says he needs a woman's touch. She likes the apology video Michael made for missing his mom's birthday but would like to forget the one he made for his condo association about swimming naked in the pool. *(Product Recall)*

- Michael loves *What a Girl Wants*, starring Amanda Bynes. *(Beach Games)*

- Michael thinks *Home Alone* is the saddest movie ever. When Pam asks why, he says, "Because the whole family forgets the kid at home. There is nothing funny about that." *(Grief Counseling)*

- Michael acts like Meryl Streep's character after watching *The Devil Wears Prada*. *(Money)*

- Michael explains how John McClane is different in *Die Hard* and in *Die Hard 4* to his coworkers at the diet pill telemarketing firm. *(Money)*

- Michael (or Jan) buys *The Muppet Show* on DVD. *(Money)*

- Jim premieres the real Dunder Mifflin commercial—the "Michael Scott Director's Cut"—in Poor Richard's Pub's DVD player. *(Local Ad)*

- Michael loves the video where the dog nurses the tiger cub. *(Baby Shower)*

- Michael learned a lot of lessons from *Scream 2*, including that having Toby come back to work is like when Neve Campbell goes to college and then the murderer comes back. *(Frame Toby)*

- Michael has difficult decisions like deciding whether or not to rent *The Devil Wears Prada* again or to finally getting around to seeing *Sophie's Choice*. *(Casual Friday)*

- Erin and Pam play *Mr. Bean* in the conference room and *The Pink Panther* in Michael's office to get ahead of his broken heart over Donna. *(The Chump)*

- Michael makes a sad video and a happy video, depending on whether Holly breaks off her engagement with A.J. *(Ultimatum)*

- While considering breaking up with Holly, Michael has an idea for a movie called *Boner Bomb*, starring Jason Statham, or going against type and starring an Eisenberg or Michael Cera. Tagline: "Saving the world has never been this hard." *(PDA)*

**The CAST**

Michael Scott.......................................................................Michael Scarn

Dwight ....................................................................... Samuel, robot butler

Darryl.........................................................................President of the USA

Stanley ................................................................................... Narrator

Creed ...................................................... Hockey trainer, Cherokee Jack

Oscar............................................................................Civilian skater #1

Jim.....................................................................................Goldenface

Ryan ...................................................................... Hockey announcer

Toby (who was a wanted animal rapist), Kevin, Kelly, Pam.............Hostages

Jan..............................................Jasmine Windsong, singer at the Funky Cat

Helene Beesly ............................................................. Hospital nurse

Troy .....................................................................Goldenface's henchman

Andy ........................................................................Billy the bartender

Karen.......................................................................Bachelorette #1

Meredith, Phyllis, Angela .........................................................Bachelorettes

Todd Packer.................................................................................Bar drunk

● Michael finally premieres *Threat Level Midnight*. It takes Michael ten years to make *Threat Level Midnight*—three years of writing, one year of shooting, four years of reshooting, and two years of editing. *(Threat Level Midnight)*

the office book of lists

## DWIGHT'S QUOTES

FACT: Dwight has some of the most memorable lines among the Dunder Mifflin staff.

- When Dwight annoys Jim, who is on the phone with a client, Dwight claims, "Retaliation. Tit for tit." *(Diversity Day)*

- Dwight is unconcerned about the health care plan, since "in the wild, there is no health care. In the wild, health care is 'Ow, I hurt my leg. I can't run. A lion eats me and I'm dead.' Well, I'm not dead. I'm the lion. You're dead." *(Health Care)*

- Dwight remarks, "One thing about deer, they have very good vision. One thing about me, I am better at hiding than they are . . . at vision." *(The Alliance)*

- Angry that someone wrote something about Michael on the bathroom stall of the women's bathroom, Dwight declares, "Having a bathroom is a privilege. It is called a ladies' room for a reason. And if you cannot behave like ladies, well then you are not going to have a bathroom." *(The Dundies)*

- Dwight declares that his purple belt is not a toy. "This is a message to the entire office so that everyone can see that I am capable of physically dominating them."

*(The Fight)*

- Dwight says, "Yankee Swap is like Machiavelli meets Christmas."

*(Christmas Party)*

- Dwight thinks, "Woman are like wolves. If you want a wolf, you have to trap it. You have to snare it. And then you have to tame it. Keep it happy. Care for it. Feed it. Lovingly, the way an animal deserves to be loved. And my animal deserves a lot of loving." *(Valentine's Day)*

- Dwight insists that Michael has to take a drug test. "That is the law, according to the rules." *(Drug Testing)*

- Despite Andy's attempt at a friendship with Dwight, Dwight insists, "I will never be your vichyssoise." *(Women's Appreciation)*

- Dwight says, "It just goes to show you—you play with fire and you are gonna singe your eyebrows. And they do not grow back the same way." *(The Merger)*

- "Are you trying to hurt my feelings?" Dwight asks. "Because if so, you are succeeding. Fortunately, my feelings regenerate at twice the speed of a normal man's." *(Lecture Circuit)*

- Dwight declares, "Do you know who the real heroes are? The guys who wake up every morning and go into their normal jobs, and get a distress call from the commissioner, and take off their glasses and change into capes and fly around fighting crime. Those are the real heroes." *(The Negotiation)*

- Dwight observes, "Your heart is a wonderful thing, Michael. But it has made some terrible decisions." *(Prince Family Paper)*

- Dwight boasts, "Nothing stresses me out. Except having to seek the approval of my inferiors." *(Stress Relief)*

- Dwight clarifies to Michael that "any really good headhunter would storm your village at sunset with overwhelming force and cut off your head with a ceremonial knife." *(Two Weeks)*

- When meeting with Dwight's biggest client and keeping Dwight on the phone to hear, Michael says, "What is that thing that Dwight always says? Paper is the soil in which the seeds of business grow?" Dwight, in his car, yells out, "It's not the soil! It's the manure! Paper is the manure! On-time delivery is the soil!" *(Heavy Competition)*

- Dwight ponders a paradox: "Jim is my enemy. But it turns out that Jim is also his own worst enemy. And the enemy of my enemy is my friend. So Jim is actually my friend. But . . . because he is his own worst enemy, the enemy of my friend is my enemy. So, actually, Jim is my enemy." *(Koi Pond)*

- Dwight speculates, "In an ideal world, I would have all ten fingers on my left hand so my right hand could just be a fist for punching." *(Scott's Tots)*

- "R is among the most menacing of sounds," Dwight points out. "That's why they call it 'murder' and not 'mukduk.'" *(Mafia)*

- Dwight tells Michael, "You couldn't handle my undivided attention." *(New Leads)*

- Dwight complains that in following in Michael's footsteps for his career path, he hitched his wagon to "a horse with no legs." *(New Leads)*

- When scheming to keep Kelly out of the minority executive program, Dwight wishes, "Just once, I would like to be a puppet master and have nothing go wrong. Is that too much to ask?" *(Body Language)*

the office book of lists

- When he gets complaints about the half-ply toilet paper he provided to the building, Dwight sneers, "I'm sorry, isn't that good enough for your anus? Don't get me started on how coddled the modern anus is." *(China)*

- After losing another chance at becoming regional manager, Dwight laments, "Always the Padawan, never the Jedi." *(Michael's Last Dundies)*

- After Deangelo yells at him, Dwight admits, "Okay, a little about me. I respond to strong leadership." *(Inner Circle)*

- Dwight asks, "Who is Justice Beaver?" *(Todd Packer)*

- When trying to inspire the others to lift things in the warehouse, Dwight says, "Grunting is scientifically proven to add more power. Ask any female tennis player. Or her husband." *(Lotto)*

- When he first sees Angela's baby, Dwight adores him. "Oh, yes. Oh, what a beautiful child. Prominent fore-head, short arms, tiny nose. You will lead millions . . . [whispers] willingly, or as slaves. That baby is a Schrute. And unless somebody taught Mose sex, that baby is mine." *(Jury Duty)*

• Dwight dismisses Ryan's presentation, saying, "PowerPoints are the peacocks of the business world. All show, no meat."

*(Special Project)*

- When deciding whether to accept Nellie as manager, Dwight says he wouldn't let her manage a celery farm. After all, "those who can't farm, farm celery." *(Get the Girl)*

• Dwight says, "I wonder if king-sized sheets are called presidential-sized in England. I really should have a Tweeter account." *(Welcome Party)*

- When teaching Erin phrases in Dothraki, Dwight explains, "People laughed at Klingon at first, and now you can major in it." *(Andy's Ancestry)*

- Dwight points out, "I can't hire Clark. Yeah, he looks like a Schrute, but he thinks like a Halpert and he acts like a Beesly." *(Junior Salesman)*

- After Pam's mural is vandalized, Dwight says, "If there's anything I hate worse than art, it's crime." *(Vandalism)*

- When Andy is gone for three months, Dwight says, "I really like Andy these days. He's pretend, and he does exactly as I tell him to." *(Couple's Discount)*

## DWIGHT'S PRANKS AND SCHEMES

Dwight never takes Jim's pranks lying down. He fights back valiantly and sometimes does get the best of Jim in their prank wars. He also continually schemes to get what is rightfully his. Whether it's obtaining the regional manager position or remaining top salesman, Dwight never hesitates to stoop to any low to achieve his goals.

- Dwight shreds paper loudly while Jim is on the phone with his biggest client. He then steals the client by offering him a discount. *(Diversity Day)*

- After Dwight's secret meeting with Jan, Michael tests him by claiming Jan demoted Michael and will be calling Dwight to make him acting manager. *(The Coup)*

- Dwight says that in order to defeat his enemy, he must become his own worst enemy so he comes to work dressed and acting like Jim. *(Product Recall)*

**DID YOU KNOW?**

Dwight institutes a system of demerits—three demerits means you receive a citation. Five citations and you're looking at a violation. Four violations and you receive a verbal warning. Keep it up and you're looking at a written warning. Two of those land you in a world of hurt, in the form of a disciplinary review written by Dwight and placed on the desk of his immediate superior. Dwight gives Jim a demerit for tardiness. Jim then wants a copy of the demerit on his desk by the end of the day, or Dwight will receive a full "disadulation," which he declines to explain to Dwight. *(Women's Appreciation)*

- Dwight puts Imodium (instead of Ex-Lax) in Toby's coffee before the fun run. *(Fun Run)*

- Michael and Dwight conspire to sell Holly an elevator pass. *(Goodbye, Toby)*

- Dwight, Meredith, and Mose put a raccoon in Holly's car to haze her. *(Goodbye, Toby)*

- Dwight buys Andy's Xterra to flip it for a profit. *(Did I Stutter?)*

- Dwight tells Holly that the office hired Kevin as part of a special work program since he was "slow, you know, in his brain." *(Goodbye, Toby)*

- To force Phyllis to burn calories for the weight loss competition, Dwight takes her to see a client and strands her at an abandoned warehouse five miles away so she has to walk. *(Weight Loss)*

- Dwight pretends he is applying to Cornell to make Andy mad. When Andy pretends he has opened Bernard Farms, which produces the "best beets in the state," Andy is unable to bite into a raw beet, though Dwight can. *(Employee Transfer)*

- Dwight offers to be the "desirable" bait to catch Toby in an act of sexual harassment. Dwight mentions it's a good thing he's wearing his mustard shirt. *(Frame Toby)*

- In his effort to frame Toby, Michael plants a caprese salad in Toby's desk. Dwight then calls the police as "Andrew Bernard" with a drug tip. *(Frame Toby)*

- To get Phyllis to give him the last signature he needs on his apology letter, Dwight tricks her into signing for a fake package. *(Stress Relief)*

65

**Dwight tells Michael a knock-knock joke:**

- Dwight tells Erin the building is haunted by the ghost of prostitute Haddie McGonagle, who taps people on the shoulder when they are the next to die. He then taps Erin on the shoulder. *(The Michael Scott Paper Company)*

"Knock, Knock."

"Who's there?"

"KGB."

"KGB—"

[Dwight slaps Michael.] "We will ask the questions!"

*(Golden Ticket)*

- Dwight offers to take Michael's company out to lunch at Alfredo's. Instead, he sneaks into their office, hides a dead fish, and steals Michael's Rolodex. *(Heavy Competition)*

- Dwight pays Erin to scream out that she won an art contest in front of Pam. *(Café Disco)*

- Dwight tricks Jim with an easily found listening device in a wooden duck so Jim doesn't find the other one in his pen. *(The Lover)*

- Dwight and Andy get into an escalating war of favors. *(Double Date)*

- Dwight has Andy suggest an Employee of the Month program as a scheme to get Jim fired. *(Scott's Tots)*

DUNDER MIFFLIN, INC.
EMPLOYEE
OF THE
MONTH
SCRANTON BRANCH

- Dwight receives Secret Santa gifts from someone and it's the same idea he planned for Osama bin Laden— pieces that, when assembled around him, form a jail! *(Secret Santa)*

- Dwight creates a "megadesk" while Jim is on paternity leave and gets hooked on it. *(St. Patrick's Day)*

- To recombine his megadesk, Dwight tries to get Jim to miss being at home with the baby by playing "Cat's in the Cradle." *(St. Patrick's Day)*

- Dwight offers to "milk" Pam when she can't find her breast pump. It turns out that Meredith took the pump, because she likes the way it feels. *(Secretary's Day)*

- After Jim hits him with a snowball, Dwight builds himself into a snowman and locks the building door, then pummels Jim with snowballs when he can't get back in the building. *(Classy Christmas)*

- Dwight rigs a present Jim thought was from Pam—addressed to "Pickles" from "Swiss Cheese"— that shoots a snowball at him. *(Classy Christmas)*

- Dwight tries to offer Packer a hot chocolate filled with laxative. *(Todd Packer)*

- Dwight tries to frame Jim for putting a porcupine in his desk. *(Christmas Wishes)*

- Dwight tries to frame Jim by painting "Jim is awesome" on his own car. He also writes "IDIOT" on his own forehead. Jim neglects to tell Dwight that Andy has decided not to penalize their bonuses for pranking each other. *(Christmas Wishes)*

- When Pam is out, Jim needs an audience to prank Dwight and thinks Stanley would work. Unknown to Jim, Stanley and Dwight have teamed up to steer Jim into meatball-based pranks that make him buy meatballs for them. *(Pool Party)*

- Pam and Dwight plan to haze Clark with plastic wrap. Pam plans for Dwight to put it on the toilet seat the next time Clark goes to the bathroom, but Dwight uses it to attempt to suffocate Clark. *(Junior Salesman)*

- When Dwight and Pam send Clark into the warehouse as a spy, Clark gets tied up with duct tape and "SPY you'll pay 4 this" is written on his chest. *(Vandalism)*

# DWIGHT'S ARMORY

Aside from being a martial arts enthusiast, Dwight loves weapons and keeps a veritable armory in his car and in the office.

- Dwight's spud gun shoots potatoes at sixty miles per hour. *(Conflict Resolution)*

- Dwight keeps a carving knife in the trunk of his car. *(A Benihana Christmas)*

- Dwight debates *nakiri* versus *usuba* knives with the chef at Benihana. *(A Benihana Christmas)*

- Dwight is unhappy that Michael didn't ask him to get his spud gun—which he keeps in a duffel bag in his car—to defend the office against the ex-convict. *(The Convict)*

- Dwight has his own crossbow range on his farm. *(Office Olympics)*

- Dwight offers to bring his bo staff in since he can't have a gun as a security officer. *(Drug Testing)*

- Every day for eight years, Dwight has brought pepper spray into the office and people have laughed at him. He finally uses it when Roy attacks Jim, so who's laughing now? *(The Negotiation)*

- After Roy attacks Jim, Jim says Roy was lucky Dwight didn't use the nunchucks or throwing stars. *(The Negotiation)*

- After Dwight pepper sprays Andy, Toby confiscates all the weapons in Dwight's desk, including a taser, nunchucks, a police baton, boomerangs, and cuffs. *(The Negotiation)*

- Dwight brings gasoline and chunks of rubber to make stink bombs (or real bombs) to prank the Utica branch. *(Branch Wars)*

**DUNDER MIFFLIN** INC.
PAPER COMPANY

Mr. A. Knife

- Dwight says he would stab the security guard in the eye with jumbo chalk if he needed to in order to defend himself. *(Branch Wars)*

- Dwight keeps a pair of *sais* behind the watercooler. *(Survivor Man)*

- Dwight keeps a knife filed under "Mr. A. Knife" in an accounting folder. *(Survivor Man)*

- Dwight unrolls a pack of knives to show Michael for Michael's camping trip. *(Survivor Man)*

- Dwight keeps a sword hidden above the ceiling tiles. *(Survivor Man)*

- The toilet tank assembly contains Dwight's blow dart. *(Survivor Man)*

- Dwight spies on Michael in the wilderness with the scope on his rifle. He says there is nothing to worry about, because the safety is on. Eventually. *(Survivor Man)*

- For his duel with Andy for Angela's hand in marriage, Andy suggests using bare hands. Dwight says he will use a sword to cut off Andy's bare hands. He ends up using a bike chain. *(The Duel)*

- Jim collects a scythe, a sword, a star-shaped thing under the kitchen table, and other weapons before Dwight's duel with Andy. *(The Duel)*

- Andy uses his car as his weapon in the duel against Dwight. By driving his Prius under five miles per hour, he is able to drive up silently behind Dwight and pin him to the fence. *(The Duel)*

- Dwight's crossbow is hidden under the reception area couch. *(The Duel)*

- Dwight keeps a knife strapped to his leg. *(Stress Relief)*

- Dwight fell on his sword once while running with it in his belt. It won't happen again. *(Golden Ticket)*

- While playing the murder mystery game, Dwight uses imaginary crossbows. *(Murder)*

- Dwight uses an "Apache persuasion hold" on Nick the IT guy. *(Whistleblower)*

- When the cast of *Sweeney Todd* invades the office, Dwight pulls his knife out. *(Andy's Play)*

- Dwight keeps his paintball gun, armor, and ammo in his trunk. *(Goodbye, Michael)*

- Nellie dares Dwight to use a cleaver to chop off her hand. *(Roy's Wedding)*

- Dwight keeps a pitchfork in his car. *(Vandalism)*

- Dwight uses a bull tranquilizer to knock Stanley out to go on a sales call. *(Stairmageddon)*

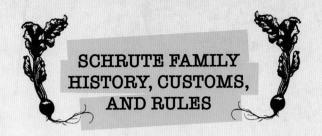

# SCHRUTE FAMILY HISTORY, CUSTOMS, AND RULES

The Schrutes are an Amish family of German descent—and that's where their connection to normalcy ends. Dwight abides strictly by the customs and traditions of his family, no matter how outlandish. Despite his upbringing—or perhaps because of it—he is one of the top salespeople at the Scranton branch, making enough money to one day purchase the Scranton Business Park building.

☛ Dwight's father's name was also Dwight Schrute and his grandfather's name was Dwide Schrude from the Amish. Dwight isn't sure where the Amish originally came from. He thinks from Amland. *(Pilot / Drug Testing)*

☛ Dwight claims to have superior genes and a perfect immune system. He can raise and lower his cholesterol at will. *(Health Care)*

☛ Dwight claims the Schrutes produce very thirsty babies. *(Hot Girl)*

☛ Dwight's grandfather left him a sixty-acre beet farm where he and his cousin Mose live. *(Office Olympics)*

☛ Dwight's grandfather was the toughest person he knew. He killed twenty men and spent the rest of World War II in an Allied prison camp. *(The Fight)*

☛ Dwight's father was also a fighter—he battled high blood pressure and obesity all his life. *(The Fight)*

☛ Dwight was a finalist in his sixth-grade spelling bee and lost to Raj Patel when he misspelled "failure." *(Dwight's Speech)*

☛ Dwight reads to the staff's daughters (and Jake) a book his grandmother read to him as a kid. *Struwwelpeter* by Heinrich Hoffman from 1864 tells the story of the tailor who cuts children's thumbs off. *(Take Your Daughter to Work Day)*

☛ Schrutes considered children very valuable. In the olden days, they could work the fields, and if there weren't enough grains and vegetables, the family could eat the weakest of the brood—but it never came to that. *(Take Your Daughter to Work Day)*

☛ A few years back, Dwight took a urine test to apply to be a volunteer sheriff's deputy and his urine was green. *(Drug Testing)*

☛ Every morning at dawn, Dwight's father made biscuits and gravy. He also cheated at the games he and Dwight played but didn't tell Dwight until years later. *(Drug Testing)*

☛ Dwight never smiles if he can help it. He explains that showing one's teeth is a submission signal in primates. *(Conflict Resolution)*

- Dwight's dad taught him how to find out who was gay and his grandfather taught him how to find communists. *(Gay Witch Hunt)*

- Dwight explains that the Schrutes are a very loyal breed. "But I also have Mannheim blood from my German grandmother. And the Mannheims knew when to cut and run. No sense going down with a losing regime. But the Schrute blood . . . It's amazing that when these two bloods mix that the whole thing didn't explode." *(The Coup)*

- Dwight wants to be frozen when he dies so he can wake up stronger and figure out how he died and what moves he could have used to defend himself better. *(Grief Counseling)*

- Dwight "resorbed" his twin as a fetus in the womb and he thinks he has the strength of a grown man and a little baby. *(Grief Counseling)*

- Dwight's grandfather was reburied in an old oil drum. *(Grief Counseling)*

- Dwight wonders if Ryan will be a slacker-loser-wiseass like Jim or part of the Dwight Army of Champions. *(The Convention)*

- Dwight says that many Schrutes were born on the farm and many ended up there. He shows Ryan the grave of his maternal grandfather, Heinrich Rolf Mannheim, and tells Ryan he was a good man who did some very bad things. *(Initiation)*

- Dwight brags that he weighed thirteen pounds, five ounces at birth and his mother couldn't walk for three months. *(The Convict)*

- Schrutes use every part of the goose. The meat has a delicious, smoky, rich flavor, plus they can save the molten goose grease in the refrigerator and avoid buying a can of expensive goose grease. *(A Benihana Christmas)*

- Dwight says it's not easy being a good mother—you need to be able to make a stew that feeds twelve and run a small schoolhouse. *(The Convict)*

- Schrutes usually marry standing in their own graves. *(Phyllis' Wedding)*

- Dwight was shunned by his family in the Amish tradition from the age of four until his sixth birthday for not saving the excess oil from a can of tuna. *(Safety Training)*

- Dwight has seen animals having sex in every position imaginable, so he thinks whoever drew the obscene watermark got it exactly right. *(Product Recall)*

- The first rule of roadside beet sales is to put the most attractive ones on top—the ones that make people pull over and say they need that beet right now. As Dwight says, "Those are the money beets." *(Product Recall)*

the office book of lists

**DID YOU KNOW?**

Dwight's Schrute Bucks idea came from his childhood. His family farm also ran a roadside store that sold irregular beets and clothing. The Schrute children got paid an allowance in Schrute Deutschmarks that allowed them to buy clothing and sundries, but the prices were terrible. Dwight still owes his great-aunt thousands of Schrute Deutschmarks, as she charged enormous interest on the debt. *(The Job)*

☞ Dwight's cousin Heimdall could have been a great athlete, but after buying an irregular pair of footie pajamas from the family store, his legs grew unevenly. Now, he can only run in broad elliptical patterns. *(The Job)*

☞ Mose's best friend was a dog. Dwight shot the dog, thinking it had rabies, but it had only eaten one of Mose's cream pies. Nevertheless, Dwight has no regrets. "That's how you deal with a thief." *(Fun Run)*

☞ Dwight's grandma Schrute lived to be 101, and his grandpa Mannheim is 103 and is still puttering around in Argentina. *(Dunder Mifflin Infinity)*

☞ Traditionally, when a Schrute male has sex with a woman, his parents reward him by leaving a bag of wild oats on his doorstep. *(Money)*

☞ Babies are one of Dwight's areas of expertise. He performed his own circumcision. *(Baby Shower)*

☞ The Schrute family believes in a five-fingered intervention: awareness, education, control, acceptance, and punching. *(Moroccan Christmas)*

☞ There are forty rules all Schrute boys have to learn by the age of five. If they didn't, they'd be eaten in their sleep. Rule #17: Don't turn your back on bears, men you have wronged, or the dominant turkey during mating season. *(The Duel)*

☞ Schrutes don't celebrate birthdays. This started as a Depression-era practicality, then moved on to an awesome tradition. *(Lecture Circuit)*

☞ Dwight wasn't given candy as a child or allowed to see movies. *(Golden Ticket)*

☞ Dwight's German is preindustrial and mostly religious. *(Two Weeks)*

☞ The massage remedy Dwight uses on Phyllis has been passed down in his family for generations. His grandfather used it on a racehorse named Diamond Dancer, who came in ninth place in the Apple Creek Derby. *(Café Disco)*

**DID YOU KNOW?**

All of Dwight's heroes are table tennis players. The first time he left Pennsylvania was to go to Andrzej Grubba's Hall of Fame induction ceremony. His other heroes include Zoran Primorac, Jan-Ove Waldner, Wang Tao, Jorg Rosskopf, Hugo Hoyama, and Ashraf Helmy. *(The Deposition)*

- Dwight says there is no Schrute book of niceness, only a survival guide. *(Double Date)*

- Dwight's family had a saying: "If 'onlys' and 'justs' were candies and nuts, then every day would be *Erntedankfest*." *(Shareholder Meeting)*

- To gain sympathy and up his sales, Dwight tells clients his cousin came down with that nasty new goat fungus. *(The Delivery)*

- Dwight had $30,000, but it was buried very deeply and he didn't want to dig past a certain someone to get it. *(The Chump)*

- In the Schrute family, the youngest child always raises the others. *(Viewing Party)*

- Every fall, Dwight's uncle Eldred would build a maze out of hay bales and call it Hay World. The kids called it Hay Place. Dwight always wanted to be Hay King, but "the world shines on Mose." At his own Hay Place, Dwight is finally crowned Hay King. *(WUPHF.com)*

- Dwight tells Deangelo he has seventy cousins—each one better than the last. *(The Inner Circle)*

- The Schrutes have a word for when everything in a man's life comes together—*perfectenschlag*. There's also a second definition for this term—"perfect pork anus." *(Special Project)*

- Dwight says Jim is like an Amish return stick when he keeps showing up. *(Last Day in Florida)*

- Dwight assumes silent auctions are like a Quaker fair, where you guess the price to win the prize, rather than bidding for it. He says it's the easiest game since Touch the Rock, which he has won three times. Almost four, but he touched the wood. *(Fundraiser)*

- As is Schrute custom for a funeral, Dwight sprinkles red, fertile dirt on people to invite them to his aunt Shirley's funeral and a dusting of black, slightly acidic soil to ask that they keep a respectful distance during his time of grief. *(The Farm)*

- Custom says that to court a woman, the man throws the beak of a crow at her, and if she's interested she destroys the beak. *(The Farm)*

- Dwight tests Phillip to see if he is his son by playing Schrute or Consequences. Phillip has to choose between two things: a check for a million dollars or a dirty old beet. Phillip chooses the beet. *(A.A.R.M.)*

- For Dwight's wedding, there is an old man to feed the bride and groom the cheese that has been fermenting since the day of Dwight's birth. *(Finale)*

- Jim is made *bestisch mensch* for Dwight's wedding. As such, he decides he will only play *guten pranken*, or good surprises, on Dwight. *(Finale)*

Dwight's cousin Mose is his self-proclaimed best friend and is often seen helping Dwight at Schrute Farms. Here's what little we know about him:

1) Mose can whittle figurines. *(Initiation)*

2) Mose has had nightmares ever since "the storm." *(Money)*

3) Mose describes Dwight going to work as him going to "the day place." *(Money)*

4) Mose doesn't know how to use a phone. *(Lecture Circuit)*

5) At Jim and Pam's wedding, Dwight worries about the farm, as Mose hates to geld the horses alone. *(Niagara)*

6) Mose can drive a moped, but thinks twice before attempting to jump it over a line of parked cars. *(Garden Party)*

7) Mose has a natural fear of paper. *(Junior Salesman)*

8) When interviewing for a job with Dunder Mifflin, Mose claims to have worked for Dow Chemical as a sales rep for fifteen years. *(Junior Salesman)*

9) Aunt Shirley implies that Mose married or had sex with his lady scarecrow. *(Moving On)*

10) Mose abducts Angela during her bachelorette party for a Brautenführung, the ceremonial bridal kidnapping. *(Finale)*

## DWIGHT'S HOBBIES

Dwight Schrute enjoys a lot of hobbies and interests. Some he names, like deer hunting, karate, and *Battlestar Galactica*, and some he demonstrates, like scheming to become regional manager and planning things like the perfect crime.

- Dwight can skin a mule deer in less than ten minutes. *(Moroccan Christmas)*

- Dwight became a *sempai*—or assistant sensei—for a while at his Goju-ryo karate dojo under Sensei Ira. *(The Fight)*

- Every year, Dwight holds a seminar updating the office on the newest developments in karate. *(Murder)*

- Dwight fancies himself a detective. He once tailed an ex-girlfriend for six nights straight and discovered she was cheating on him with a couple of guys. *(The Secret)*

- Dwight has a wig for every person in the office in case he needs to bear a passing resemblance to someone. *(Classy Christmas)*

- Dwight belongs to the Knights of the Night volunteer crime patrollers. *(Ultimatum)*

- Andy says "animal rankings" is one of Dwight's hobbies, along with survival skills. *(Mrs. California)*

- Dwight used to have an arctic wolf but lost it when he used a chain with three weak links. *(Special Project)*

- Dwight writes a lot of *X-Men* fan fiction. One character, Captain Mutato, is half man and half mermaid. *(Angry Andy)*

- Dwight plays the recorder. *(The Dundies)*

- Dwight plays laser tag on a team. *(Performance Review)*

- Dwight listens to heavy metal, especially when he prepares for important things like his reviews. *(Performance Review)*

- Dwight has a diary to keep secrets from his computer. *(Golden Ticket)*

- Dwight teaches Erin the Dothraki language from *Game of Thrones*. *(Andy's Ancestry)*

- Dwight used to collect cat turds, as each one is very different, like snowflakes. *(Suit Warehouse)*

- Dwight claims to play both soccer and clarinet, though both may just be excuses he gives Michael. *(Email Surveillance)*

- Dwight played Mutey the Mailman in his seventh-grade production of *Oklahoma*. *(The Client)*

- Dwight says he was the youngest pilot in Pan Am history. He explains, "The pilot let me ride in the cockpit and fly the plane with him." *(Booze Cruise)*

- Dwight won't tip for things he can do himself, like cut his own hair. He does tip his urologist because he can't pulverize his own kidney stones. *(Michael's Birthday)*

- Dwight orders deer urine over the internet. *(Conflict Resolution)*

- Dwight believes he'd do well in prison, as it is all about dominance and dominance is one of his fortes. *(The Convict)*

- When Dwight quits, he gives Ryan his *Farmers' Almanac*, Stanley his modified staple remover, Pam his pencil sharpener with a replaced motor, and Phyllis his ball of rubber bands since he knows she's had her eye on that. He gives Angela his chair that has great lumbar support. The rest of his belongings, except his bobbleheads, he gives to Michael. *(Traveling Salesman)*

the office book of lists

## DID YOU KNOW?

Dwight divides his résumé up into three separate ones: Professional Résumé; Athletic and Special Skills Résumé; and Dwight Schrute Trivia. *(The Return)*

- Dwight thinks Cornell is an excellent school, as without its agricultural program, modern cabbage wouldn't exist. *(Employee Transfer)*

- Dwight plans out the perfect crime: Steal the Tiffany's chandelier and make love to Tiffany, whose father owns the company. Escape disguised as a cop and flee to Canada. Thirty years later, he will find out he has a son who is chief of police. He will tell Tiffany, who waited for him all these years, to meet him in Paris, but instead he will go to Berlin, where he stashed the chandelier. *(Frame Toby)*

- While Dwight knows several ways to kill a zombie, the most satisfying method is to stab it in the brain with a wooden stick. *(Moroccan Christmas)*

- Dwight claims to a woman at the Lonely Hearts mixer that he can untie any knot. *(Blood Drive)*

- Dwight makes a homemade sunscreen / insect repellent with DEET. *(Company Picnic)*

- Dwight volunteers at the animal shelter and one Sunday he had to put down 150 pets all by himself. *(The Lover)*

- After Jo tells Dwight to invest in real estate, he buys the building at 1725 Slough Avenue . . . the Scranton Business Park building. *(Whistleblower)*

- Dwight decides to open a daycare in the building as a new revenue stream—the Sesame Avenue Daycare Center for Infants and Toddlers. It is located in the old Michael Scott Paper Company office. One of its main selling points is that the doors lock from the outside and escape is impossible. *(Counseling)*

- Dwight opens the pricey Dwight's Caffeine Corner in the entry of the building as he considers it a waste of space. *(China)*

- Dwight substitutes half-ply toilet paper in the building to cut costs. *(China)*

- Dwight opens Dwight Schrute's Gym for Muscles. *(Mrs. California)*

- Operation: Phoenix is Dwight's plan to determine whether he is the father of Angela's baby. *(Free Family Portrait Studio)*

- There's a phrase in German—*Bildenkinder*—used exclusively by childless landlords to console themselves and express that everyone in their building is kind of like their children. *(Work Bus)*

- When Dwight becomes regional manager, he installs a new security system, which makes steam blast out from above the door. *(A.A.R.M.)*

Dwight loves to make lists of things for various reasons. Many he keeps in a journal that he once shared with Pam. Here is a sampling of his many list-making activities:

- Dwight makes a "hot girl" checklist. *(Hot Girl)*

- Dwight compiles a list of marijuana symptoms that also applies to Kevin. *(Drug Testing)*

- When Dwight tries to figure out what his Secret Santa gift is, he makes a list. *(Secret Santa)*

- Dwight gives Jo a list of people who should be fired for leaking the malfunctioning printer information to the press, and apparently scores them in order of importance. *(Whistleblower)*

- Dwight lists the people who have had sex in the office. *(PDA)*

- Dwight has lists in his notebooks for both "If we were all on a cruise ship and had to divide into life boats" and "If we were all on a cruise ship and had to divide into life rafts," as well as "Who would eat who in an *Alive* situation," and compares them to Robert California's lists. None match. *(The List)*

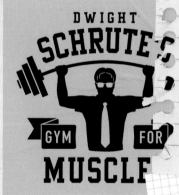

Dwight tricks everyone into signing a loyalty pledge, making them think it's their coffee order:

PHYLLIS: Banana fruit smoothie

STANLEY: Decaf (small)

DP: Double Latte (lotsa latte!)

OSCAR: Venti chai tea misto, half soy

KEVIN: Cap'n Chino

PETE: Cappuccino with cinnamon

CLARK: Tall & Black (like my women!)

NELLIE: Black Tea (any) with lemon (like my men!)

ERIN: Vanilla blendy thing (5 sugars)

M: Irish coffee, extra Irish!

CREED: Pastrami on rye, fries, coke, nothing to drink

*(Customer Loyalty)*

# JIM'S PRANKS AND SCHEMES

Jim has more time and energy to play elaborate pranks on Dwight (and sometimes others) than he does to do his work. As Jim tries to mature in his job, one thing that never gets old is pranking Dwight. Ultimately, he plays a prank that brings Dwight to tears . . . of happiness.

- When Dwight insists Jim keep his papers from overlapping onto his desk, Jim retaliates by placing a barrier of sharpened pencils in the crack between their desks. *(Pilot)*

- When Jim puts Dwight's stapler in Jell-O, it's the third time he's done that to Dwight's things. *(Pilot)*

- After Michael fake fires Pam, Jim puts Michael's "Best Boss" mug in Jell-O. *(Pilot)*

- Jim locks Dwight in the conference room he was using as his workspace. *(Health Care)*

- Jim pretends to have an alliance with Dwight so they can survive the potential downsizing. He convinces Dwight to hide in a box in the warehouse to overhear another alliance's plans. He also tries to convince Dwight he needs to dye his hair blonde and go to Stamford to spy on that branch. *(The Alliance)*

- Jim encourages Dwight to buy a purse. *(Hot Girl)*

- Pam and Jim write up Dwight's résumé and post it on Monster.com. It includes his "dog-like obedience to authority." *(Halloween)*

- Jim moves Dwight's entire desk into the men's room. *(The Fight)*

- Jim steals Dwight's purple belt. *(The Fight)*

- After learning its cost, Jim pops Dwight's exercise ball. *(Performance Review)*

- Jim takes advantage of Dwight's confusion and leads him to believe it's Friday when it's actually Thursday. *(Performance Review)*

- Jim places all of Dwight's desk supplies (including his nameplate, pencil cup, stapler, bobblehead, wallet, and photo frame) in the vending machine so he has to pay to get them back (but Pam buys the pencil cup first). *(Booze Cruise)*

- For Dwight's speech, Jim tells him to wave his arms and pound his fists to emphasize his point. He also "wrote up some talking points" for Dwight taken from speeches from some of history's famous dictators like Mussolini. *(Dwight's Speech)*

- Pam points out that Jim does the best impressions, including Stanley saying, "I enjoy the tangy zip of Miracle Whip," and Phyllis. *(Drug Testing)*

- When Dwight interrogates Jim about drug use, Jim turns it around on Dwight, reminding him that marijuana is a memory loss drug so Dwight wouldn't remember smoking it. *(Drug Testing)*

the office book of lists

- Jim types "Fart" as Dwight's middle name on his ID badge and identifies him as a security threat. *(Conflict Resolution)*

- Jim replaces all Dwight's pens and pencils with crayons. *(Conflict Resolution)*

- Jim pays everyone $5 to call Dwight "Dwayne" all day. *(Conflict Resolution)*

- Jim places a bloody glove in Dwight's desk drawer and tries to convince Dwight he's a murderer. *(Conflict Resolution)*

- Jim tells Dwight there's an abandoned infant in the women's room after Dwight sees Meredith going into the bathroom. *(Conflict Resolution)*

- Jim adds weight to Dwight's phone handset with nickels until he is used to the weight, then plans to take them out so Dwight will hit himself in the head. *(Conflict Resolution)*

- Jim makes a macro so that every time Dwight types his name it says "Diapers." *(Conflict Resolution)*

- Jim moves Dwight's desk an inch every time he goes to the bathroom. *(Conflict Resolution)*

- Jim convinces Dwight he's telekinetic. *(Casino Night)*

- On Casino Night, Jim makes Dwight think his tell during poker is coughing. *(Casino Night)*

- Jim tells Dwight he can buy "gaydar" online at Sharper Image. He then makes one and sends it to Dwight. *(Gay Witch Hunt)*

- Jim puts Andy's calculator in Jell-O. *(Gay Witch Hunt)*

- Sometimes, Jim and Pam hum the same high-pitched note and try to get Dwight to see an ear doctor for "pretendonitis." *(The Coup)*

- With their very limited free time (and very limited budget), Jim and Pam get a nanny and take a class on a very outmoded and very unnecessary form of communication, just so they can learn Morse code and talk about Dwight in front of him. *(The Cover-Up)*

- Jim takes a box of Dwight's stationery and from time to time sends him faxes claiming he is Dwight from the future sending faxes to Dwight in the past, with warnings like "Dwight, at 8 a.m. today, someone poisons the coffee." *(Branch Closing)*

- When Andy wants to ask Pam out, Jim tells him that Pam likes Frisbee-based competitions, hunting, the ads for Six Flags with the old guy, and pig Latin. He later tells Andy to play the banjo and sing "Rainbow Connection" to Pam. *(The Convict)*

- Jim takes Karen's chair and leaves her the squeaky chair. *(Initiation)*

- For months, Pam has been sending Dwight letters from the CIA to "recruit" him for a mission. Her Christmas gift to Jim is to have him decide which mission Dwight should go on. Ultimately, they make him go to the roof to wait for a helicopter. They then text Dwight and tell him the mission has been compromised and to destroy his phone, which he does. *(A Benihana Christmas)*

- While Michael is in Jamaica, Jim glues Dwight's desk drawers together, changes Dwight's voicemail so he sounds like a chipmunk, and tells him there is a meeting at 4 a.m., which only Dwight shows up for. *(Back from Vacation)*

- When Dwight was on vacation once, Jim had his desk shipped to him in Roswell. *(Back from Vacation)*

- Jim puts Andy's cell phone in the ceiling so when it rings Andy can hear it but can't find it. *(The Return)*

- Instead of getting a male stripper from Banana Slings, Jim calls Scholastic Speakers of Pennsylvania and gets a "Ben Franklin" to come to Phyllis's luncheon shower. Jim tells Dwight that the Ben Franklin speaker is really Ben Franklin, but Dwight is 99 percent sure it isn't the real Ben Franklin after questioning him. Maybe 98 percent. *(Ben Franklin)*

- Jim performs a Pavlovian experiment on Dwight to train him to want a mint whenever he hears the sound of a rebooting computer. *(Phyllis' Wedding)*

- Jim puts Dwight in charge of smoking out the crashers at Phyllis's wedding. *(Phyllis' Wedding)*

- Jim convinces Dwight that he has been bitten by the bat in the office. Dwight believes Jim has begun an "eternal journey" and is becoming a vampire. *(Business School)*

- Jim stencils a mustache on the bathroom mirror so that when Dwight looks in it he will realize the sketch Pam did of the sex predator is him with a mustache. *(Women's Appreciation)*

- Jim directs Karen into the lake when she is blindfolded during the egg and spoon race. *(Beach Games)*

- Jim makes Dwight think the new Dunder Mifflin website has come to life and is trying to destroy him when it comes to selling paper. *(Launch Party)*

- Jim pairs Dwight's cell phone to his headset (and forwards Dwight's desk phone to Jim's) and then impersonates Dwight on the phone to take some paper orders. *(Goodbye, Toby)*

Jim keeps everyone from telling Andy the answer to what candy bar jingle he's singing. Andy thinks it might be:

- Applesauce
- Chrysler car
- Football cream
- Lumbar tar
- Snickers bar
- Grey Poupon
- Claude Van Damme
- Hair for Men
- Poison gas
- NutraSweet

Andy decides it's actually Fancy Feast cat food. He never figures out it's actually a jingle for Kit Kat bars. *(Local Ad)*

the office book of lists

- Once Holly discusses time theft, Jim clocks how much time Dwight wastes yawning or having a conversation Jim deems personal. Jim later starts a conversation with Andy and mashes up the plots of *Battlestar Galactica* and *Lord of the Rings*. It makes Dwight crazy, but he's afraid to join in. *(Business Ethics)*

- Jim wraps Dwight's desk and everything on it in Christmas wrapping paper. However, when Dwight puts his briefcase down, the desk itself is gone and the paper collapses. *(Moroccan Christmas)*

- Jim sets up five hundred feet of red wire and Dwight follows it from his computer up to a telephone pole. *(Prince Family Paper)*

- When Michael learns that the phone has a PA function, he can't stop broadcasting to the office. Jim bends over, pretending he dropped something, and cuts the wire. Michael doesn't realize he's no longer broadcasting to the office. *(Lecture Circuit)*

- When Dwight sends out a memo about the dress code, Jim wears a tuxedo to work and Michael starts taking him more seriously. *(New Boss)*

- After Michael passes out from eating chicken potpie, Jim gets the entire office to change the clocks and convince Michael it's five o'clock so they can all leave. *(Company Picnic)*

- Jim plans a prank to make Dwight play out the plot of *National Treasure* but doesn't follow through. *(The Lover)*

- Jim convinces Dwight to show him how he would beat himself in karate. Dwight ends up punching himself in the groin. *(Murder)*

- Jim outdoes Dwight's megadesk with a quad-desk. *(St. Patrick's Day)*

- Jim plans to add a key to Dwight's key ring every day until his pants fall down at Christmas, but Pam accidentally messes it up. *(Nepotism)*

- To test how much Stanley doesn't notice things, Jim slips a cardboard box with a paper printout of a computer screen over Stanley's computer. *(Costume Contest)*

- Jim edits Jo's audiobook to insult Gabe, then calls Gabe to make him think it's actually Jo reading changes to her book. *(WUPHF.com)*

- Jim eggs Dwight on when he practices picking things up with his toes, until Dwight spills hot coffee on his crotch. *(China)*

- Jim gives Dwight a list of four hundred ideas to prank Packer when, really, he's trying to prove his original idea—of jamming Packer's desk drawer so he can see in but not reach anything—is best. *(Todd Packer)*

- Jim and Dwight convince Packer that Jo is going to give him a job in Tallahassee and that he should just hop the fence at Jo's house and wait at the pool. *(Todd Packer)*

- At the garage sale, Jim tricks Dwight into thinking Professor Copperfield's Miracle Legumes are real. *(Garage Sale)*

- After Dwight's gun goes off, the whole office blackmails him. Jim makes him do jazz hands any time he coughs. **(Dwight K. Schrute, (Acting) Manager)**

- Jim tells Dwight that Erin wants a hot chocolate tea when he can't remember her order. **(Lotto)**

**DID YOU KNOW?**

Jim's book on garden parties convinces Dwight to shout out people's names as they arrive. It also advises that he perform a courtly dance, put on a *tableau vivant* of *The Last Supper*, and end with a closing ceremony of a dance with torches. Jim also tricks Dwight into saying that Jim is the best salesman in the office. **(Garden Party)**

- Jim eggs Dwight on to stand all the time at his standing desk, then pushes him over when he sees a pole supporting Dwight. **(Mrs. California)**

- Trying to tempt Dwight into pranking him so Dwight will lose his bonus, Jim recites his credit card and security code out loud. Dwight uses it to send a $200 bouquet to Pam. **(Christmas Wishes)**

- Jim defaces a photo of Cece to frame Dwight, until Andy says that kind of damage is fireable. **(Christmas Wishes)**

- Jim tricks Dwight into going to LA by making him think he's won a walk-on part on *NCIS*. **(Jury Duty)**

- When Dwight comes to wake Jim up in his Florida hotel room, Jim stages the room to appear like he's involved with some "bad apples" and was murdered by Dwight. **(Tallahassee)**

- Jim finds out where Dwight gets his clothes dry-cleaned, then custom orders the same suit and makes it with tear-away Velcro, then rips it off Dwight as he walks into the office building. **(Free Family Portrait Studio)**

- Jim makes Dwight believe the new guy has a belt above black in karate. **(New Guys)**

- Jim makes Dwight think the electromagnetic areas in the office can cause sterility. **(Work Bus)**

Jim stays late for a month crafting a prank on Dwight, which sets him off on the quest for the Holy Grail following these clues:

1) A letter from Robert Dunder describing a valuable item—"a golden chalice of immeasurable historical and religious significance"—he has hidden on the property (Glenn actually uses the gold chalice as a coffee mug)

2) Invisible ink on the letter

3) The message "Higher than numbers go," which leads to a ceiling tile

4) An X on a key

5) A scroll with the words Sedes Introitti (seat of entrance)

6) A poker flush, which leads to the men's room

7) A miniature forklift in a plastic bag, which leads to the warehouse

**(Customer Loyalty)**

the office book of lists

- Jim rigs the A.A.R.M. challenge so the only person suitable to be Dwight's assistant is Dwight. *(A.A.R.M.)*

As Dwight's *bestisch mensch*, Jim vows to play only good pranks on Dwight:

Guten Prank #1: Jim schedules Dwight's wedding on a weekend to make sure Darryl and Andy can come.

Guten Prank #2: Dwight gets to fire a bazooka in a field while smoking a cigar.

Guten Prank #3: Jim takes Dwight to Kevin's bar so they can bury the hatchet.

Guten Prank #4: Jim claims he can no longer be Dwight's best man . . . and reveals that Michael is there to do it. Jim says it's his best prank ever. *(Finale)*

## PAM'S ART

Pam longs to have a career as an artist but struggles to know where to start. Her fiancé, Roy, is never supportive. Jim encourages her, however, and she eventually goes to art school in New York. Her confidence grows, and by the time the documentary is released, she is getting paid to paint murals.

- Pam tells the camera crew she likes to do illustrations, mostly watercolors and a few oil pencils. As she says this, she's using Wite-Out on a form. *(Pilot)*

- Jan encourages Pam to take the company's design training program in New York. *(Boys and Girls)*

- After Pam calls off her wedding to Roy, she starts taking art classes. *(The Convention)*

- When Michael heads to a convention, Pam has a date with a local cartoonist. *(The Convention)*

- Pam does a lot of doodling at the office. She once sketched a clock tower. She also masters doodling the ten-sided cube, the intricate maze, and the sea serpent that keeps popping his head out of the water. *(The Convict)*

**DID YOU KNOW?**

Pam has her series of watercolors called *Impressions* hung at her art show. The works include a stapler, a vase of flowers, a building, a coffee mug, a bowl of fruit, and the Dunder Mifflin office building. *(Business School)*

- Pam's watercolor of the Frances Willard Elementary School wins a contest and she receives $100 as a prize. *(Traveling Salesman)*

- Roy claims he finds Pam's art sexy, not strippers. *(Ben Franklin)*

- Pam is taken aback when the female stripper says she isn't going to strip forever and that she's taking art classes. *(Ben Franklin)*

- Pam sketches a tape dispenser on the day of her art show. *(Business School)*

- Pam sketches the flasher based on Phyllis's description. It looks exactly like Dwight with a mustache and no glasses. *(Women's Appreciation)*

- After Pam sees Michael's "dangling participle," he reminds her she's an artist and she should just think of him as one of her models. *(Fun Run)*

- When Ryan suggests Pam do some mock-ups for the Dunder Mifflin Infinity logo, he's only trying to hit on her. *(Dunder Mifflin Infinity)*

- At her dinner party, Jan dismissively calls Pam's art her "doodles." *(Dinner Party)*

- At the job fair, Pam asks about an entry-level graphic design job at Creative Impulse Design. The person there suggests she take an adult education class in New York or Philadelphia to learn the basic computer programs needed for design. *(Job Fair)*

- Pam's "summer project" is an ASCII computer drawing of Dwight. *(Weight Loss)*

- Pam loves Chuck Close's photo-realist paintings. *(Customer Survey)*

- Dwight isn't surprised Pam failed art school. He points out that her painting of the building has shadows coming from two different directions. After all, "it's not an office building in the Andromeda galaxy with two suns." *(Business Trip)*

- Pam draws some office doodles that someone anonymously captions. This leads to a contest to caption Pam's cartoon drawing of two dogs on a desert island. *(The Search)*

- Pam has an idea for a series of young adult novels about a quirky tenth grader who finds a wounded Pegasus and becomes the Horse Flyer. *(The Inner Circle)*

- When Jim sarcastically suggests Pam draw the ghost she saw, she draws a hand with a middle finger up. *(Spooked)*

- To apologize for Jim lying about jury duty, Pam and Jim bring in drawings they claim Cece did, but they're too sophisticated for a two-year-old. *(Jury Duty)*

- Pam sketches Lloyd Gross, the fictional salesman Jim and Dwight invent to circumvent the commission cap. He looks like a composite of everyone on the sales team. Toby takes on the role of Lloyd in front of a rival branch's salesperson. *(Turf War)*

- Pam paints a mural in her children's room of a hippo leading five children. *(New Guys)*

- Pam paints a mural for Angela's son. The lion has a tuxedo, as Angela insists all the animals be fully clothed. *(Andy's Ancestry)*

- Senator Lipton helps Pam submit a design for a mural on a downtown building. She initially thinks a nobody like her won't be selected over a big name like Tracy Fleeb. However, Pam gets the job. *(Customer Loyalty)*

- Frank defaces Pam's mural in the warehouse. *(Vandalism)*

- At the documentary reunion panel, Pam has just finished a mural for the Irish Cultural Center. *(Finale)*

- Pam reveals the final mural she painted in the Dunder Mifflin warehouse. Originally, it was supposed to depict the history of paper. Instead, she made it about the history of "us," all working together in the office. *(Finale)*

- Pam takes the watercolor of the office when they leave. *(Finale)*

## RYAN'S LOOKS

Michael consistently gives Ryan the Hottest in the Office Dundie—except for the year Danny Cordray gets it—and part of Ryan's appeal is probably due to his style. Though it starts nondescript and business casual, Ryan goes through a number of looks over the years.

- When Ryan is hired as a temp, he wears off-the-rack business casual shirts and ties, and his hair is slightly long on the sides. *(Basketball)*

- By the time he attends his first Dundies, Ryan's hair is cut back slightly. *(The Dundies)*

- When Ryan interviews for Jan's job, he uses product in his hair and wears more tailored suits. *(The Job)*

- Once Ryan becomes vice president, he wears mostly black, has a beard (or half beard, depending on the day), and gets a $200 haircut. *(Dunder Mifflin Infinity)*

- Ryan wears his shirt unbuttoned when he gives Jim a warning about his job. *(Did I Stutter?)*

- After he gets out of jail and gets sober, Ryan continues to wear dark colors, and for a while he sports a goatee, which Michael copies. *(Weight Loss)*

- After his supposed trip to Thailand, Ryan bleaches his hair. *(Dream Team)*

- As a salesman for the Michael Scott Paper Company, Ryan lets his hair return to normal and wears typical business clothes again. *(The Michael Scott Paper Company)*

- After Ryan has been made a temp again at Dunder Mifflin, he begins to adopt hipsterish styles, including glasses, bow ties, sweaters, scarves, and suspenders. *(Murder / The Manager and the Salesman)*

- When Ryan moves to Ohio to seek his fortune in the "Silicon Prairie," he leaves on a bus in a disheveled suit and carries his clothes in a trash bag. *(New Guys)*

- When Ryan shows up at Dwight's wedding, he is wearing a formal suit with a cutaway shirt collar. *(Finale)*

Ryan keeps a list of excuses on his BlackBerry for why he can't go somewhere with Michael. The list includes:

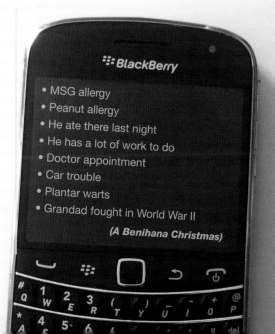

- MSG allergy
- Peanut allergy
- He ate there last night
- He has a lot of work to do
- Doctor appointment
- Car trouble
- Plantar warts
- Grandad fought in World War II

*(A Benihana Christmas)*

## KELLY'S CRUSHES

One of Kelly's main goals is to have a dramatic romance and get married. While Ryan is her most consistent relationship target, she often has crushes on other people in the office or people she encounters.

♥ When the staff plays Who Would You Do? during the fire, Kelly says she would definitely do Jim. *(The Fire)*

♥ Kelly kisses Dwight at the Christmas party under the mistletoe. *(Christmas Party)*

♥ Kelly first shows an attraction to Darryl when he defends her. They end up dating for a while. *(Launch Party)*

♥ Kelly thinks Dwight has a crush on her. *(The Job)*

♥ Kelly (as well as Angela and Meredith) has a crush on Charles Miner. *(New Boss)*

♥ Kelly and Andy have a dirty "dance-off" in Michael's Café Disco. She then tries to pierce his ear. *(Café Disco)*

♥ Kelly thinks Andy likes her due to his Valentine's card, which surprises her—she never thought of him that way since he's annoying or possibly homosexual. *(The Manager and the Salesman)*

Kelly makes a list of people (or things) she would rather make out with than Michael Scott:

- A turtle
- A fridge
- Anyone from the warehouse
- A woodchipper
- Kevin
- A candle
- Lord Voldemort

*(Stress Relief)*

### DID YOU KNOW?

Kelly begins bringing personal issues to Charles. When he hires a receptionist, who is also named Kelly, Kelly Kapoor hangs out near Jim's desk to try and answer whenever Charles calls for a Kelly. *(The Michael Scott Paper Company)* After Angela brings Charles a brochure on an accounting seminar, he tells the camera he's aware of the effect he has on women. *(Two Weeks)*

♥ When Andy says that he doesn't like Kelly, it makes her like him even more. **(The Manager and the Salesman)**

♥ Kelly is instantly taken with Danny Cordray. **(The Sting)**

♥ It appears as though Kelly has a relationship with her Yale University adjunct professor in management, Scott Powell. **(The Seminar)**

♥ While Kelly chooses Ravi over Ryan, she reverts to her old ways when Ryan shows up at Dwight's wedding, and they run off together, leaving Ryan's baby behind. **(Finale)**

# ANGELA'S MORALS

Angela has strict, unyielding views on everything from party streamer colors to how breastfeeding causes gayness. While her behavior (especially with Dwight) doesn't always match her words, Angela's moral compass never wavers . . . at least when she's judging others.

† When Pam suggests green streamers for a party, Angela says she thinks green is kind of whorish. *(The Alliance)*

† Angela tells Katy the colors she likes are gray, dark gray, and charcoal. *(Hot Girl)*

† Pam guesses Angela is the one in the neighborhood who gave trick-or-treaters toothbrushes. *(Halloween)*

† Angela really enjoys being judged and believes she holds up very well to even severe scrutiny. *(Performance Review)*

† Angela is a vegetarian. *(Email Surveillance)*

† Angela feels it's okay for her to drink wine since Jesus drank wine. *(Email Surveillance)*

† Angela disputes Phyllis's claim that she is good at computer stuff. *(Boys and Girls)*

† During the Women in the Workplace seminar, Angela says that when Jan talks about wearing clothes that reflect what you aspire to be, Jan looks like she's aspiring to be a whore. *(Boys and Girls)*

† Kevin has never seen Angela take a sick day. Angela says she's seen Kevin take enough for the both of them. *(Dwight's Speech)*

† Angela never misbehaved in front of her father since he was a strict disciplinarian. She hopes her mate will have similar qualities. *(Take Your Daughter to Work Day)*

† Angela will not give permission for Dwight to give Michael his urine for the drug test. *(Drug Testing)*

† Pam doesn't want to invite Angela to her and Roy's wedding since she doesn't want anyone there who has called her a hussy. *(Conflict Resolution)*

† Looking at her poster of babies playing saxophones makes Angela feel like the babies are the true artists and God has a really cute sense of humor. *(Conflict Resolution)*

† While happy to get a save-the-date for Pam and Roy's wedding, Angela thinks the invitation isn't to her taste. *(Conflict Resolution)*

† Even though the proceeds from Casino Night go to charity, Angela feels that the staff might as well deal drugs or prostitute themselves and donate that money. *(Casino Night)*

† Angela doesn't like *Will & Grace* (it's terribly loud) unless Harry Connick Jr. is guest-starring. *(Gay Witch Hunt)*

† In the Martin family, "Looks like someone took the slow train from Philly" was code for "Check out the slut." *(The Convention)*

† Angela doesn't approve of Movie Mondays. *(The Coup—deleted scene)*

† Angela knows that patience and loyalty are good and virtuous traits. "But sometimes," she says, "I just think you need to grow a pair." *(The Coup)*

† Angela thinks the guests will be eating monkey brains at the Diwali party. *(Diwali)*

† Angela doesn't think Diwali is a real holiday since Hallmark doesn't have a card for it. *(Diwali)*

† Angela is appalled when the server at the Diwali party gives her naan bread and touches it with his hands. *(Diwali)*

† Angela is incredibly offended when Michael shows everyone the *Kama Sutra*. *(Diwali)*

† Angela is outraged about canceling Christmas—not for herself but on behalf of baby Jesus. He wouldn't cancel Christmas because he got dumped. *(A Benihana Christmas)*

† Angela changes her mind about green streamers by Christmas. She then says orange is whorish, not green. *(A Benihana Christmas)*

† Angela had a disagreement with her sister and hasn't spoken to her in sixteen years. *(A Benihana Christmas)*

† When the nude photo of Jan circulates to the whole company, Angela tells the camera crew, "Your body is a temple. You have to respect it. You can't just whore it out." *(Back from Vacation)*

† Angela tells Pam she's not like her, walking around in her provocative outfits and saying anything that pops in her head. *(The Return)*

† Angela says that under no circumstances should a man strip in the office. Meredith disagrees. *(Ben Franklin)*

† Angela says her eyes are burning from the whiteness of Phyllis's wedding dress. *(Phyllis' Wedding)*

† Despite the obscenity of the watermark, Angela doesn't think it will be the most distasteful part of her day. *(Product Recall)*

† Angela won't lie and say she's sorry about the watermark, because the company didn't do anything wrong. Apologizing would be immoral and ridiculous. *(Product Recall)*

† Angela thinks the clothes at Gap Kids are sometimes too flashy, so she is forced to go to American Girl and order clothes for large colonial dolls. *(Women's Appreciation)*

† Angela tells Dwight, "Cat Heaven is a beautiful place, but you don't get there if you're euthanized." *(Fun Run)*

† Angela finds the mystery genre of fiction disgusting, as she hates being titillated. *(Local Ad)*

the office book of lists

† Angela considers first base allowing a kiss on the forehead. *(Business Trip)*

† Everyone thought Angela wrote the note on the microwave. It was rude, condescending, and a little snotty. She wished she had written it. *(Frame Toby)*

† When Pam asks Angela why she would think Pam would draw a penis on her own microwave note, Angela responds with "Why do you wear bright colors? For attention, Pam." *(Frame Toby)*

† Angela says she won't judge Phyllis for desecrating Christmas. She adds, "There is one person who will, though, and Phyllis just stuffed him into a drawer." *(Moroccan Christmas)*

† Angela is disgusted that at Christmas Andy would sing a song about nudity and France. *(Moroccan Christmas)*

† Angela claims she had another pair of men duel over her years ago when she lived in Ohio—John Mark and John David. *(Blood Drive)*

† Angela doesn't like the general spirit of music, but even she ends up moving her foot to the beat of "Y.M.C.A." at Michael's Café Disco. *(Café Disco)*

† Angela reminds Pam that a baby conceived out of wedlock is still a bastard. *(Gossip)*

† When a pregnant Pam tries to go to the hotel bar, Angela offers to save her some time and kick her in the stomach instead. *(Niagara)*

† When she has to play a voodoo priestess in the dinner murder mystery, Angela claims her dalliance with the dark arts comes from being exposed to *Harry Potter*. *(Murder)*

† Angela is anxious to get off work so she can go protest St. Patrick's Day. *(St. Patrick's Day)*

† Angela scolds Pam and says, "Jesus is not your caterer." *(The Christening)*

† Angela says porcupines don't have souls. They're like dogs. *(Christmas Wishes)*

† Angela claims she doesn't need a long, luxurious Parisian maternity leave. *(Jury Duty)*

† Angela says jazz is stupid and she thinks they should just play the right notes. *(The Target)*

† Angela tells her pastor that gayness came from breastfeeding. *(The Target)*

† Angela feels it would be immoral for Erin to cheat on Andy. She knows because she did it and he didn't like it. *(Customer Loyalty)*

† Angela calls a lawyer every time someone watches a YouTube video of animals doing it. *(Vandalism)*

† Angela thinks that loose braids reflect a loose character. *(Moving On)*

# STANLEY'S WASTES OF TIME

Stanley is devoted to one thing above all others—not working any harder than he has to. Though he is a good enough salesman to almost get poached by the Utica branch, ultimately he wants to do little more than run out the clock until he is ready to retire. As such, he indulges in many nonwork activities at the office, including doing his beloved crossword puzzles.

- Stanley does crossword puzzles. *(multiple episodes)*

- While unloading boxes in the warehouse, Stanley doesn't take Ryan's suggestion to be more efficient and says this is a "run-out-the-clock situation. Just like upstairs." *(Boys and Girls)*

- Stanley bets Karen $5 that Bob Vance will call Phyllis three times in ten minutes. He wins the bet. *(Safety Training)*

- Stanley likes to eat pink snowballs. *(Gay Witch Hunt)*

- Pam agrees to do Stanley's faxes so he can go to the bird funeral. *(Grief Counseling)*

- Stanley doesn't mind waiting in line for a long time on Pretzel Day. *(Initiation)*

- There are four things Stanley loves: his wife, his daughters, Pam Grier, and a hot, chewy roll of buttered dough. *(Initiation)*

- While Stanley doesn't want to do inventory, he comes to the warehouse because he doesn't want to miss the show when Jan shows up. *(Back from Vacation)*

- Stanley says he will work out today—"I will work out a way to avoid running for a stupid cause." *(Fun Run)*

- Stanley dances to the music that plays while the new website loads, but claims he isn't dancing. *(Launch Party)*

- Stanley looks up "accomplices" while Oscar and Kevin look up "kidnapping" and "jail time" when Michael forces the pizza delivery guy to stay in the conference room. *(Launch Party)*

- At home, Stanley likes to relax in his sweats, drink some red wine, and enjoy his mystery stories. *(Money)*

- When trying to lose weight, Stanley does leg lifts at his desk with a ream of paper. *(Weight Loss)*

- Stanley starts to gather his things every day at a quarter to five. *(Business Ethics)*

- Charles, ironically, makes Stanley his productivity czar. *(Two Weeks)*

- Stanley dreams of living in a decommissioned lighthouse where no one knows he lives and he can press a button to launch it into space. *(WUPHF.com)*

- Stanley has always wanted to be on jury duty so he can sit in an air-conditioned room, judging people, while his lunch is paid for. *(Classy Christmas)*

- Ironically, Stanley asks Deangelo if he needs help, when Stanley never offered to do more than the bare minimum before. *(Training Day)*

- In addition to his crossword puzzles, Stanley does sudoku. *(Goodbye, Michael)*

- Stanley's new joke is to give a long description of something and then end with "and shove it up your butt." *(The List)*

- Andy can't believe Stanley is working for the incentive plan, as he's sat next to him for years and at a certain time of day Stanley would go into open-eye naptime. *(The Incentive)*

- After he retires, Stanley fills his time whittling wooden birds. *(Finale)*

## OSCAR'S OBSERVATIONS

Jim laughingly says Oscar lives up to the "old stereotype of the smug, gay Mexican." Oscar may not appear to be as judgmental as Angela, but nevertheless, he often has something caustic to say about the shenanigans he observes around the office.

- Oscar knows Michael can't be two-fifteenths Native American, as that fraction doesn't make any sense. *(Diversity Day)*

- Oscar thinks the Dundies are like a kid's party. There's nothing there for you to do, but the kid is having a good time, so you're kind of there. *(The Dundies)*

the office book of lists

- Oscar knows the smelly mess left in Michael's office is wrong but laughs about it and understands why someone did it. *(The Carpet)*

- Oscar goes to the office early every morning to set the thermostat to 66 degrees. It makes him more productive and he doesn't care if others don't like it as cold as he does. Kevin likes to put it at 69. *(Dwight's Speech)*

- Oscar thinks that if Jesus saw Angela's poster of the babies dressed as musicians, he'd freak out. *(Conflict Resolution)*

- Kelly thinks that the fact that Oscar is gay is cool. Oscar says it's super-cool to be an accountant at a failing paper supply company, much like Sir Ian McKellen. *(Gay Witch Hunt)*

- While Oscar hopes the office learned something from his discrimination settlement, part of him hopes they keep talking because he'd really love a home theater. *(The Return)*

- At Phyllis's wedding, Oscar says he'd like to get married, but he's "afraid" it would threaten the marriages of the heterosexual people around him. *(Phyllis' Wedding)*

- At Pam's art show, Oscar and his boyfriend Gil critique her art, and Oscar points out that courage and honesty aren't Pam's strong points. *(Business School)*

- Oscar wonders how many phone calls Kelly is missing while she teaches the staff how to answer phone calls. *(Safety Training)*

- Oscar disputes *Uptown Girls* as being neither a romance nor a comedy. *(Safety Training)*

- At Beach Day, Oscar claims that turkey is a healthy meat. *(Beach Games)*

- After Jim and Pam secretly begin dating, Oscar observes that there is no evidence of intimacy between them other than that they've both been in remarkably good moods. *(Fun Run)*

- Oscar points out that there is a very big difference between the two pizza places with Alfredo in the name in both quality of ingredients and overall taste. *(Launch Party)*

- When Ryan is arrested, Oscar notes that it's because he was recording sales twice, which is what they refer to in business as "misleading the shareholders or fraud." He adds that Ryan's real crime was his beard. *(Goodbye, Toby)*

- When Andy begins to question his sexuality due to Michael's made-up rumor about him, Oscar wonders what exactly his responsibility is here—to comfort insecure heterosexual men? *(Gossip)*

- Oscar says besides having sex with men, the Finer Things Club is the gayest thing about him. *(Branch Wars)*

- Oscar sarcastically asks his coworkers how any organization thrives with two leaders and challenges them to name a country that doesn't have two presidents. *(The Meeting)*

- The Dunder Mifflin stock symbol is DMI, and Oscar says it stands for "dummies, morons, and idiots." *(Shareholder Meeting)*

- Oscar makes a video of Kevin's voice coming out of Cookie Monster. Everyone loves it. *(Secretary's Day)*

- After seeing the video intro to Michael's last Dundie Awards, Oscar observes that the analytical part of him wants to examine it but he knows it has no content. *(Michael's Last Dundies)*

- Oscar is horrified overall by Angela's engagement to a gay man in the closet, but as a lover of elegant weddings he's a little excited. *(Search Committee)*

- When the stakes are high, there's only one computer Oscar trusts and it's powered by Thai food and Spanish red wines—his brain. *(Doomsday)*

- When the senator gives Oscar his cell phone number, it confirms three things to Oscar: he's right about the senator, he's still got his looks, and poor Angela. *(Fundraiser)*

- Oscar laments that he doesn't really know Dwight. Then he realizes he has known him twelve years. "Time is a son of a bitch." *(The Farm)*

- Oscar notices the Schrutes are a "descriptive people" at Dwight's aunt's funeral. *(The Farm)*

- Oscar says the office has an unusually large number of unusually large people. *(Stairmageddon)*

- After Angela moves in with Oscar, he notes that it is ironic that Angela is now literally in a closet. *(A.A.R.M.)*

- Noting the saddle shoes and denim Angela has for Phillip, Oscar threatens to call child services. *(A.A.R.M.)*

- Oscar says, "You take something ordinary, like a piece of paper. It's not much. But if you see it in the right way . . . And that's what you did with this documentary. But seriously, you made a nine-year documentary and you couldn't once show me doing my origami." *(Finale)*

- Oscar runs a blog called *There's No Accounting for Taste*—it features anecdotes about accounting and decorating tips. *(Webisode: The Podcast)*

# KEVIN'S SNACKS

Kevin loves his snacks—to the point that he can do complex calculations about pie portions. These skills fail him when it comes to salad, however. Kevin has enjoyed many snacks over the years at Dunder Mifflin.

- Angela points out to Kevin that he has Danish on his face as he's eating. *(Pilot)*

- Kevin eats an Italian sub with what Jim calls the "works." *(The Alliance)*

- Michael wanted one of the skillets of cheese at the Dundies the previous year and someone (namely Kevin) had eaten them all. *(The Dundies)*

- Stanley steals Kevin's pretzel out from under him. *(Initiation)*

- Kevin tells Jim his M&Ms are under the desk, hidden from *them* (presumably the Stamford staff). *(The Merger)*

- Kevin debates going to Angela's party because while it has double-fudge brownies, it also has Angela. *(A Benihana Christmas)*

- Kevin says, "I just want to lie on the beach and eat hot dogs. That's all I've ever wanted." *(Beach Day)*

- Holly helps Kevin decide what to get from the vending machine with 75 cents—pretzels or chips. *(Goodbye, Toby)*

- Kevin swallows the brownies whole and eats them so fast that Angela wonders if they are even touching his tongue. *(Frame Toby)*

- When Dwight starts a fire, Kevin breaks the vending machine open with a chair and grabs a bunch of snacks. *(Stress Relief)*

- The day after Michael's roast, Kevin uses a sock puppet to say, "He is so dumb that he tried to put his M&Ms in alphabetical order." *(Stress Relief)*

- To cheer Kevin up, Jim and Pam get him a party pack of M&Ms, sixty-nine Cup of Noodles, and a DVD of *American Pie 2* (his favorite movie). *(Michael's Birthday)*

- Kevin eats ice cream and a popsicle when he doesn't eat all of his lunch. *(Lecture Circuit)*

- At least once a year, Kevin brings in his famous chili. The secret is to undercook the onions. Unfortunately, the time he brings in his chili after Michael returns to Dunder Mifflin, Kevin spills it on the carpet. *(Casual Friday)*

- Kevin crawls into bed at Gabe's apartment so he can eat a pig in a blanket in a blanket. *(Viewing Party)*

- Kevin says, "Oh, yeah" every time he eats a candy bar. He can't help it—it's just really good. *(Trivia)*

- Kevin talks himself out of eating cats, even though Angela's are so cute. *(New Guys)*

- Kevin can do complex math when pies are involved. Salads, not so much. *(Work Bus)*

- When Nellie suggests mini cupcakes, Kevin gets angry. He doesn't want mini versions of regular cupcakes, which are already a mini version of cake. *(Dwight Christmas)*

- During the weight loss competition, Kelly and Creed see Kevin putting peanut butter on a bagel. *(Weight Loss)*

- Kevin thinks Angela's opening with puff pastries at Phillip's first birthday is a bold play. *(Vandalism)*

- Kevin has been enjoying Andy's "chunky lemon milk" while Andy has been on his boat trip. *(Vandalism)*

## DID YOU KNOW?

When his fiancée, Stacy, forgets to give Kevin food, he has to cook stuff in the office with only a toaster oven and microwave, as he thinks Meredith stole the blender. Kevin gets ingredients from the vending machine, or as he calls it, "the supermarket that only takes quarters." To make quesadillas, he uses chips and squeezy cheese (that he keeps in his desk drawer). For crème brûlée, he gets tapioca pudding and sugar and evenly distributes the sugar on top. He takes the label off the pudding can so it doesn't start a fire and leaves it in the toaster until it gets nice and brown all over the top. Since there is a rule against bringing beer into the office, Kevin makes his in the office. Oscar calls it bacteria-filled yeast water. *(Web Short—Kevin Cooks Stuff in the Office)*

## "CREED THOUGHTS"

Creed asks Ryan to set up a blog for him. In order to protect the internet from Creed's innermost thoughts, Ryan opens a Word document on Creed's computer and types "www.creedthoughts.gov.www/creedthoughts" at the top of the page. While we will never be able to read Creed's actual entries, we have a pretty good idea of what they might be.

➔ Creed knows some conversational Chinese and says "hi" to his friends in China. *(Dwight's Speech)*

➔ Creed has a foot with four toes (the hair covers most of it) and offers to show the kids visiting the office. *(Take Your Daughter to Work Day)*

➔ Creed knows his marijuana. When Dwight shows him a photo of pot, Creed correctly identifies it as "Northern Lights, *Cannabis indica.*" *(Drug Testing)*

➔ Creed loves to steal things and stopped caring a long time ago. *(Casino Night)*

➔ Creed wins a mini fridge at Casino Night and says he's never owned a refrigerator before. *(Casino Night)*

➔ Creed isn't offended by homosexuality. He made love to many women in the 1960s in the mud and rain and it's possible a man slipped in there. *(Gay Witch Hunt)*

➔ Creed reintroduces himself to Meredith and explains, "Andrea's the office bitch. You'll get used to her." *(The Convention)*

➔ Creed says a human can go on living several hours after being decapitated. Dwight says he's thinking of a chicken. *(Grief Counseling)*

➔ When Michael shows everyone the *Kama Sutra*, Creed recognizes the union of the monkey position. *(Diwali)*

→ The *Scranton Times* obituary writer recognizes Creed as the guitar player for Grass Roots in the late 1960s, who supposedly died. Creed congratulates him on writing a good obituary. He then explains that ten years ago he faked his own death and collects the benefits as his own widow. *(Product Recall)*

→ Creed wonders why anyone would throw away a perfectly good bird's nest. *(The Job)*

$150

→ Four nights a week Creed sleeps at his desk, and the other three nights he sleeps in Toronto, as it is a welfare state and they don't know about this job. *(The Coup)*

→ Creed starts selling the office's equipment when he thinks the branch is closing. *(Branch Closing)*

→ Creed was in prison, which is where he got the name Creed. He misses the pruno wine he made in prison. They made it in the toilet from fruit, sugar, and ketchup. *(The Convict)*

→ Creed doesn't care which Christmas party he goes to. After he danced naked at a hash bonfire with the spirits of the dead, all parties have seemed pretty much the same to him. *(A Benihana Christmas)*

→ Creed says the only difference between him and a homeless man is his job, and he will do whatever it takes to survive like he did when he was a homeless man. *(Product Recall)*

→ Creed says if what happened to Phyllis was flashing, they better lock him up. *(Women's Appreciation)*

→ Creed says he blogged about Pam's outburst at the beach. *(The Job)*

→ Creed uses the copier to make 2.1 million Schrute Bucks and asks Dwight for the cash value. *(The Job)*

When visiting Meredith in the hospital, Creed asks which of these painkillers she's on:

- CODEINE
- VICODIN
- PERCOCET
- FENTANYL
- OXYCONTIN
- PALLADONE

→ When Creed has money trouble, he transfers his debt to William Charles Schneider, one of his alter egos. He claims, "Bankruptcy is nature's do-over." *(Money)*

→ Creed is offended when Holly asks what he does in the office. He's sure it's something close to "quabity assuance." *(Goodbye, Toby)*

→ Creed says since a lot of jazz cats are blind, he'd like to put a piano in front of Pam without her glasses and see what happens. He'd also like to see her topless. *(Did I Stutter?)*

→ When the office is broken into, Creed vows that no one steals from Creed Bratton and gets away with it. The last person who did, disappeared. His name was . . . Creed Bratton. *(Crime Aid)*

→ Creed can get a permit for a controlled burn in a well-ventilated area in an hour. *(Moroccan Christmas)*

→ Creed tells Andy he got Squeaky Fromme not with small talk but by showing her who's boss and going right in and kissing her. *(Lecture Circuit)*

→ Creed wonders, if he can't scuba, what is he even working toward? *(Gossip)*

→ Creed calls in a review of Andy's play, saying, "Unfortunately, in this ham-fisted production of *Sweeney Todd*, the real terror comes from the vocal performances. New paragraph." *(Andy's Play)*

→ Creed can understand pirate code, but he can't speak it. *(China)*

→ Creed's interpretation of the day Dwight did a high-wire act was that it was like a circus. Which wasn't bad for a day in the life of a dog food company. *(New Guys)*

# PHYLLIS'S GIRL TALK

Phyllis loves gossip and rumors and never minds instigating things or snooping into people's business. She isn't often shy about revealing what goes on between her and Bob Vance, Vance Refrigeration. As she went to school with Michael, she also has dirt on him, much to his chagrin.

- Phyllis tells Dwight what was written about Michael in the ladies' room. *(The Dundies)*

- Pam asks Phyllis if she's heard anything about a secret office romance, thinking Dwight and Angela have started a relationship. Phyllis assumes she's asking about Pam and Jim. *(Email Surveillance)*

- Phyllis is excited about the Women in the Workplace meeting, because she loves girl talk. *(Boys and Girls)*

- Phyllis says that in high school everyone thought Michael was gay due to his ties and matching socks. *(Gay Witch Hunt)*

- Phyllis tells Pam she heard Jim is coming back from Stamford. *(Branch Closing)*

- Phyllis tells Karen she's glad Karen is with Jim since he was hung up on Pam for so long. *(Traveling Salesman)*

- Phyllis pointedly reminds Pam she can't get all the sales leads just because of who she's sleeping with "this week." *(Dunder Mifflin Infinity)*

- Phyllis Googles how to deal with difficult people and tries it out on Angela. *(Launch Party)*

- Phyllis smirks when she relays that Michael wasn't invited on Ryan's camping trip—but Toby was. *(Survivor Man)*

- Phyllis catches her nemesis, Angela, having sex with Dwight in the office while Angela and Andy are still together. *(Goodbye, Toby)*

- After Phyllis hurts her back dancing, she wonders if Bob Vance, Vance Refrigeration, is cheating on her with his secretary. Then she laughs because that would be ridiculous. *(Café Disco)*

- Phyllis tells Angela she thinks Pam ran off from her wedding because she knew deep down she wouldn't be a good wife. Angela agrees. *(Niagara)*

- Dressed as Santa, Phyllis promises Andy not to tell Erin he is her Secret Santa. He ends up telling her anyway. *(Secret Santa)*

- When Michael leaves, Phyllis is afraid he might mention that she had a baby she put up for adoption. Instead, he talks about how caring she is. *(Goodbye, Michael)*

- Phyllis tells Andy she will try to find out if Gabe and Erin are having sex. *(Viewing Party)*

- Phyllis never had an orgasm until she was forty-two. She got nothing done the year she was forty-three. *(Angry Andy)*

the office book of lists

- The plants are gonna love this.
- I sure don't want to get stuck in this on the way home.
- Raining cats and dogs out there.
- The humidity is going to make my hair freak.
- Roads are actually slickest in the first half hour.
- I actually sleep better in the rain.
- We're paying for all the sun we got this year/summer.
- The rain makes me want to stay at home curled up with a good book.
- If we lived in Seattle, every day would be like this.
- I wish I were allowed one rain check.
- I love the smell after it rains.
- Nobody knows how to drive in the rain.

Over the years, the staff realizes Phyllis has said the same twelve things every time it rains. Jim promises to buy everyone hot chocolate if she says all twelve by noon, but in attempting to get her to say how nice it would be to stay at home and curl up with a good book, they prevent her from saying her last cliché. *(Angry Andy)*

## DID YOU KNOW?

Phyllis has a list of people that are on her "hall pass," and even her husband is okay with Jim being on her list. The complete list includes Jim, George Clooney, Leo DiCaprio, and the British guy who got in trouble with the prostitute. *(Beach Games)*

# TOBY'S GUIDELINES

Toby is intensely disliked by Michael, mainly for not letting Michael have fun. As the Corporate HR rep, Toby doesn't have an easy time of things at the Scranton branch, but he does his best. On the side, Toby pursues his dream of writing mystery novels and moving to Costa Rica.

- When the CFO at Corporate resigns due to sexual harassment, Toby has to give a refresher seminar in the Scranton office. It goes as well as expected, with the reappearance of serial offender Todd Packer, inappropriate email forwards, and a blow-up doll. *(Sexual Harassment)*

- Toby points out to Michael that they are not supposed to serve alcohol at the Christmas party. *(Christmas Party)*

- Toby threatens to take Michael's corporate credit card away again after Michael takes Jim to Hooters for lunch. *(The Secret)*

- Toby reminds Michael that when you sign your job application you agree to comply with random drug testing. *(Drug Testing)*

- Every Friday at four, Dwight has a standing appointment with Toby to file a grievance against Jim, which Toby puts in a "special file in New York," which is actually just a box under his desk. *(Conflict Resolution)*

- Toby has a separate folder for complaints against Michael and shows a large folder for January through March of the current year. *(Conflict Resolution)*

- After Michael outs Oscar, Toby and Jan get involved. Oscar ends up getting a company car, time off, and a settlement. *(Gay Witch Hunt)*

- Toby puts an end to the Indian Cultural Seminar and takes the copies of the *Kama Sutra* from everyone. *(Diwali)*

- Toby warns Michael he needs to disclose his relationship with Jan to HR. *(Back from Vacation)*

- Toby writes up Angela for slapping him. *(A Benihana Christmas)*

- Toby is certain that Michael's raise negotiation will be a groundbreaking case when it goes to trial. It will be the first time a male subordinate attempts to get a modest, scheduled raise by threatening to withhold sex from a female superior. *(The Negotiation)*

- Angela questions everyone about how Dwight stopped Roy. Kelly says she should just read the report Toby wrote—he took everyone's stories. *(The Negotiation)*

- Toby sends a memo around about PDA in the office after he sees Jim and Pam kissing. *(Dunder Mifflin Infinity)*

the office book of lists

Michael reviews many
office complaints that Toby
has gathered, including:

## COMPLAINTS FILED:

1) Stanley used Kevin's Miracle Whip without asking.

2) Meredith said everyone talked too loud in the morning and the lights were too bright.

3) Creed was sick of looking at the redhead all day and wanted a seat facing Pam.

4) Someone complained that Pam should do her wedding planning at home. (Pam thought Angela wrote the complaint, but Jim later admitted he wrote it.)

5) Kelly complained Ryan never returned her calls.

6) Jim joked and claimed Dwight tried to kiss him.

7) Creed complained the bathroom was "whites only" because of the white stickman figure on it.

8) Stanley said Phyllis cries too much.

9) Ryan complained Creed has a distinct "old man smell."

10) Angela complained Kevin made sexually suggestive remarks that made her feel uncomfortable. (Michael suggested she do it back to him.)

11) Phyllis complained Angela gave her dirty looks and she couldn't get off the Party Planning Committee.

12) Dwight had numerous complaints about Jim's pranks.

- Toby tries to dissuade Jim and Pam from signing a "we're dating" thing for the company, as he hopes it's casual and not a relationship since he has a crush on Pam. *(Dunder Mifflin Infinity)*

- After the brainstorming meeting where Stanley asks Michael, "Did I stutter?" Toby tells Michael he needs to address Stanley's insubordination. *(Did I Stutter?)*

- Toby says Ryan's formal warning to Jim about his job performance was mainly about goofing off with Pam. Jim thinks it's more likely because he talked to David Wallace behind Ryan's back. *(Did I Stutter?)*

- Toby threatens to write Dwight up when he won't sit down during the Casual Friday discussion. Toby then cancels Casual Fridays. *(Casual Friday)*

### DID YOU KNOW?

Dwight makes Toby suspicious of Darryl's broken ankle. They spy on Darryl and mistake his sister, who is not on crutches, for Darryl. Darryl then threatens to call Corporate and file a complaint against them. Dwight wants to file a complaint against Darryl for lying. Toby ends up having to do all the paperwork. *(The Meeting)*

- After Michael spanks the new assistant (his nephew), he has to have six hours of counseling with a certified counselor—Toby. *(Nepotism)*

- When Dwight's gun goes off, Toby looks excited to get the accident report binder, as he's never used the gun violence forms before. *(Dwight K. Schrute, (Acting) Manager)*

- To protect his secret about his affair with the senator, Oscar frames Kevin for his old gambling problem so Toby will send him home. *(The Boat)*

## MEREDITH'S KINKS AND DRINKS

Meredith enjoys sex and drinking to the point that it sometimes affects her job performance. She appears to have few boundaries, even giving her son advice on stripping. She also seems to suffer a list of disastrously unlucky accidents.

- Meredith is allergic to dairy. *(The Alliance)*

- Meredith drinks at the Christmas party since she made a New Year's resolution not to drink during the week anymore. *(Christmas Party)*

- Meredith goes into the "crew only" part of the ship with Captain Jack. She is seen later wearing only a skirt and a life preserver. *(Booze Cruise)*

- Meredith keeps a bottle of booze under the seat in her minivan. *(The Injury)*

- During spring cleaning, Meredith throws out an empty liquor bottle. *(The Secret)*

- During the Women in the Workplace seminar, Meredith introduces herself and starts to say, "And I'm an alcoholic." *(Boys and Girls)*

- Meredith's goal is to be five years sober in five years. *(Boys and Girls)*

- Meredith appears to fix a gin and tonic in a soda cup in the break room. *(Valentine's Day)*

- Meredith sometimes drinks hand sanitizer. *(Gay Witch Hunt)*

- Meredith thinks she and Michael agreed to sleep together on their last day of work. *(Branch Closing)*

- Meredith runs inside to get a large drink cup for the bus ride once she sees the "No Alcohol" sign. *(Beach Games)*

- Meredith opens her blouse to flirt with Dwight once it appears he's the new boss. *(The Coup)*

- If Pam doesn't want to go to the Diwali party, Meredith offers to have her over to drink appletinis and watch *Sex and the City. (Diwali)*

- Meredith has the same thermos as Karen, and she offers Karen some of the booze from her flask. *(The Merger)*

- Meredith says you can't get drunk off Kahlúa. "It's just a kind of coffee." *(Fun Run)*

- Meredith lifts up her shirt and starts belly dancing at the Moroccan Christmas party. *(Moroccan Christmas)*

- Meredith says she does have an addiction, but not to alcohol—to porn. *(Moroccan Christmas)*

- Meredith has had two men fight over her before, usually to see who gets to hold the camcorder. *(The Duel)*

- Creed asks why they've never . . . and Meredith says they have. *(The Promotion)*

- Meredith looks forward all morning to her afternoon cigar and she's not stopping for anybody. *(Niagara)*

- Meredith claims she had sex with a terrorist. *(Koi Pond)*

- Meredith is a hoarder. *(Christmas Wishes)*

- Someone got Meredith's phone number wrong on the men's room wall. Creed says that number was also a good time and there was less mileage. *(Vandalism)*

- Meredith says if it wasn't for the documentary, she would have done some truly vulgar crap. *(A.A.R.M.)*

- Meredith claims she was getting her PhD in school psychology for the first seven years of the documentary. *(Finale)*

## DARRYL'S DELIVERIES

As the warehouse foreman, Darryl is efficient and conscientious and has innovative ideas that lead Jo to promote him. However, his best deliveries are often the insults and comebacks he provides with no shipping fee.

> • Darryl refers to Michael's tight pants and says, "Man, we can see all your business coming around the corner, okay? Good thing you don't have a lot of business to start with." *(Sexual Harassment)*

- When Michael asks Darryl his biggest fear, he says it's that someone will distract him from getting his shipments out on time. *(Boys and Girls)*

- Darryl points out that the warehouse staff and office staff are compensated very differently, which leads to talk of unionization. *(Boys and Girls)*

- Darryl teaches Michael fake urban slang for his "interracial conversations," like "fleece it out," "dinkin' flicka," and "going mach five." He also teaches him a weird handshake. *(Casino Night)*

- When Michael asks if Darryl can promise to make the warehouse into a sexy venue in less than thirty minutes, Darryl tells him he only promises things to his three-year-old daughter. *(Ben Franklin)*

- When Michael negotiates for a raise, Darryl teaches him, "Bippity boppity, give me the zoppity." *(The Negotiation)*

- Darryl tells Michael he needs to ask Jan for a raise and he's gotta "get out there and earn, son." *(The Negotiation)*

- When the warehouse workers attend the office's safety training and contrast the dim lighting with the danger of the baler, Darryl tells Michael he is living a sweet, little Nerfy life sitting on his biscuit, never having to risk it. *(Safety Training)*

- To get Michael off the roof, Darryl says he's a very brave man and it takes courage just to be him. *(Safety Training)*

- When Dwight yells at Kelly for ordering paper online, Darryl tells him to stop yelling at our sweet little Miss Kapoor over five hundred sheets of paper and to get back to his desk and start selling multiple reams like a man. *(Launch Party)*

When Michael asks if Darryl has been in a gang, he says he's been in the following:

CRIPS

BLOODS

LATIN KINGS

WARRIORS

NEWSIES

*(Did I Stutter?)*

- Darryl tells Michael the way gangs handle people getting in their face is to use "fluffy fingers." They tickle each other until they are laughing and hugging and then forget the whole thing. *(Did I Stutter?)*

- Freaked out about the five golden tickets going to one customer, Michael goes to the warehouse and calls Darryl an idiot. Darryl calmly tells Michael to start over. *(Golden Ticket)*

- Darryl tells Andy, "Man up, alright? You will win this in the end. It's all about heart and character. Be your best self." He doesn't know what Andy's problem is—it's just his standard advice. *(Sex Ed)*

- When Darryl dates Kelly, he has to tell her to access her uncrazy side. *(Money)*

- When Michael accidentally purchases a woman's suit and wears it, Darryl says he has to call Roy. This is going to make him feel better. This is too good. *(The Negotiation)*.

- When Oscar passive-aggressively tries to invite Matt to happy hour by going through Darryl, Darryl says, "Look, just be straight with me, man. You can be gay with Matt, just be straight with me." *(Happy Hour)*

- When Jim brings Darryl into his sports marketing company and tells him Pam doesn't know about it, Darryl tells him it's not real until his wife is on board. *(Andy's Ancestry)*

# ANDY'S ANGER MANAGEMENT

Poor salesperson, a capella band member, and Angela's former fiancé, Andy Bernard (the 'Nard Dog) has a lot of pent-up anger and a short fuse, especially when his coworkers play practical jokes on him. Andy works hard to deal with his anger, especially after his ten-week anger management course.

- Andy says he's gonna lose his frickin' mind if he doesn't find out who put his calculator in Jell-O. *(Gay Witch Hunt)*

- Andy threatens to shoot Jim for real when he thinks Jim is sabotaging the team in *Call of Duty*. *(The Coup)*

- Andy gets angry when Karen switches her squeaky chair with his chair. *(Initiation)*

- Andy growls and punches napkins in the break room after it is announced that the Stamford branch is closing. He composes himself when Josh comes to say goodbye. *(Branch Closing)*

- Andy gets so angry when he can't find his freaking phone (that Jim put in the ceiling) that he punches a hole in the wall. He admits it's an overreaction. *(The Return)*

- Andy is sent to a ten-week anger management program. He thinks he can be done in five weeks. *(The Return)*

- After Andy graduates anger management, he says he has a bunch of new techniques for dealing with "the grumpies." *(Safety Training)*

- Andy tries to have everyone call him "Drew" upon his return from anger management. He points out that when people think of "Andy," they think of hate and anger. By leaving out cookies with a note saying "Compliments of Drew," he hopes to make people think of Drew when they think of baked goods. *(Safety Training)*

- A device Andy learned to diffuse tension is to be the first to make fun of yourself, because if others make fun of you first, you might lose your mind. *(Safety Training)*

- When Kevin takes the last of the coffee, Andy says it's okay. He notes, "I can't always have what I want, but I can want what I have." Kevin responds, "A cup of no coffee?" *(Safety Training)*

- Andy says he can't achieve anger anymore and he has a new car—a Prius. Andy doesn't care about fuel efficiency, but Drew has seen *An Inconvenient Truth* . . . nearly twice. *(Safety Training)*

- Andy struggles not to react when he sees that Angela keyed his new car. *(Safety Training)*

- Andy is okay losing every contest on Beach Day as it will give him the opportunity to demonstrate what a good sport he is. *(Beach Games)*

- Angela tells Dwight she plans to misunderstand everything that Andy says on Beach Day until he goes insane. *(Beach Games)*

- Andy doesn't win the sumo wrestling contest but claims it's because he recently learned it's better to work things out with words. *(Beach Games)*

- Dwight tells Andy to ignore Jim, but Andy acknowledges he's had a hard time letting things go. *(Launch Party)*

- Andy "jokingly" yells at Dwight to take the Cornell sweatshirt off, then tells him those colors are sacred and he shouldn't wear them. *(Employee Transfer)*

- Andy loses it after Dwight puts up a Cornell banner, Creed mispronounces it as "colonel," and Dwight puts a Big Red bobblehead bear on his desk. *(Employee Transfer)*

- Andy gets irritated when Jim won't pour the coffee out of the *America's Got Talent* finale mug with Andy's face on it. Jim pretends he doesn't see the resemblance between Andy's face and the photo on the mug. *(Customer Survey)*

- Andy gets angry at Pam and Jim's advice to Kevin about Lynn, saying two hot people with a perfect relationship can't understand what he or Kevin goes through. *(Golden Ticket)*

- Andy yells at Erin for missing the volleyball, asking if she's blind, but then pretends he was yelling at someone wearing sunglasses. *(Company Picnic)*

- Andy gets angry with a kid who says he's bad at working on a car. *(Mafia)*

- Andy gets mad at Michael when he calls Erin a rube. *(Secretary's Day)*

- Andy threatens to break the temples off Phyllis's glasses and stick them in her eye sockets if she tells Jo he was the whistleblower. *(Whistleblower)*

- During his discussion on the pros and cons of sex, Andy gets angry when no one appreciates what he's doing and he throws a pizza at the wall. *(Sex Ed)*

- Andy gets angry when his old bandmate Broccoli Rob gets to record a song about milk awareness. *(The Sting)*

- After his interview with the search committee, Andy sits in his car and screams. *(Search Committee)*

- To soothe Andy when he gets mad, Erin puts her hand on his arm and sings him a lullaby about the state of Pennsylvania watching over her. *(Angry Andy)*

- After Erin yells at Nellie, it triggers Andy, who yells at Erin (then apologizes) and at his father. He throws a chair, rips Nellie's portrait down, and punches the same wall he punched years earlier. *(Angry Andy)*

To try and show Robert up at the fundraiser, Andy adopts all the dogs there. While being told about all the special needs each one has, Andy gets frustrated. Luckily, some of the staff later adopt the dogs:

- Andy attends Outward Bound (along with David Wallace's son) to learn to be more decisive and confident. *(New Guys)*

- Andy gets incensed when the comments on the documentary promos are not flattering. *(Promos)*

BELLA

DAISY

HUEY

MOJO

KENNY

PEPPER

RUBY (who everyone assumes has died)

*(Fundraiser)*

Since his days with Here Comes Treble, Andy has been a natural performer. Unfortunately for his colleagues, almost anything can cause him to break into song. These are a few of his stand-out performances:

1) A drunk Andy and Jim sing "Closer to Fine" when they have to work late in Stamford. *(Diwali)*

2) At the Integration Celebration, Andy and Michael sing "What Is Love?" *(The Merger)*

3) Andy and Jim sing "The Lion Sleeps Tonight" in the car. *(Product Recall)*

4) Andy calls two friends on speakerphone to help him sing Abba's "Take A Chance on Me" to Angela during the launch party. *(Launch Party)*

5) At the end of every workday, Andy sings "Closing Time." *(Doomsday)*

6) When Andy and Erin arrive at the office, they sing "My Girlfriend's Back." *(Angry Andy)*

7) Andy auditions for America's Next A Capella Sensation with the Cornell fight song and a hobo song, "Dapper Dan." He doesn't make it, but he becomes a viral sensation. *(A.A.R.M.)*

the office book of lists

## "I HAVE AN ANNOUNCEMENT TO MAKE"

It seems like every day someone needs to make an announcement to the entire office. From Michael getting everyone's attention for avian funeral services, to Erin asking if she's earned the right to make an announcement yet, the Scranton employees make sure to inform one another about a lot of things.

- Dwight just wants to announce that the women in the office are terrible. *(The Dundies)*

- Michael tells everyone Toby has an announcement he insists on making right now in the middle of the day. Michael also tells the staff he can no longer be their friend and this can be considered his "retirement from comedy." *(Sexual Harassment)*

- Dwight tells everyone the cause of the fire is that some "smart, sexy temp left his cheese pita on 'oven' instead of timing it for the toaster thing." *(The Fire)*

- Dwight tells the staff his uncle bought him some fireworks. *(The Client)*

- Michael announces their "weekly" suggestion box meeting. *(Performance Review)*

- Jim makes a "quick announcement" about where the drinks are at his barbecue. *(Email Surveillance)*

- On the cruise, Roy asks for everyone's attention to set a date for his and Pam's wedding. *(Booze Cruise)*

- When Michael burns his foot, he asks if anyone knows what it's like to be disabled. *(The Injury)*

- In order to show Dwight how to hold people's attention by saying something they care about, Michael announces to the staff that they are all getting $1,000 bonuses. But they aren't. *(Dwight's Speech)*

- Dwight tries to hold everyone's attention by saying there has been an accident on 84 West and Brad Pitt was in it. There will be no bonuses. Also, this branch is closing. *(Dwight's Speech)*

- Michael announces that they are taking Kevin to a place that will make him happy and is far, far away from the evil sun. *(Michael's Birthday)*

- Michael asks how many people have complained to Toby about other employees. *(Conflict Resolution)*

- Michael tells everyone Dwight is replacing him as their leader in order to test Dwight's loyalties. *(The Coup)*

- Michael announces that Ed Truck died. He later announces how Ed was decapitated. *(Grief Counseling)*

- Dwight tells everyone to get rid of Ed Truck's contacts since he died, and adds that Pam's shredder will be available. *(Grief Counseling)*

- Michael announces that at 4 p.m. they will hold the funeral service for the bird that flew into the window. *(Grief Counseling)*

- Michael announces that the branch is being shut down after Jan tells him to be discreet. *(Branch Closing)*

- Josh tells everyone in Stamford he knows rumors are going around about the Stamford branch closing, but until things are official they should just keep working. *(Branch Closing)*

- Michael announces that Martin is an ex-convict, declares publicly that he trusts him, and gives examples of Black people he trusts more than any white person anyone else can name. *(The Convict)*

- Michael announces that anyone who gets the "very PG-13 picture" of him and a woman should delete it, sight unseen. *(Back from Vacation)*

- Michael announces that Christmas is canceled because he and Carol broke up. *(A Benihana Christmas)*

- Pam announces that her and Karen's party is starting in the break room. Angela then makes an announcement about their paychecks arriving on time to stall until she can officially announce that her party is starting. *(A Benihana Christmas)*

- Dwight announces that if they work hard at inventory, they should be done in seven hours, and that whoever finds the deck of cards can redeem it for a free soft drink. Jim has already found it during the announcement. *(Back from Vacation)*

the office book of lists

- Dwight makes an announcement that he's quitting "to spend more time with his family," even though he is quitting to prevent anyone from finding out about him and Angela. *(Traveling Salesman)*

- Michael and Dwight announce the formation of the Emergency Anti-Flashing Task Force. Jim wonders if it will interfere with Dwight's other task forces. *(Women's Appreciation)*

- Dwight announces that he is removing all bananas from the kitchen. *(Women's Appreciation)*

- On the bus to Beach Day, Michael announces that they will be participating in mandatory "funtivities." *(Beach Games)*

- After she does the coal walk, Pam wants to say some things to the group, because she's been trying to be more honest lately. *(Beach Games)*

### DID YOU KNOW?

After he takes over as regional manager, Dwight introduces Schrute Bucks. Doing something good allows an employee to receive a Schrute Buck. One thousand Schrute bucks equals an extra five minutes for lunch. The cash value of a Schrute Buck is one-hundredth of a cent. Dwight then announces that Michael wasted an enormous amount of the group's time and patience with non-work-related ethnic celebrations and parades of soft-minded do-goodedness, and now there will be no more meetings, only lectures designed to increase everyone's knowledge of the world of paper. *(The Job)*

- When Michael doesn't get the job at Corporate, he makes an announcement to say he officially withdrew his name from consideration. And then he asks why his office is black. *(The Job)*

- After Michael hits Meredith with his car, he announces that he wants to plant a tree to take everyone's mind off the unavoidable tragedy. *(Fun Run)*

- Before the fun run starts, Michael says a few words about rabies. *(Fun Run)*

- Ryan tells everyone he knows that he used to be the temp, but now he's the boss and wants his staff's respect. *(Dunder Mifflin Infinity)*

- Michael announces that in the last year they lost seven clients to the big chains and they're giving them gift baskets to get them back. *(Dunder Mifflin Infinity)*

- Michael announces that the office will not be using any new technology ever, starting now. Ryan says this is not correct. *(Dunder Mifflin Infinity)*

- Michael lets everyone know he is heading to New York to attend the launch party with sushi and important people. Also, if anyone has interesting and easy-to-memorize anecdotes, they should stop by his office. *(Launch Party)*

- Michael shouts out, "I DECLARE BANKRUPTCY!" not understanding there is more to it than that. *(Money)*

- Michael tells everyone Stanley is transferring to the Utica branch for more money, and they misinterpret his tone as one of congratulations. *(Branch Wars)*

- Jim asks who has problems with the communal birthday party idea and finds out everyone hates the idea. *(Survivor Man)*

- Michael tells everyone the chair model on page 85 of a catalog is the template for the woman he'd like anyone to fix him up with. He then formally requests that people help him fall in love, and says that if they don't give him the names of an eligible woman, they are fired. *(Chair Model)*

- After putting his hand on Pam's knee in front of everyone, Toby announces he is finally moving to Costa Rica. *(Night Out)*

- Michael runs in and asks what he should write in the drying cement outside. *(Did I Stutter?)*

- Michael announces to everyone he is fake firing Stanley to discipline him, and he's telling everyone so they will behave as though he is actually getting fired. *(Did I Stutter?)*

- At Toby's goodbye party, Michael says Holly is the best thing that's happened to the company in fifty years. *(Goodbye, Toby)*

- Andy asks for Angela's hand in marriage just as Jim is about to propose to Pam. *(Goodbye, Toby)*

- Dwight points out that most of the people in the office have not lost any weight during the weight loss competition. *(Weight Loss)*

- On a call with Pam, Jim lets her know he hasn't announced their engagement yet. She tells him to and people are mainly unimpressed, except Michael, who tackles Jim with a hug. *(Business Ethics)*

- Holly announces that the staff needs to finish the ethics seminar and she has to get everyone's signatures to show they completed the training. *(Business Ethics)*

- Michael introduces Jan's baby, Astrid, to everyone. He then reenacts the *Lion King* scene and holds the baby up high. *(Business Ethics)*

- Phyllis announces to everyone that she caught Angela and Dwight having sex after Toby's going-away party. *(Moroccan Christmas)*

- Pam announces that with the new year there is new candy at her desk—hot tamales. *(The Duel)*

- Andy asks everyone if he can have the floor to announce that no one has RSVP'd to his and Angela's wedding. What he doesn't know is that Phyllis told everyone else seventeen days earlier that Angela was cheating on him. *(The Duel)*

- Michael tells everyone that Dwight has to issue a formal apology to everyone. Dwight then says, "I state my regret." *(Stress Relief)*

- Michael announces that he knows why everyone is stressed—they are too intimidated to tell him what they really think, so he wants to have a roast of Mr. Michael Scott. *(Stress Relief)*

- Michael announces that he just told Jim to suck it and he's having a special Lonely Hearts Convention on Valentine's Day. *(Blood Drive)*

- Michael announces that he and Dwight have returned from a wonderful stroll together and he had fun. *(Golden Ticket)*

- David Wallace tells the staff the golden ticket idea is one of the most brilliant signs of initiative he's ever seen at the company. *(Golden Ticket)*

- Pam lets everyone know the new copier is ready, and then it has a G-44 error. *(Two Weeks)*

- As he is being walked out of the office by security, Michael tries to say goodbye to the office with an announcement, but Charles stops him. *(Two Weeks)*

- Andy announces that Jim Halpert is very upset and disturbed and wants people to be nicer to him. Jim was messing with him. *(Heavy Competition)*

- David Wallace announces that he knows the Michael Scott Paper Company has siphoned off a large chunk of their business and it's only a temporary setback. *(Broke)*

- When Michael returns to Dunder Mifflin, Pam and Ryan hold up a paper hoop with a question mark and Michael bursts through it. *(Casual Friday)*

- Dwight asks who is planning a trip to the superior court in Youngstown, Ohio, and takes the staff's silence to mean they are hiding something. Pam and Jim are planning to sneak away and get married quietly. *(Café Disco)*

- As Dwight makes an announcement about Darryl's false injury claim, Michael interrupts to announce Jim is now co-manager of the Scranton branch. *(The Meeting)*

- Jim announces that there is not enough money for raises for everyone and raises are only going to the sales staff. *(The Promotion)*

- Dwight and Jim announce "Merry Christmas" to the staff on behalf of themselves. *(Secret Santa)*

- Erin isn't sure she's earned the right to make announcements yet, but she needs to stop her Secret Santa from giving her all twelve days of Christmas. *(Secret Santa)*

- Michael forces a vote on who should be Santa, him or Phyllis. *(Secret Santa)*

- Michael announces that he shouldn't have distributed the new machines from Sabre to everyone. *(Sabre)*

- Michael announces that he is giving the new leads to Creed, Angela, and Meredith. *(New Leads)*

- Andy announces at happy hour that he and Erin Hannon have been on two dates and there will probably be more. *(Happy Hour)*

- Gabe announces that everyone has to stop laughing about the Cookie Monster video. *(Secretary's Day)*

- Andy congratulates Angela for the party she put together for Secretary's Day. *(Secretary's Day)*

- Andy asks if everyone is coming to his play. *(Andy's Play)*

- Andy asks for everyone's attention about Michael's herpes, but everyone tells him it feels like he is always asking for their attention, like when he got his new phone and he was announcing scores for the World Cup. *(Sex Ed)*

- Michael makes an announcement that he's hired Danny Cordray. *(The Sting)*

- Michael announces "sex" then "money" to help Ryan get people to invest in WUPHF.com. *(WUPHF.com)*

the office book of lists

- Michael tells everyone to stop working and imagine that America is not the number-one superpower and they need to come up with a big idea. *(China)*

- Kelly and Ryan make an announcement that they were in the Poconos and got a divorce and never told anyone they'd gotten married a week earlier. *(The Search)*

- Michael announces to Holly in front of the staff, "Love you, love you." And she says the same. *(PDA)*

- On Valentine's Day, Michael and Holly announce that they are moving in together. *(PDA)*

- Michael announces that Todd Packer is going to apologize to Kevin. *(Todd Packer)*

- Michael asks everyone to start clapping to meet the new manager, Deangelo Vickers, who then rolls down the blinds in Michael's office to reveal himself. *(Training Day)*

- Andy says to listen up, as he wants Michael's job. *(Search Committee)*

- Andy and Jim confess they were lying about Jim's jury duty. *(Jury Duty)*

- Angela announces that her cat Comstock is still up for adoption. *(New Guys)*

- Dwight announces that the new guys aren't so cool because they can slackline and pedal over a trapeze wire from the roof across the parking lot. *(New Guys)*

- Darryl announces that there is a voluntary meeting to talk about Erin's looks for her news audition. *(Roy's Wedding)*

- Pam raises the lift in the warehouse to ask who vandalized her mural. She then claims David Wallace gave her clearance to hold a super-secret classified conference room meeting in the office, where she also talks about the vandalism. *(Vandalism)*

- Andy announces that he is leaving Dunder Mifflin to pursue his dream of being famous. He later announces that he is staying on in sales. *(Livin' the Dream)*

## STAFF RELATIVES

When people work together as long as the employees at the Dunder Mifflin Scranton branch have, eventually they start meeting one another's relatives. Over the years, through weddings, births, and even bird funerals, the coworkers meet or hear about many of their office family's extended families.

- Teri is Stanley's wife, until he has an affair with his nurse, Cynthia. *(The Dundies)*

- Pam's mom, Helene, briefly dates Michael after her divorce. *(Sexual Harassment)*

- Stanley's daughter, Melissa, hits on Ryan. *(Take Your Daughter to Work Day)*

- Mose Schrute is Dwight's cousin and best friend for a while. *(Office Olympics)*

- Larisa Halpert is Jim's sister. *(The Fight)*

- Kevin's fiancée, Stacy, has a daughter named Abby. *(Take Your Daughter to Work Day)*

- Meredith's son, Jake, is suspended for a week and she gets permission to bring him to work and not pay for a sitter. He later becomes a stripper and Meredith gives him tips during Angela's bachelorette party. *(Take Your Daughter to Work Day / Finale)*

- Toby's daughter is named Sasha. *(Take Your Daughter to Work Day)*

- Oscar's great-grandmother in Mexico died when he was five. *(Drug Testing)*

- Roy's cousin Billy has twins. *(Grief Counseling)*

- Mehetabel Schrute's grave is seen behind Heinrich Rolf Mannheim's at Schrute Farms. *(Initiation)*

Dwight explains what each of his cousins is known for:

Johann is the handsome one.
Mose is the artsy one.
Helga is the outlaw.
Dwight is Joe Cool.
Heimdall is the runt.

*(The Convict)*

- Michael's mom marries a man named Jeff. *(Phyllis' Wedding)*

- Roy brings his brother, Kenny, to Pam's art show. *(Business School)*

- Jan has a baby girl, Astrid. *(Baby Shower)*

- Jim's brother Pete lives in Boston and his brother Tom lives in New Jersey. *(Employee Transfer)*

- Jim buys the house he grew up in to help his mom, and for him and Pam—without telling her. *(Frame Toby)*

- Pam's parents get divorced after Jim tells her dad how much he loves Pam, and Pam's father realizes he doesn't love Pam's mother like that. *(Stress Relief)*

- While Stanley's wife Teri goes out of town a lot, Stanley starts having an affair with Cynthia, the nurse who helped him during his rehab. *(Gossip)*

- Pam's mee-maw, Sylvia, is eighty and very conservative. *(Niagara)*

- Pam's sister is named Penny. *(Niagara)*

- Michael's aunt blocked him on Instant Message. *(The Lover)*

- Jim and Pam's daughter is named Cecelia Marie Halpert and is nick-named Cece. *(The Delivery)*

- Erin's foster brother's name is Reed. *(St. Patrick's Day)*

- Michael hires his nephew, Luke Cooper, as an assistant and ends up having to spank and fire him. *(Nepotism)*

- Cece's godfather is Pam and Jim's friend Seth, not Michael. *(The Christening)*

- Darryl's daughter is named Jada and his ex-wife is named Justine. *(Classy Christmas)*

- Darryl's grandmother dies, and when Pam circulates a sympathy card, everyone thinks it's his birthday and writes inappropriate birthday-type greetings. *(PDA)*

- Michael calls Holly's father about asking for her hand in marriage. Unfortunately, her father can't seem to focus. *(Garage Sale)*

**DID YOU KNOW?**

Ryan claims his mom makes the best pesto in the world, so he tries to sell it at the garage sale. He uses Phyllis's picture on the Mama Sally's Kosher Homemade Pesto label, as it has the mom look he wants. He uses Oscar's photo for her Señor Chico's Hot Cha Cha Salsa. *(Garage Sale)*

- Phyllis takes a test to see if she is Erin's mom, but it turns out she isn't. They remain close, though. *(Search Committee)*

- Pam and Angela both plan to name their sons Phillip. *(Garden Party)*

- Andy's mother and father are Ellen and Walter. His younger brother is Walter Jr., as his parents felt he more exemplified the name than Andy did. *(Garden Party)*

- Robert California's son is named Bert. He comes to the office dressed as a zombie. *(Spooked)*

- Robert California's wife, Susan, tries to get hired at the Scranton branch. *(Mrs. California)*

- Andy's grandmother is named Ruth and he is extremely close to her. *(Christmas Wishes)*

- Angela marries Senator Robert Lipton and has a son (that is actually Dwight's), Phillip Halstead Lipton. *(Jury Duty)*

- Toby claims his ex-wife used to demolish him in fights. *(Test the Store)*

- Darryl admits on camera that his daughter is chubby and then apologizes to her on camera. He adds that they will exercise more. *(Last Day in Florida)*

- Andy believes he is a distant blood relative of Michelle Obama when Nellie pretends she looked up his ancestry online. *(Andy's Ancestry)*

- Dwight has a brother named Jeb, who no longer comes back for Christmas. *(Dwight Christmas)*

- Dwight's aunt Shirley is on her last legs. *(Couples Discount)*

- When Aunt Shirley dies, Dwight's brother, Jeb, and sister, Fannie, come home for the funeral. Fannie's son is named Cameron. Fannie writes a poem, "A Willing Ignorance," that is published in the *Hartford Women's Lit Quarterly*. **(The Farm)**

- Stanley's wife, Teri, knows about Cynthia, but neither of them know about Lydia. **(Promos)**

- Angela's big sister is Rachel. They haven't spoken in over sixteen years due to a disagreement Angela doesn't remember. **(Finale)**

## OFFICE GIFTS

Christmas and Valentine's Day aren't the only times presents get exchanged in the office. There are a handful of notable gifts over the years, including Michael's infamous going-away present for Toby.

### DID YOU KNOW?

Stanley gets Pam and Roy a toaster. When they call off their wedding, they give it back to him. He can't return it, so now his house has two toasters. **(Gay Witch Hunt)** He gives one to Phyllis for her nuptials and then tries to give Jim and Pam a toaster for their wedding. **(Niagara)** Karen and Jim also give Phyllis a toaster for a wedding gift. **(Phyllis' Wedding)**

- Dwight gives Michael a hockey jersey that reads on the back "FROM DWIGHT." **(Michael's Birthday)**

- The staff gives Michael the Night Swept collection of fragrances—most likely from the drugstore. **(Michael's Birthday)**

- Corporate sends everyone Dunder Mifflin bathrobes. The shipment is one bathrobe short and Dwight steals Toby's. Later, Pam gives Toby one. **(A Benihana Christmas)**

- Ryan gives Kelly a CD for Christmas. She gets him a present but throws it away when she doesn't think Ryan is giving her a present. She then searches through the dumpster for it. **(A Benihana Christmas)**

- Dwight wins walkie-talkies in the Christmas raffle. **(A Benihana Christmas)**

- For Toby's going-away present, Michael gives him a rock with a Post-it note that says "Suck on this." When everyone shames Michael for this, he claims it was a "psych" and the real gift is his watch. **(Goodbye, Toby)**

- Everyone chips in and gives Jan a stroller for her baby shower. **(Baby Shower)**

the office book of lists

- After Meredith's intervention, Phyllis doesn't want to give out the gifts from Corporate, as they aren't appropriate—shot glasses. *(Moroccan Christmas)*

- Andy gives Michael a bottle of wine for a farewell present. *(Two Weeks)*

## DID YOU KNOW?

When Michael returns from Jamaica, he gives some of the staff gifts, including a Rasta wig for Dwight, a Bob Marley (who Michael thinks is Milli Vanilli) T-shirt for Andy, a lei for Angela, a coconut bra for Pam, and a coffee for Stanley that he tells him is ganja. *(Back from Vacation)*

- Phyllis gives Jim and Pam a romantic birdhouse mailbox that her cousin made for their wedding gift. *(The Promotion)*

- For his wedding gift to Pam, Ryan convinces Pam to give him $50 to invest in an opportunity for a $5,000 gift a year from now. *(The Promotion)*

- Michael paints a portrait of Jim and Pam for their wedding gift. He paints one of them in the nude as well, but that's for him. *(Niagara)*

- Dwight gives Jim and Pam a set of turtle-boiling pots, a shell hammer, and bibs for their wedding. *(Niagara)*

- Jim and Pam bring back a bottle of Oscuro rum from their honeymoon to give to Michael. *(The Lover)*

- Michael gives Helene a scrapbook of their first memories for her birthday. *(Double Date)*

- Andy frames a newspaper of the day Cece was born, but since she wasn't born until the next day, he has to replace the newspaper. The new headline reads "Scranton Strangler Strikes Again." *(The Delivery)*

- Michael gives Jo a piece of coal from the Anthracite Heritage Museum when she leaves to go back to Tallahassee. *(St. Patrick's Day)*

- Val gives all the warehouse workers knitted beanies. Darryl thinks it's a special gift for him. *(Special Project)*

- Darryl gives Nate the cashmere gloves he wanted to give Val for Valentine's Day. *(Special Project)*

- Nate gives Darryl a coupon for one free tickle monster attack. *(Special Project)*

- Clark donates his espresso maker as a gift from Jan to the office. *(Suit Warehouse)*

- "Phillip" gives Kevin a $25 iTunes gift card (with $7 left) for letting him hang out in Accounting. *(A.A.R.M.)*

- Stanley carves a statue of Phyllis that has flamingo legs. *(Finale)*

## OFFICE DISPUTES

Put any group of people together for long enough and conflicts are bound to arise. Over the years there are definite conflicts among the staff, but ultimately everyone gets along, well, except for Toby and Michael.

- Michael hates Toby and looks for any reason to dislike him more. *(multiple episodes)*

- Jim and Dwight wage a never-ending prank war against each other. *(multiple episodes)*

- Dwight and Andy instantly become rivals when they meet, though over time they bond. *(multiple episodes)*

- Dwight is determined to prove Oscar lied about calling in sick. When he catches him, he agrees not to tell Michael in exchange for one great big, giant favor, redeemable by Dwight at a time and place of his choosing. *(The Secret)*

- Dwight generally likes everyone he's worked with, except for four people. *(Conflict Resolution)*

- Oscar hates Angela's poster of babies playing saxophones. It makes him think of the horrible, frigid stage mothers who force their babies into it. *(Conflict Resolution)*

- When Dwight finds out that four years of his reports on Jim's malfeasance haven't been shared with Corporate, he demands that either he or Jim be out of there by the end of the day. *(Conflict Resolution)*

the office book of lists

- Even though there is no assigned parking, Angela is mad that Phyllis parked in "her" spot, and Phyllis whispers that she doesn't like Angela. *(Conflict Resolution)*

- Angela dismisses Karen from the Party Planning Committee. *(A Benihana Christmas)*

- After Pam and Karen ask Angela if they can merge their Christmas parties, Angela agrees and then reveals she hid their karaoke machine power cord. *(A Benihana Christmas)*

- When Stanley refuses to do anything before the $100 missing from his bonus shows up, he won't tell Phyllis where the list of exchanges was saved. She claims that she really likes Stanley, but then tells the camera crew she doesn't really like him. *(Back from Vacation)*

- When the whole office staff disputes the correct usage of "whomever" versus "whoever," an angry Michael tells Toby to take a letter opener and stick it in his skull. *(Money)*

- When Darryl starts beating Jim at ping-pong, Kelly starts smack-talking Pam. Pam then attempts to get Jim to get better so he can defend her honor. When Jim doesn't get better at ping-pong, Pam and Kelly play each other (badly). *(The Deposition)*

- When Phyllis takes over the planning for Toby's party, she asks for Angela's list of vendors, but Angela says she shredded it. Phyllis knocks some things off Angela's desk in retaliation. *(Goodbye, Toby)*

- Phyllis likes being head of the Party Planning Committee and not being under Angela's heel, while keeping hers on Angela's "little grape head." *(Business Ethics)*

- Phyllis decides she doesn't think it would be blackmail to threaten to reveal Angela is cheating on Andy. She thinks that in order for it to be blackmail, there would have to be a formal letter. *(Moroccan Christmas)*

- For Michael's fifteenth work anniversary party, both Jim and Dwight suggest an ice sculpture surrounded by chocolate-covered fruits, but Jim says it while wearing a tuxedo and in a classier way, so Michael loves the idea coming from him. *(New Boss)*

- Ryan and Pam argue over who should make copies of the "Unparalleled Customer Service" coupons. *(The Michael Scott Paper Company)*

- When Pam becomes a salesperson at Dunder Mifflin, Phyllis is angry that Pam stole her clients by telling them she didn't have enough time for them. *(Casual Friday)*

- Once they become co-managers of the branch, Jim and Michael begin butting heads about having meetings. *(The Promotion)*

- Ryan sends an email around that says Jim is not as much in charge as Michael is. *(Shareholder Meeting)*

- Andy and Darryl wrestle over a pencil when Andy is on a sales call. *(New Leads)*

- Two years ago, Andy blamed the warehouse for a late shipment and Darryl got in trouble. He waited, knowing Andy is a fool and there would be an opportunity to get even. *(The Cover-Up)*

- Michael scoffs at the thought that people consider Gabe the boss. *(Viewing Party)*

- When Michael knows a fact about the populations of cities in China and proves Oscar wrong, no one lets Oscar forget it. *(China)*

- Nate gives Pam information on how Dwight is breaking the law by not adhering to suitable standards for comfortable temperatures and adequate lighting in the building. *(China)*

- Erin dislikes Holly, thinking she's not good enough for Michael. *(The Search)*

- After Erin breaks up with Gabe, he bullies Andy in the bathroom. *(Goodbye, Michael)*

- Phyllis doesn't think people should tell Angela they think Robert is gay. *(Search Committee)*

- Pam and Ryan snap at each other when Ryan says he liked seeing Pam back at the reception desk. *(Lotto)*

- Darryl takes Val with him on a coffee run when Gabe tries to impress her by sending Darryl for coffee. *(Doomsday)*

- Pam plainly tells Ryan she doesn't think he's a good person and she doesn't like him. The rest of the office agrees. *(Angry Andy)*

- Pam realizes Phyllis is a bully when she insults Jim and Pam's house and takes the floral arrangement from the table at the fundraiser. *(Fundraiser)*

- When Jim and Darryl share an apartment, they clash over Jim's messy behavior. *(Vandalism)*

## OFFICE ALLIANCES

Just as crowding coworkers into a confined space day after day can lead to office disputes, it can also lead to some staff alliances and bonds—sometimes surprising ones.

- When paranoia in the office leads to downsizing rumors, Jim and Dwight form an unlikely alliance against their coworkers. *(The Alliance)*

- Andy and Kevin bond over how awesome Ryan is once he moves to New York. *(Dunder Mifflin Infinity)*

- Andy muses that he had to go all the way to Canada to get to know Oscar, who sits twenty feet away from him and is delightful. *(Business Trip)*

- Dwight and Andy were once sexual competitors and Dwight hated him. Dwight's study of Andy to understand why he hated him so much blossoms into a very real friendship. *(The Michael Scott Paper Company)*

the office book of lists

- Charles likes Dwight's work ethic and wants to give him more responsibility. *(Heavy Competition)*

- When Michael needs help because Pam is mad at him for sleeping with her mom, he hugs Toby and likes him briefly for trying to help him with Pam. *(The Lover)*

- Ryan finds a copy of Dwight's plan to take Jim down and tells him he wants in. *(Scott's Tots)*

- Toby and Michael actually bond when Michael makes fun of Gabe. *(Counseling)*

- Michael realizes Erin looks at him as a father figure. *(Viewing Party)*

- After trying to be Darryl's friend for a while, Andy finally sends a text Darryl likes—he tells him to come see two pigeons eating out of an ice cream cone in the parking lot. *(China)*

- Dwight and Jim bond to get rid of Todd Packer when he gets a desk job in the office. *(Todd Packer)*

- Deangelo has an inner circle of Jim, Kevin, Gabe, and Darryl. Andy replaces Jim after Jim calls out Deangelo's sexism. *(The Inner Circle)*

- Kelly agrees to pretend Ryan is her boss to impress Deangelo. *(The Inner Circle)*

- Angela suggests she and Pam take neonatal walks each day as recommended by *Parenting* magazine. *(The Incentive)*

- Oscar tells Toby he should join his wine-tasting club. *(Pool Party)*

- Angela, Pam, and Oscar rotate siding with each other and against each other regarding treating dogs as if they are the same as babies; babies walking; and having two babies versus one. They all unite, however, when Andy tries to show off his brother's new sailboat. *(After Hours)*

- Dwight makes a temporary alliance with Gabriel Susan Lewis to keep Packer from sleeping with Nellie for the VP job. *(After Hours)*

the office book of lists

- Pam does online shopping with Kelly to keep her from getting back together with Ryan. *(Angry Andy)*

- Nellie keeps trying to bond with Darryl. He finally relents when he gets them tacos and he has to teach her how to eat them. *(Fundraiser)*

- Darryl gets Dwight and Nellie to bond by making them watch *127 Hours*. *(Roy's Wedding)*

- Oscar realizes Angela makes a lot of sound points after she hires someone to shatter his kneecaps for sleeping with her husband. *(Dwight Christmas)*

- After most of the office gets lice, Pam and Meredith have a drink, bond over motherhood, and sing "Girls Just Want to Have Fun" karaoke. *(Lice)*

- Dwight plans a "Dwight and a friend axis" against Pam for when he hires the new junior salesman. *(Junior Salesman)*

- Erin is excited to help Darryl "sneak" out of the office to go work at Jim's company in Philly. *(Vandalism)*

- Kevin calls out the senator for stringing Angela and Oscar along. *(Vandalism)*

- To get the Valentine's couples discount, Darryl pretends to be Oscar's partner. When they get discriminated against, Darryl aggressively stands up for gay rights. *(Couples Discount)*

- After Angela is evicted from her apartment, Oscar invites her to move in with him. *(Livin' the Dream)*

- Dwight and Jim finally truly bond over Jim's advice that Dwight go after Angela since he loves her. *(A.A.R.M.)*

- Phyllis vows Angela will get to the altar. *(Finale)*

- Dwight says Pam is his best friend. *(Finale)*

## OFFICE QUOTES

While Dwight and Michael seem to get some of the best one-liners, there are many hilarious and memorable quotes and sayings from the rest of the staff.

- Jim: "If I advance any higher in this company, then this would be my career. And, uh, well, if this were my career, I'd have to throw myself in front of a train." *(Health Care)*

- When Michael asks Stanley what his "injured" foot looks like in its makeshift bubble-wrap "cast," Stanley says, "Mailboxes, etc." *(The Injury)*

- Pam: "It's just good to stop a Michael train of thought early before it derails and destroys the entire town." *(Sex Ed)*

- Meredith: "For my New Year's resolution, I gave up drinking . . . during the week." *(Christmas Party)*

- Kevin: "So, me think, why waste time say lot word, when few word do trick." *(Incentive)*

- Jim: "As it turns out, Dwight finding drugs is more dangerous than most people using drugs." *(Drug Testing)*

- Pam: "It's like Mommy and Daddy are fighting. Except Mommy outranks Daddy and Mommy is way scarier." *(Initiation)*

- Phyllis: "Close your mouth, sweetie. You look like a trout." *(Casual Friday)*

- Robert: "If I invited you to lunch, I think you're a winner. If I didn't, I don't. But I just met you all. Life is long; opinions change. Winners prove me right. Losers prove me wrong." *(The List)*

- Ryan: "I miss the days when there was only one party I didn't want to go to." *(A Benihana Christmas)*

- Andy: "My heart belongs to music. But my ass belongs to these people." *(The Incentive)*

- Kevin: "I got six numbers. One more and it would have been a complete phone number." *(Niagara)*

- Robert: "There's something about an underdog that really inspires . . . the unexceptional." *(The Incentive)*

- Darryl: "My future's not gonna be determined by seven little white lotto balls. It's gonna be determined by two big black balls. I control my destiny. I do." *(Lotto)*

- Phyllis: "We have a gym at home. It's called the bedroom." *(Mrs. California)*

- Kelly: "I talk a lot, so I've learned to tune myself out." *(Counseling)*

- Andy: "Do not bring Shakespeare into this. How dare you play the bard card?" *(Free Family Portrait Studio)*

- Creed: "Everywhere I look it's Betty White this and Betty White that. Finally, a kid that's not talking about Betty White. Of course, I follow him." *(Nepotism)*

- Toby: "Michael is like a movie on a plane. You know it's not great but it's something to watch. And when it's over you're like, how much time is left on this flight? Now what?" *(Two Weeks)*

- Andy: "Women cannot resist a man singing show tunes. It's so powerful, even a lot of men can't resist a man singing show tunes." *(Andy's Play)*

- Pam: "AND I FEEL GOD IN THIS CHILI'S TONIGHT." *(The Dundies)*

- Jim: "I miss Dwight. Congratulations, universe. You win." *(The Return)*

the office book of lists

- Jim: "I've never been a kissup. It's just not how I operate. I mean, I've always subscribed to the idea that if you really want to impress your boss, you go in there and you do mediocre work, halfheartedly." *(Dream Team)*

- Creed: "You ever notice you can only ooze two things? Sexuality and pus. Man, I tell ya." *(Body Language)*

- Kevin: "*C* is for suspension." *(Secretary's Day)*

- Stanley: "I would like the memory of a day uninterrupted by this nonsense." *(Café Disco)*

- Phyllis: "I'm glad Michael is getting help. He has a lot of issues and he's stupid." *(Counseling)*

- Creed: "I've been involved in a number of cults, both as a leader and a follower. You have more fun as a follower, but you make more money as a leader." *(Fun Run)*

- Stanley: "I took an extra shot of insulin in preparation for this cake today." *(Survivor Man)*

- Jim: "Oh God, now I can't drink at this thing . . . I get really pranky when I drink." *(Christmas Wishes)*

- Angela: "If you pray enough, you can change yourself into a cat person." *(New Guys)*

- Stanley: "Life is short. Drive fast and leave a sexy corpse. That's one of my mottos." *(Tallahassee)*

- Oscar: "I didn't realize how many of Angela's opinions I agreed with until she tried to have my kneecap shattered for sleeping with her husband. She makes a lot of very sound points." *(Dwight Christmas)*

- Kelly: "Ravi makes me incredibly happy. And Ryan put me through so much drama. So I guess I just have to decide which of those is more important to me." *(Angry Andy)*

- Kelly: "Don't dump me while I'm in the dumpster!" *(A Benihana Christmas)*

- Stanley: "I always knew my coworkers were annoying. I never realized I could profit from it." *(Safety Training)*

- Kevin: "Oscar, I'm now going to be prone to surges." *(Crime Aid)*

- Stanley: "I've got a golden ticket idea. Why don't you skip on up to the roof and jump off?" *(Golden Ticket)*

- Kelly: "I mean, who says exactly what they're thinking? What kind of game is that?" *(Money)*

- Darryl: "I wanted to leave quietly. It seemed dignified. But having Kevin grind up on my front while Erin pretends to hump me from behind is a more accurate tribute to my years here. I'm gonna miss these guys." *(A.A.R.M.)*

- Andy: "I wish there was a way to know you're in the good old days before you've actually left them. Someone should write a song about that." *(Finale)*

- Pam: "There's a lot of beauty in ordinary things. Isn't that kind of the point?" *(Finale)*

## MICHAEL SAYS GOODBYE

It is bittersweet for Michael to leave the office he's been part of for so long to move to Colorado with Holly. Uncharacteristically, he doesn't make a big deal about it. He even leaves a day early, before his goodbye party. Still, he manages to say goodbye to everyone in his own way.

- Michael gives Phyllis a windup mouth toy so she can speak her mind more.

- Michael gives Stanley a toy pool table with no balls.

- Michael gives Andy his ten most important accounts.

- Michael rips up a poster of Kevin as a pig and tells him, "Never settle for who you are."

- Michael gives Oscar a pathetically made ragdoll, knowing Oscar's low opinion of him and that Oscar would accept that he worked hard to make it for him.

the office book of lists

- Michael admits he thought he and Angela would have sex one day.

- Michael gives Darryl his unfinished manuscript of *Somehow I Manage*.

- Michael shoots hoops with the warehouse staff until he makes one and says, "Catch you on the flippity-flop." They ignore him.

- Michael gives Erin advice and his phone number.

- Michael gives Dwight a glowing and personal letter of recommendation and then plays paintball with him in the parking lot.

- Michael tells Creed, Gabe, and Meredith not to worry about dying; it will be okay.

- Both Michael and Jim get emotional, as Jim is the only one who realizes Michael is leaving early. They make lunch plans for the following day.

- Michael gives Toby nothing.

- Michael walks away from Kelly when she's talking to him.

- Michael gives Ryan his neon St. Pauli Girl sign.

- Michael and Pam hug and share a sweet moment at the airport.

*(Goodbye, Michael)*

# Chapter Three:
# Office
# Romances

# PAM AND ROY

Roy and Pam are engaged for three years when the documentary begins filming.

♥ Roy gets angry when he thinks Jim and Pam are planning pranks on Dwight, thinking Jim is trying to "cop a feel." *(The Alliance)*

♥ Roy and his brother once went to a hockey game and left while Pam was in the bathroom, forgetting all about her. *(The Client)*

♥ Roy publicly sets a date for his wedding with Pam on the booze cruise. *(Booze Cruise)*

♥ Michael tries to make a Brangelina-type reference out of Roy and Pam's names, calling them Ram. *(Boys and Girls)*

♥ Roy tells Jim he is cool about knowing Jim used to have a crush on Pam. He's glad she has someone to talk to so she doesn't talk a lot at home. *(Boys and Girls)*

♥ Roy has a connection at the VA and wants to have his and Pam's wedding reception there. Pam explains it's nicer than you'd think there. *(Dwight's Speech)*

♥ After Pam kisses Jim on Casino Night, she calls off her wedding to Roy, moves out, and starts taking art classes. Roy grows a beard, gets arrested for drunk driving, and starts working out. *(Gay Witch Hunt)*

♥ Roy comes to the Diwali celebration, but when he sees Pam dancing, he leaves before anyone sees him. *(Diwali)*

♥ At Phyllis's wedding, Roy pays Scrantonicity $20 to play his and Pam's song. *(Phyllis' Wedding)*

♥ After Phyllis's wedding, Roy and Pam get back together. Pam thinks they have a solid foundation. *(Business School)*

♥ Pam tells Roy that if they're going to be a couple, he has to come to stuff with her, like happy hour at Poor Richard's with the office. *(Cocktails)*

♥ At Poor Richard's, Pam tells Roy about the time she kissed Jim. Roy gets mad and starts breaking things. He later threatens to kill Jim. *(Cocktails)*

♥ Roy attacks Jim, but Dwight pepper sprays him. Roy is then fired. *(The Negotiation)*

♥ After Roy is fired, he and Pam have coffee and he says he doesn't get Pam. She says she knows. *(Product Recall)*

♥ Roy invites Jim and Pam to his wedding to Laura at their mansion at 8 a.m. on a weekday. *(Roy's Wedding)*

# JIM AND PAM

Pam and Jim's love story becomes the defining relationship of nearly a decade of the documentary filming. Even the documentary crew admits they are following Pam and Jim to see what will happen.

♥ During a long meeting, Pam falls asleep with her head on Jim's shoulder. *(Diversity Day)*

♥ Jim admires Pam's idea to trick Dwight into getting into a box in the warehouse. *(The Alliance)*

♥ Pam almost asks Jim a serious question at the Dundies but changes her mind. *(The Dundies)*

♥ While playing Who Would You Do?, both Jim and Pam avoid saying each other. *(The Fire)*

♥ Pam sarcastically calls Katy's car "adorable." *(The Fire)*

♥ After forwarding Katy's call to Jim, Pam tells Jim he can just give Katy his direct extension. *(Halloween)*

♥ Pam and Jim playfully start a fight at Dwight's karate dojo. *(The Fight)*

♥ Jim and Pam watch Dwight's fireworks from the roof. Jim says they've now had their first date, but Pam brushes it off. *(The Client)*

♥ Phyllis assumes Pam and Jim are having a secret office romance, because they hang out all the time. *(Email Surveillance)*

♥ Pam trades Dwight the iPod for the Secret Santa present she was supposed to get from Jim. Jim takes back the card inside the teapot

for Pam, in which he professes his feelings to her, before she can read it. *(Christmas Party)*

♥ Jim admits on the cruise that if there were a fire in the office, he would save the receptionist. *(Booze Cruise)*

♥ Jim breaks up with Katy on the cruise. He then admits to Michael that he "used to have a big thing for Pam." Michael is shocked, as he usually has a radar for stuff like that. *(Booze Cruise)*

♥ Michael, unable to keep Jim's confession that he has a crush on Pam a secret, blurts out the details and Kelly realizes he's talking about Pam. *(The Secret)*

♥ Jim admits to Pam that he liked her but claims it was a long time ago. Michael later tells Pam it was as recent as the booze cruise. *(The Secret)*

♥ Jim calls and asks Brenda from Corporate out. *(The Carpet)*

♥ Pam leaves Jim seven voicemails about things happening when Michael takes over Jim's desk. *(The Carpet)*

♥ When Roy dismisses Pam's desire to take the graphic design internship in New York, Jim rebukes Pam for listening to Roy, which ends up creating tension between them. *(Boys and Girls)*

♥ Jim observes that Pam tries not to "bother" Roy with things like her thoughts and feelings. *(Conflict Resolution)*

♥ On Casino Night, Jim tells Pam he's in love with her. She says he has misinterpreted her feelings for him. When Pam is on the phone telling her mom, she and Jim kiss. *(Casino Night)*

♥ When Jim returns to Scranton, he tells the camera crew he and Pam are friends and that's where things stand. *(The Merger)*

♥ When the Stamford and Scranton branches merge, Jim tells Pam he's seeing someone. *(The Merger)*

♥ Pam asks Ryan to set her up with one of his business school friends after Karen asks her if she is still interested in Jim. *(Ben Franklin)*

♥ Jim and Pam lock eyes while Jim dances with Karen at Phyllis's wedding. *(Phyllis' Wedding)*

♥ On Beach Day, after Pam walks across hot coals, she tells everyone she called off her wedding for Jim and that it sucks that things are weird between them now. *(Beach Games)*

♥ Jim sees the Office Olympics medal Pam left him in his quarterly numbers and he decides not to take the job at Corporate. *(The Job)*

♥ When Jim comes back from his interview with Corporate, he asks Pam out on a date. *(The Job)*

♥ Toby's memo on PDA causes Jim and Pam to admit to the office they're dating. *(Dunder Mifflin Infinity)*

the office book of lists

♥ After their relationship is made public, Jim asks Pam if the "magic" is gone. She jokes that it is and says she now finds Jim repulsive. *(Dunder Mifflin Infinity)*

♥ While eating pizza on the roof, Jim says the moment he knew Pam was the one was on his first day when Pam warned him he could never go back to the time before he met Dwight. Pam knew Jim was the one when he told her not to eat the mixed berry yogurt that had expired. *(Launch Party)*

♥ After seeing Dwight devastated by his breakup with Angela, Jim kisses Pam passionately and makes a date to go to dinner at the new Italian place. *(Money)*

♥ After Pam sets Michael up on a date with his landlady, Jim says Pam's going to get kicked out of her apartment. They discuss living together and getting engaged. Jim promises the engagement will "kick her ass." Jim shows the camera crew the ring he bought a week after they started dating. *(Chair Model)*

♥ Jim plans to propose at the office during Toby's going-away party and gives Phyllis money to buy fireworks. However, Andy steals his thunder when he takes the moment to propose to Angela. *(Goodbye, Toby)*

♥ Unable to wait any longer, Jim meets Pam halfway between Scranton and New York at the Exit 17 rest stop, where soda explodes on him. He proposes to her in the rain. She says yes. *(Weight Loss)*

♥ Jim and Pam have an off day in communication when the office holds Jan's baby shower. They leave each other voicemails retelling the same anecdote and saying how they miss each other. *(Baby Shower)*

♥ After running into Roy at a bar and being reminded that Roy used to think Jim was just Pam's friend, Jim drives to New York to see Pam, who has been hanging out all night with her friends. Then he turns around, as he is not "that guy" and they are not "that couple." *(Crime Aid)*

♥ When Pam fails one of her classes, Jim supports her decision to stay another three months and retake it, telling her to come home "the right way" after she follows her dream. When he leaves work, Pam is in the parking lot. She came back the "wrong way" but says it's not because she misses Jim. *(Business Trip)*

♥ Jim tells Pam's father how he feels when Pam walks in a room and how he never doubted for a second that she's who he wants to spend the rest of his life with. *(Stress Relief)*

♥ Jim and Pam decide one morning to go to Youngstown, Ohio, where they can get a marriage license without a three-day waiting period. Later, while dancing in Michael's Café Disco, Pam decides she wants a "wedding" wedding. *(Café Disco)*

♥ After prepping the rest of the office not to spill the beans about Pam's pregnancy at the wedding, Jim accidentally does when making a toast. *(Niagara)*

♥ When Pam's veil rips, Jim cuts his tie in half to make her feel better. They end up running off to a Niagara Falls tour boat, getting married there, and then coming back to the church. *(Niagara)*

♥ Pam's family and the office staff perform a flash mob dance to "Forever" up the aisle at Jim and Pam's wedding. *(Niagara)*

♥ Pam had two dates with Danny Cordray four years earlier, which everyone blows out of proportion when Danny gets hired. *(Costume Contest)*

♥ After Robert divides the office into winners and losers, Jim makes a list that has "Pam, Cece, and new baby" in the winners column and "everything else" in the losers column. Pam weeps and decides to frame it. *(The List)*

♥ Pam loves when Jim gets excited about her good news and says "Beesly!" excitedly. *(Customer Loyalty)*

♥ Pam and Jim get into an argument when Pam isn't able to film Cece's recital and Jim loses Bridgeport Capital. *(Customer Loyalty)*

♥ Jim gets angry that Brian, the sound guy, knows more about his marriage than he does. *(Couples Discount)*

♥ When Jim gives Pam a framed sketch she did of people in a café, it heads off their argument on Valentine's Day. *(Couples Discount)*

♥ Pam likes her life with Jim in Scranton and is reluctant to get a job in Philadelphia. *(Moving On)*

♥ Pam and Jim go to marriage counseling. Jim wants Pam to be patient until his sports marketing company is big, and Pam wants Jim to stop making decisions without telling her. *(Stairmageddon)*

- ♥ In counseling, Jim and Pam are told to appreciate each other at every opportunity. *(Paper Airplane)*

- ♥ Pam and Jim argue about their truths and Clark thinks they might be high. *(Paper Airplane)*

- ♥ Jim is about to leave for Philly after he and Pam fight. Pam runs to Jim in the rain to give him his umbrella. They tell each other, "I love you." *(Paper Airplane)*

- ♥ Pam confesses to Jim that she thinks she's not enough for him. *(A.A.R.M.)*

- ♥ Pam's conversation with Darryl makes her wonder if she was wrong to try and keep Jim in Scranton. *(A.A.R.M.)*

- ♥ Jim finally gives Pam the teapot note and the camera crew's DVD of their relationship highlights. Pam finally realizes she has always been everything to him. *(A.A.R.M.)*

- ♥ At the reunion panel, someone asks what romantic things Pam is doing to pay Jim back. He interrupts and says she paid him back every day by being his wife. *(Finale)*

- ♥ Pam hires Carol Stills to sell their house so she and Jim can go anywhere they want. She tells Jim that since he bought the house without telling her, she thought she could sell it without telling him. *(Finale)*

## MICHAEL AND JAN

Michael and Jan's passionate romance begins in the parking lot of Chili's and ends after a tempestuous dinner party.

- ♥ Once Michael closes a deal with a difficult client, the newly divorced Jan is thrilled and lets Michael kiss her. That night, they talk and she falls asleep on Michael's arm. *(The Client)*

- ♥ Michael is about to register his relationship with Jan with HR when Jan calls him to say it was a mistake and wonders if he slipped her something. They then have their first fight. *(The Client)*

- ♥ Michael asks Pam to analyze a voicemail Jan left him. *(Performance Review)*

- ♥ Jan won't discuss the kiss during Michael's review, yet he considers Jan his girlfriend now. *(Performance Review)*

- ♥ Jan admits Michael is sweet and that he cried with her during their night together. *(Performance Review)*

- ♥ After Michael tells David he was only joking about having slept with Jan, Jan tells Michael "thank you" in the elevator and they kiss again. *(Valentine's Day)*

- ♥ Michael invites Jan to Casino Night, calling her the Eva Perón to his Cesar Chavez and suggesting that they remain good friends with privileges. *(Casino Night)*

♥ Michael is flustered when both Jan and Carol are at Casino Night. He tells Jan that he understands they have an open relationship. *(Casino Night)*

♥ Michael asks Jan if she wants to go to Sandals with him. *(A Benihana Christmas)*

♥ Jan goes to Sandals with Michael and they have sex. *(Back from Vacation)*

♥ After a salacious photo of Jan and Michael is accidentally emailed out, Jan comes to the office and tells Michael she wants to find some kind of happiness, even if it means lowering her expectations. *(Back from Vacation)*

♥ At the mall, Michael admits he's unhappy with Jan. She makes him dress up as the schoolgirl when they have sex and she videotapes their sex to watch it back and show Michael how to improve his form. She also shows the tape to her therapist. In Michael's pros and cons list, he writes, "I'm unhappy when I'm with her." He also says he's happy with Jan sometimes when they scrapbook or right toward the end of sex. *(Women's Appreciation)*

♥ Jan comes to see Michael just as he leaves her a voicemail breaking up with her. *(Women's Appreciation)*

♥ Michael assembles the women in the office in the conference room to support him during "DEFCON 20"— when Jan wants to get back together. *(The Job)*

♥ Even though Michael is scared of Jan and doesn't want to get back together with her, when she shows up at the office with breast implants, he says, "It's a sign of maturity to give people second chances. So I am going to hear her out." *(The Job)*

♥ When Jan doesn't want to go to the website launch party, Michael asks if he can invite Carol. Jan says no. *(Launch Party)*

♥ Jan tells Michael he was there for her when her world collapsed and that he is worth staying beside during his debt crisis. *(Money)*

♥ At Michael and Jan's dinner party, Jan tells Pam that Michael claimed he and Pam dated. Both Jan and Angela remark that they've seen Pam look at Michael in the office. *(Dinner Party)*

♥ Jan has "space issues," so Michael sleeps on a bench at the foot of the bed. *(Dinner Party)*

♥ Michael tries to get Jim and Andy to invest $10,000 in Jan's candle company. *(Dinner Party)*

♥ Michael lets everyone know he had a vasectomy and reversed it three times because Jan couldn't decide if she wants kids or not. *(Dinner Party)*

♥ Michael and Jan's fight at their dinner party escalates when she points out that dipping his veal in his wine is disgusting. Michael then rehangs his St. Pauli Girl neon beer sign and Jan throws a Dundie Award at his plasma TV. *(Dinner Party)*

♥ After Michael and Jan's dinner party, Michael swears off women. But maybe just one woman—Jan. *(Chair Model)*

♥ Instead of telling Jan he might have herpes, Michael engages her in a postmortem of their relationship. *(Sex Ed)*

# PHYLLIS AND BOB VANCE

Phyllis proudly talks up Bob Vance, Vance Refrigeration, to her coworkers and the two end up engaged and happily married.

♥ Bob thinks Phyllis is thirty-one and wants lots of babies. *(The Convict)*

♥ When Oscar comes out, Phyllis announces that she and Bob Vance, Vance Refrigeration, are getting married. *(Gay Witch Hunt)*

♥ Phyllis doesn't want any more drama at her wedding. She already has baby-mama drama with Bob's other family coming in from Ho Chi Minh City. *(Ben Franklin)*

♥ On a lunch double date with Pam and Jim, Phyllis and Bob go into the handicapped bathroom and have sex. *(Blood Drive)*

♥ When Dwight massages her hurt back, Phyllis admits she thinks Bob Vance, Vance Refrigeration, is going to cheat on her with his secretary. When she says it out loud, she giggles, knowing it sounds silly. *(Café Disco)*

♥ When Michael shows up as Santa when Jim promised Phyllis that she could be Santa, she threatens, "Don't make me get Bob involved." *(Secret Santa)*

♥ Phyllis likes to go to bars with Bob, wear something low-cut to get men to flirt with her, and then watch as Bob beats them up. *(Happy Hour)*

♥ Phyllis claims that when she was wooing Bob, she showed up in his office every day for two weeks— naked, except for kitty-cat ears. Then Bob showed up naked, except for a dog nose. *(Search Committee)*

## KELLY AND RYAN

Kelly and Ryan's on-again, off-again relationship takes many twists and turns, with the pair running away together in the series finale.

♥ After Kelly asks Jim to see if Ryan likes her, Ryan asks Jim to see if Kelly is looking for something long-term or if she's okay just hanging out. Kelly responds to Jim that she wants to fall in love, have babies, and spend every second together, but that he shouldn't tell Ryan that. *(The Carpet)*

♥ Ryan and Kelly first hook up on February 13. *(Valentine's Day)*

♥ Kelly tells Jim she would be so psyched to date Ryan forever. Jim tries to tell Kelly Ryan isn't into her, but she doesn't listen. *(Valentine's Day)*

♥ Ryan tells Kelly he can't see himself ever getting married. *(Dwight's Speech)*

♥ Ryan explains he and Kelly agreed to just have fun, but he's finding out fun for Kelly means getting married and having babies—immediately—with him. *(Take Your Daughter to Work Day)*

the office book of lists

- ♥ On their double date with Pam and Alan, Kelly keeps feeding Ryan. *(The Convention)*

- ♥ At the Diwali celebration, Kelly's mom wants her to date Wali, who is a "whole" doctor, not a temp like Ryan. *(Diwali)*

- ♥ When it appears the Scranton branch is closing, Ryan suggests he and Kelly not see each other anymore as it doesn't make sense. When Jan says Stamford is closing instead, Kelly says it's the best day of her life. *(Branch Closing)*

- ♥ While Kelly looks in the dumpster for the present for Ryan she threw away, Ryan suggests they may need to break up. She cries that he can't dump her while she's in a dumpster. They end up having sex in the dumpster. *(A Benihana Christmas)*

- ♥ When stuck with Kelly in the annex, Ryan asks Toby about a rule against interoffice dating, but Toby refuses to do his "dirty work" for him. *(Cocktails)*

- ♥ Ryan calls Kelly in the middle of the night whenever he thinks his apartment has been broken into. Kelly calls him in the middle of the night to say she loves him. *(The Negotiation)*

- ♥ Kelly wants to name her and Ryan's potential baby Usher Jennifer Hudson Kapoor. *(The Negotiation)*

- ♥ At the mall, Kelly says things with her and Ryan are awesome. "Um, awful, I mean. But sometimes awesome." *(Women's Appreciation)*

- ♥ When Ryan gets the job at Corporate, he tells Kelly they're done. *(The Job)*

- ♥ When Ryan comes back to the office to introduce Dunder Mifflin Infinity, Kelly claims she's pregnant by him. After he yells at her for lying about being pregnant, he says they will never get back together and she asks, "Why not?" *(Dunder Mifflin Infinity)*

- ♥ Ryan suggests to David Wallace that they should downsize Kelly and outsource the customer service to India. *(Dunder Mifflin Infinity)*

- ♥ Kelly slaps a piece of pizza on the TV when it shows Ryan's face during the launch party broadcast. *(Launch Party)*

- ♥ After Ryan is arrested, Kelly can't wait to visit him in prison, wearing her hottest track suit and making the prisoners say he has a hot ex-girlfriend and they wouldn't have treated her so bad on the outside. *(Goodbye, Toby)*

- ♥ When Pam is due back from New York, Ryan has to move back to the annex next to Kelly. Although she is dating Darryl now, after Ryan does a few pushups, they begin making out. *(Business Trip)*

- ♥ Ryan writes a text on Kelly's phone for her to use to break up with Darryl and they press "send" together. Darryl replies, "It's cool," which then makes Ryan have second thoughts. *(Business Trip)*

♥ Ryan tells Kelly he needs to break up with her because he's going to Thailand with some friends from high school. Well, *a* high school. She mentions she broke up with Darryl for him, and Ryan says not to put that on him. *(Frame Toby)*

♥ Kelly wants to come to Jim and Pam's wedding, but not unless Ryan is coming. *(The Meeting)*

♥ Inspired by Michael's attitude of taking what he wants, Ryan asks Erin to sleep with him, then gets cold feet. *(The Chump)*

♥ Kelly makes Ryan take her and her mother out to dinner. *(The Inner Circle)*

♥ Ryan tries to give Jim and Pam baby advice, as they're laughing with Kelly's new pediatrician boyfriend, Ravi. Ryan realizes he loves Kelly once she starts dating Ravi. Ryan dresses up in Indian garb and gets on a horse and recites poetry to propose to Kelly. She chooses Ravi instead. *(Angry Andy)*

♥ When Ryan shows up at Dwight's wedding, he and Kelly make eyes at each other. He causes his baby to have an allergic reaction to strawberries so he can talk to Kelly. They kiss and decide to take off, leaving the baby with Ravi, who then lets Nellie take it. *(Finale)*

## MICHAEL AND CAROL

This short-lived relationship ends when Michael Photoshops his head onto Carol's ex-husband's head in a photo of their family on a ski vacation.

♥ Michael runs into Carol at the ice rink and is great with her kids. *(Michael's Birthday)*

♥ Michael invites Carol to Casino Night when he doesn't think Jan is coming. *(Casino Night)*

♥ After Casino Night, Michael sees Carol seven times, calls her son Thomas "Tomas," and doesn't remember her daughter's name. *(Gay Witch Hunt)*

♥ Michael tells Carol the Diwali party is a costume party. She dresses as a cheerleader. He then proposes to Carol on what is only their ninth date. She leaves him at the party to find his own way home. *(Diwali)*

♥ When Michael tells Carol he might have herpes, she tells him he makes relationships bigger than they are. *(Sex Ed)*

the office book of lists

# MICHAEL AND HELENE

Pam is none too thrilled when Michael dates her mom.

♥ Michael meets Pam's mom, Helene, at Jim and Pam's wedding and they bond over their rough weekend. *(Niagara)*

♥ While Jim and Pam are on their honeymoon, Michael and Helene begin having an affair. *(The Lover)*

♥ Michael feels like he is "robbing the grave" when he finds out Helene is fifty-eight. At her birthday lunch, Michael breaks up with Helene because of her age. *(Double Date)*

♥ Michael calls Helene a jerk after she tells him he's self-deluded. *(Sex Ed)*

# DWIGHT AND ANGELA

The two have a whirlwind of a relationship over the years that ends happily when Dwight realizes that he's the father of Angela's son. Angela and Dwight get married following traditional Schrute customs.

♥ A concussed Dwight says Angela is sweeter than candy and pats her behind. *(The Injury)*

♥ Dwight and Angela share a meaningful look that Kevin notices when they both think that Oscar's absence on Spring Cleaning Day is unacceptable. *(The Secret)*

♥ Angela is the only one to wish Dwight good luck on his speech. *(Dwight's Speech)*

♥ Angela looks approvingly at Dwight when he calls Meredith's son "a horrible little latchkey kid who got suspended from school." *(Take Your Daughter to Work Day)*

♥ Dwight and Angela argue over who should bring Michael's ice cream cake to him. Angela relents, but says Dwight will get no cookie later. *(Michael's Birthday)*

♥ Dwight has to interrogate Angela about the half a joint found in the parking lot, and when he asks where she was the night before, she smiles. *(Drug Testing)*

♥ Six months prior to discussions about complaints in the workplace, Angela withdraws all her complaints about Dwight, and Toby redacts her name. *(Conflict Resolution)*

♥ Angela goes to the hotel at the convention and asks if a key for Dwight's room was left for Jane Doe. *(The Convention)*

♥ Angela defends Dwight to Kelly, saying he's not weird—he's just individualistic. *(Initiation)*

♥ Dwight pretends to be single before the Diwali party, and Angela overhears it. *(Diwali)*

- ♥ Dwight takes the tax forms to Corporate when Angela misses the deadline. *(Traveling Salesman)*

- ♥ Angela breaks up with Dwight after he euthanizes her sick cat, Sprinkles. *(Fun Run)*

- ♥ Dwight tries to give Angela a feral barn cat named Garbage to make up for killing Sprinkles. Garbage has already killed an entire family of raccoons. *(Dunder Mifflin Infinity)*

- ♥ Dwight tells Angela he wants to be just friends, plus a little extra. She doesn't go for it. *(Dunder Mifflin Infinity)*

- ♥ Dwight brings his old babysitter as his date to Michael's dinner party to make Angela jealous. *(Dinner Party)*

- ♥ While everyone is out or at the job fair, Dwight and Angela work alone in the office and are civil to each other. *(Job Fair)*

- ♥ Phyllis catches Dwight and Angela kissing right after Angela accepts Andy's marriage proposal. *(Goodbye, Toby)*

- ♥ When showing off the farm to Andy and Angela as a wedding venue, Dwight uses a German-speaking Mennonite minister to trick Angela into marrying him right then. She later has the legal issue "taken care of." *(The Surplus)*

- ♥ During their duel, Andy and Dwight discover Angela is sleeping with both of them. *(The Duel)*

## DID YOU KNOW?

Dwight confronts Angela and says that he knows Phillip is his son. At first, she denies it and then finally admits it. Dwight pulls Angela over in her car and expresses his love with a megaphone, then proposes to her with the ring taken from the buttocks of his grandmother, put there by the gangster patriarch of the Coors dynasty, melted in a foundry run by Mennonites. Angela and Phillip move in with Dwight. *(A.A.R.M.)*

♥ After the duel over Angela, Dwight throws away the bobblehead Angela had made of him. *(The Duel)*

♥ At the company picnic, when Rolf belittles Angela for what she did to Dwight, Dwight tells him to knock it off, as he and Angela exchange glances. *(Company Picnic)*

♥ Dwight and Angela make a parenting contract for her to bear his child, for business reasons. *(The Delivery)*

♥ Angela says that it would be permissible for Dwight to develop feelings for her under item 7C, clause 2, of their procreation agreement. *(Andy's Play)*

♥ Angela hole-punches the card for their procreation agreement without having sex on the night of Andy's play. *(Andy's Play)*

♥ When Dwight stands Angela up during the Hay Place event, she meets Senator Robert Lipton and flirts with him. *(WUPHF.com)*

♥ Angela leaves the voided procreation agreement on the door where she and Dwight always met in the warehouse. *(WUPHF.com)*

♥ Dwight vomits up his beet runoff power drink when he finds out he is not the father of Angela's baby. *(New Guys)*

♥ After she helps his aunt Shirley, Dwight kisses Angela and says he wants to spend the rest of his life with her. *(Moving On)*

♥ Dwight starts thinking Phillip is his son after all when he demonstrates that he likes the same paper Dwight does and looks at the *Battlestar Galactica* model the same way Dwight does. *(A.A.R.M.)*

♥ Angela and Dwight get married one year after the documentary airs. *(Finale)*

## OSCAR AND MATT

Oscar has a secret crush on Matt the warehouse guy.

♥ At Christmas, Pam discovers Oscar is interested in Matt, the "gay warehouse guy." She tries to set them up. *(Secret Santa)*

♥ When Matt leaves the party, Oscar deliberately calls him by the wrong name. Oscar tells Pam he knows what he's doing. *(Secret Santa)*

♥ Oscar comes in early to run into Matt. *(Happy Hour)*

♥ At happy hour, even though Darryl tells Oscar that Matt is a dummy and they have nothing in common, Oscar is still excited when Matt asks him to play hoops. *(Happy Hour)*

## JIM AND KAREN

Jim meets Karen when he transfers to the Stamford branch and the two begin a relationship.

♥ Karen pranks Jim and tells him not to be a suck-up. *(Gay Witch Hunt)*

♥ After playing *Call of Duty*, Jim tosses an imaginary grenade at Karen and she pretends it explodes on her desk. *(The Coup)*

♥ To find the chips Karen likes, Jim calls the manufacturer, who refers him to the distributor, who refers him to the vending machine company, who tells him that they sell them in the machines in the building next door. *(Grief Counseling)*

♥ Karen says Jim has a nice basket . . . on his bike. *(Diwali)*

♥ When an extremely drunk Jim falls off his bike after working late, Karen drives him home. *(Diwali)*

♥ When the Stamford branch closes, Jim decides to go back to Scranton. He tells Karen she should go if she's offered a job there. She tells the camera crew she doesn't think Jim is into her, but she's kind of into him. *(Branch Closing)*

♥ The staff goes outside to see all their slashed tires. When Karen and Jim go back inside, Pam sees Karen touch Jim's back. *(The Merger)*

♥ When Jim is hesitant about Karen getting an apartment near him, she avoids sitting next to him at Michael's presentation on Jamaica. After Pam talks to Jim, the conversation convinces him to have Karen move into a place only a few blocks from him. *(Back from Vacation)*

the office book of lists

♥ Jim finally tells Karen he used to have a crush on Pam, but says he's glad Karen moved to Scranton. *(Traveling Salesman)*

♥ At Oscar's party, Karen asks Jim if he still has feelings for Pam and he admits he does. *(The Return)*

♥ Jim and Karen have long talks, every night for five nights, after he admits he still has feelings for Pam. *(Ben Franklin)*

♥ At the CFO's party, Karen tells Jim she used to date Drake. Karen also says she was seeing another coworker, whose wife was staring daggers at her during the CFO party. She then claims David Wallace might still have feelings for her—then admits she's pranking Jim. *(Cocktails)*

♥ Karen and Jim break up after her job interview. After saying she isn't going anywhere because she worked really hard for her career, Karen transfers out of the Scranton branch. Later, Jim asks Pam out on a date. *(Fun Run)*

♥ After Michael, Dwight, and Jim visit Utica, Karen says, "I cried for weeks over that guy, so yeah, seeing him climb out of a PT Cruiser in a ladies' warehouse uniform felt pretty good."
*(Branch Wars)*

## ANDY AND ANGELA

This mostly one-sided relationship ends when Dwight proposes to Angela and Angela and Dwight end up together.

♥ Andy steals an ice sculpture to impress Angela. *(Launch Party)*

♥ Andy moonwalks past Accounting like ten times, but Angela doesn't react. Pam can't believe it's not working. *(Money)*

♥ Andy claims to Jim and Dwight that he's dying of lovesickness and horny sickness. *(Money)*

♥ Andy asks Angela out to see the Scranton University varsity lacrosse team scrimmage with the JV squad. *(Money)*

♥ Andy boxes up a stray cat and gives it to Angela to replace her dead cat, Sprinkles. *(Money)*

♥ Angela allows Andy to take her out to dinner, but nothing fancy or foreign, no barns, no patios, no vegetables, and no seafood. *(Money)*

♥ Andy calls his plan to get Angela to first base "Operation: Fallen Angel." *(Local Ad)*

♥ Andy tells Dwight that when he kisses Angela, she closes her eyes and says, "Oh, D., oh, D." Andy thinks this means "*D for Andy.*" *(Local Ad)*

♥ Andy brings flowers to Jan's dinner party but holds back one for his flower, Angela, as a gesture. Angela questions what she's supposed to do with a flower. *(Dinner Party)*

♥ After Michael's dinner party, Andy and Angela get ice cream. He playfully takes a bite of hers and then she mashes the rest of it against the door of his car. *(Dinner Party)*

♥ When Michael and Dwight head to New York to meet women, Andy says his "old ball and chain's been a lot more chain than ball lately" while Angela is standing right there. *(Night Out)*

♥ Andy steals Jim's moment (and fireworks) when he proposes to Angela during Toby's goodbye party. *(Goodbye, Toby)*

♥ Andy hires the best "tentist" on the East Coast to create a two-story "Shangri La tent" for him and Angela to get married in. It's heated and has a bridal suite, but Angela says she doesn't want to be married in a tent like a hobo. She demands that the wedding be in a hand-plowed field and describes Schrute Farms. *(Customer Survey)*

♥ In Canada, Oscar asks Andy how he can stand Angela. Andy says he sees through her hard exterior to a little jelly in the middle and he can't wait to have sex with her. Oscar dares him to call her, and when he does, Dwight is with her. *(Business Trip)*

♥ Moments after Phyllis has announced she caught Angela cheating on Andy, Andy comes out to play a Christmas carol for Angela on his sitar. When no one reacts, he says, "Tough room." *(Moroccan Christmas)*

♥ Michael is the one to finally tell Andy that Angela and Dwight have been having an affair. *(The Duel)*

♥ When Andy confronts Angela about her affair with Dwight, she asks if she would have said yes to formal chrysanthemums if she didn't want to get married. *(The Duel)*

After Andy and Angela break up, Andy goes on all the honeymoons he made nonrefundable deposits for, like hot-air ballooning. *(Blood Drive)*

the office book of lists

# ANDY AND ERIN

Andy has a crush on Erin, which leads to the two dating, and ends when Erin falls for Pete.

♥ Andy notices Erin is sweet and cute and she smells like his mom. *(Niagara)*

♥ Erin offers Andy her scarf to sit on after his scrotum is damaged. *(Niagara)*

♥ As Andy and Pam come back from cold-calling, he tells her that he likes Erin. *(Koi Pond)*

♥ Pam finds out Erin thinks Andy is, like, the coolest person ever. *(Koi Pond)*

♥ Andy asks Erin out as their Belles, Bourbon, and Bullets characters, and is unsure if Erin knows he's really asking her out. *(Murder)*

♥ Andy and Erin both think that the "asking each other out ball" is in the other's court after the whole "drum line thing" at Christmas. *(Sabre)*

♥ Andy gets Erin a Snoopy Valentine's card sprayed with Roger Federer for Men. Erin doesn't know who Snoopy is. *(The Manager and the Salesman)*

♥ Andy claims he is waiting for the stars to align to ask Erin out—literally, as he has a skylight in his bedroom and he wants the moon to be visible when he does. *(The Delivery)*

♥ Michael tries to set Erin up with Kevin, but she is not interested. Michael claims Kevin might die if she doesn't go out with him, as Andy spies on them. *(The Delivery)*

♥ Andy tells Erin to fax something important and adds that if she doesn't send it immediately, she'll be fired. The fax says, "Erin, will you have dinner with me?" and it is from Andy. *(The Delivery)*

♥ Andy and Erin have their first kiss in the dump while looking for the lost leads. *(New Leads)*

♥ Andy and Erin pretend to yell at each other to keep their relationship secret from the office. *(Happy Hour)*

♥ Secretary's Day is Andy and Erin's three-week anniversary. *(Secretary's Day)*

♥ Michael tells Erin that Andy and Angela were engaged. *(Secretary's Day)*

♥ Andy asks Darryl why Erin likes Gabe. Darryl says that between Andy and Gabe, he would choose Andy. *(Viewing Party)*

♥ Knowing Gabe keeps making Erin watch horror films she doesn't like, Andy stops by her desk and gives her *Shrek 2*. *(The Seminar)*

♥ Andy is going out with a woman he met at Darryl's cousin's party, but he still pines for Erin. *(PDA)*

♥ When Erin uses a puppet to ask for a date, Andy thinks they shouldn't date again. *(Search Committee)*

♥ Angry at Andy, Erin wants to use her Christmas wish for Jessica to be dead. *(Christmas Wishes)*

♥ At Robert's pool party, Erin tries to make Andy jealous by flirting with Dwight. Annoyed, Dwight pushes her into the pool. *(Pool Party)*

♥ Dwight asks Andy if he is completely okay with him dating Erin, as he doesn't want another Angela situation. Andy claims they're over, and Dwight calls him an idiot. *(Pool Party)*

♥ Erin still pines for Andy and is distraught when Andy and Jessica are still carpooling. *(Special Project)*

♥ Erin decides not to come back to Scranton when she visits Florida. *(Special Project)*

♥ Erin video chats with Andy and tells him she has a job in Florida and isn't coming back. *(Last Day in Florida)*

♥ When Andy shows up at Irene's to bring Erin back, they argue over whose heart has been broken more recently and more often. *(Get the Girl)*

♥ Erin plans to break up with Andy when he returns from the boat sale. *(Vandalism)*

**DID YOU KNOW?**

After Andy's three-month sabbatical, Erin lets him know she doesn't love him anymore. He convinces her to stay and fake it. She almost does. Then after kissing Pete, she breaks up with Andy, inadvertently letting David Wallace know that Andy has been gone three months. *(Couples Discount)*

## OSCAR AND SENATOR ROBERT LIPTON

Oscar and Senator Lipton have an affair while the senator is still married to Angela.

♥ Senator Robert Lipton gives Oscar his personal cell phone number. When Oscar doesn't call, Robert encourages him to use it. *(Fundraiser / Free Family Portrait Studio)*

♥ Oscar adopts Robert's favorite cat when Angela discovers their baby is allergic to it. This way, Robert can see the cat whenever he has dinner with Oscar. *(New Guys)*

♥ The camera crew catches Oscar and the senator kissing outside on Halloween. *(Here Comes Treble)*

♥ Oscar asks the camera crew to be discreet and Kevin overhears it. *(The Boat)*

♥ While Oscar and Angela are spying on Robert at yoga, Oscar tells her that Robert isn't gay. Then Robert calls Oscar's cell phone. *(The Whale)*

♥ Oscar is angry that Robert invited him to Phillip's birthday party only to be his token Mexican friend. *(Vandalism)*

♥ After the senator comes out as gay and announces he's in love with his chief of staff, his affair with Oscar ends. *(Stairmageddon)*

the office book of lists

# DARRYL AND VAL

Darryl and Gabe both vie for the warehouse foreman's affection, which mostly includes a lot of awkward flirting.

♥ After Val is hired, Gabe is attracted to her, but Val says she doesn't date coworkers. Darryl hears this and decides he shouldn't pursue a relationship with her. *(Doomsday)*

♥ When Val shows up at the Christmas party dressed too formally, Darryl puts on a tux. *(Christmas Wishes)*

♥ After he receives a beanie Val knitted, Darryl thinks it's a special present for him. He gets her cashmere gloves, but when he goes to the warehouse he realizes she made them for everyone. *(Special Project)*

♥ While part of the staff is in Florida, Val's boyfriend caters the late-night working session and accuses Darryl of coming on to Val with texts. They both deny it. *(After Hours)*

♥ When Glenn and Hide come back to work, Darryl raves about Val as the new foreman. Brandon hears and asks if Darryl is flirting with Val and Darryl says yes. He later takes a family portrait with his daughter and has Val join them. *(Free Family Portrait Studio)*

♥ Darryl manipulates Val into breaking up with him so he's free to go to Philadelphia and work for Jim's new sports marketing company. They get back together briefly after Kevin asks her out. *(Lice)*

161

## GABE AND ERIN

Although Gabe and Erin start dating, Erin says she's only dating him because he's her superior. She mostly finds him boring.

♥ Gabe and Erin begin dating over the summer. *(Nepotism)*

♥ Gabe and Erin host a *Glee* viewing party. *(Viewing Party)*

♥ Gabe and Erin play Scrabble to see who gets to pick the movie for the night. Gabe always wins and makes Erin watch horror films with him like *The Shining*, *Rosemary's Baby*, and *The Ring*. *(The Seminar)*

♥ Erin starts eating lunch in her car to have time alone, without Gabe. Pam encourages her to break up with him. *(Michael's Last Dundies)*

♥ Gabe holds a meeting with Andy and breaks down crying, saying he needs to not be alone. *(Dwight K. Schrute, (Acting) Manager)*

♥ Gabe makes a passionate speech to Erin about not believing in anything but their love. Erin tells the camera crew he's a great guy but it's a challenge being touched by him. *(Dwight K. Schrute, (Acting) Manager)*

♥ Erin asks Gabe for advice on getting more pizzazz for the Halloween party. *(Spooked)*

## KELLY AND DARRYL

Kelly and Darryl have a short relationship before Kelly goes back to Ryan.

♥ Kelly orders paper from the new website. When Darryl delivers it, he asks if she still misses Ryan. She says not so much anymore. *(Launch Party)*

♥ Kelly kisses Darryl during Ryan's presentation meeting on using Power-Point. *(Money)*

♥ Kelly gives Darry an ultimatum—renting *Charlotte's Web* with his daughter or going out with her. *(Money)*

♥ Darryl knows Kelly is dating him only to get back at Ryan, but he likes it so much and is excited when he sees Ryan come into the office. *(Money)*

♥ Kelly doesn't understand what game Darryl is playing with her—he always says exactly what he's thinking. *(Money)*

♥ Kelly is excited to see Darryl in a tie and claims she's dating Barack Obama. *(Job Fair)*

♥ When Ryan rejoins Dunder Mifflin, he convinces Kelly to break up with Darryl via text. *(Business Trip)*

the office book of lists

## MICHAEL AND HOLLY

After replacing Toby as the human resources representative for the Scranton branch, Holly dates Michael and eventually accepts his proposal.

♥ Michael falls in love with Holly at first "see" with his "ears." He decides to make a mix CD that works on two levels—"Welcome to Scranton" and "I love you." *(Goodbye, Toby)*

♥ Michael and Holly impersonate Yoda as they put her chair together and find they both have the same sense of humor. *(Goodbye, Toby)*

♥ Jim tells Michael to be friends with Holly first, instead of lovers first. Michael thinks this is bad advice. *(Weight Loss)*

♥ When Holly's date for Counting Crows doesn't call, Michael offers to buy the tickets. *(Weight Loss)*

♥ Michael pretends to hate Holly when Jan comes in for her baby shower. Then he hugs Holly and asks her out. *(Baby Shower)*

♥ Michael and Holly play Putt-Putt golf on their second date. *(Crime Aid)*

♥ When Michael and Holly have sex for the first time, they forget to lock the doors to the office, allowing it to get robbed. *(Crime Aid)*

♥ On the way to Nashua, Holly starts crying, worrying that the distance will break her and Michael up. When she tries to end things, Michael breaks down, saying he's not strong and will go back to Jan. "And I hate Jan!" *(Employee Transfer)*

WELCOME TO SCRANTON
I LOVE YOU

♥ Before heading back to Scranton from Canada, Michael tells David Wallace it's sucky to send Holly away. *(Business Trip)*

♥ Michael plans to tell Holly they should be together whenever he finds the perfect moment at the company picnic. He ends up not telling her, but he knows even if it takes a long time, one day it will be perfect. *(Company Picnic)*

♥ Michael tells Jo he wants Holly to be transferred back to Scranton and she says she'll see. *(Whistleblower)*

♥ Michael is supposed to let Holly know he has herpes. He doesn't tell her and she tells him he romanticized their affair and made it more than what it was. Michael later leaves her a message that he never felt anything like he did with her—and to talk to a doctor, because she might have herpes. *(Sex Ed)*

♥ When Holly temporarily returns to Scranton, she and Michael discuss *Toy Story* and Michael discovers she and A.J. are living together. *(Classy Christmas)*

♥ The women in the office convince Holly to give A.J. an ultimatum to propose by the end of the year. *(Classy Christmas)*

♥ Michael claims to have a girlfriend in New York City named Tara, who gave him a toy taxi. *(Classy Christmas)*

♥ Michael ruins the toy A.J. gave Holly because he's jealous and wants Holly back. *(Classy Christmas)*

♥ Holly breaks up with A.J. the week before Andy's seminar. *(The Seminar)*

♥ When Holly finds Michael on the roof, they tell each other how much they've missed each other, and kiss. *(The Search)*

♥ On their first Valentine's Day, Michael and Holly realize they still face the challenge of a long-distance relationship when Holly has to go back to Nashua. They decide to move in together. *(PDA)*

♥ Michael has several ideas for proposing to Holly: He could write the question in gas in the parking lot and set it on fire. Or he could throw a corpse off the roof, and when the head pops off, he could say, "I lost my head when I fell in love with you." *(Garage Sale)*

♥ Michael thinks Holly is about to propose to him in the break room, and he stops her. *(Garage Sale)*

## DID YOU KNOW?

To propose to Holly, Michael walks her through all the spots in the office that mean something to their relationship. They end up in the kitchen, where everyone is holding a candle. Each man (and Angela) asks if Holly will marry him. Finally, Michael proposes in a Yoda voice, as the hundreds of candles set off the fire sprinklers. *(Garage Sale)*

# ANGELA AND SENATOR ROBERT LIPTON

Their short marriage ends when Angela finds out the senator has been having an affair with Oscar.

♥ Robert and Angela meet at Dwight's Hay Festival on a bale of hay. *(WUPHF.com)*

♥ Robert goes to the classy Christmas party at the office and meets Oscar, who instantly knows Robert is gay. *(Classy Christmas)*

♥ Angela suspects Oscar is having an affair with Blake, a yoga instructor. Oscar, incensed that Robert is also cheating on him, goes with her to the gym and spies on Robert. *(The Whale)*

♥ After Angela and Oscar spy on Robert, she asks Dwight to also spy on Robert for her. *(The Target)*

♥ During a press conference with Angela, Robert comes out as gay. He then announces he's in love with his chief of staff, Wesley Silver. *(Stairmageddon)*

# Chapter Four:
# Corporate Culture

# CLIENTS

No business can exist without its clients, and notwithstanding its many challenges, Dunder Mifflin retains a lot of clients, despite its sometimes questionable customer service interactions and day-to-day office drama.

- When Jim can't close a deal with the library, Michael gets on the phone and mistakenly calls a woman a "gentleman and a scholar." *(Pilot)*

- Michael and Jan meet with Christian from Lackawanna County, and Jan is so impressed when Michael closes a sale, she kisses him. *(The Client)*

- Michael uses the excuse of the Saint Andrew's account to ask Dwight if he can use his urine for a drug test. *(Drug Testing)*

- Fairfield County Schools is one of the Stamford branch's clients that Karen needs to generate a price list for. *(Grief Counseling)*

- Ryan and Dwight try to get business from Axelrod Ltd. for Ryan's initiation. When they don't get it, they egg the building. *(Initiation)*

- Michael makes a huge sale to Brent Koselli, calling him the "Cos" and talking about Jell-O Pudding Pops. *(Initiation)*

- Michael tries to give Barbara Allen a novelty check to make up for the obscene watermark, but she's furious and wants Michael to resign. *(Product Recall)*

- Karen closes a six-month deal with a law firm while Michael is on vacation. *(Back from Vacation)*

- Jim and Dwight make a sales call to Halsey-Pierce Accounting and Dwight shows a client how difficult it is to get one of their big guy competitors on the phone for customer service. *(Traveling Salesman)*

- Phyllis and Karen get makeovers that resemble a client's wife in order to make a sale. *(Traveling Salesman)*

- Dunmore High School uses the obscenely watermarked paper for their prom invitations. *(Product Recall)*

- Larry Meyers is one of the former clients Michael brings gift baskets to, trying to show that ordering from a website lacks the personal touch. *(Dunder Mifflin Infinity)*

- Stone, Cooper, and Grandy, attorneys at law, is another former client Michael and Dwight bring a gift basket to. After Michael and Dwight drive into the lake, they angrily go back to retrieve the gift basket. *(Dunder Mifflin Infinity)*

- On the way to deliver a gift basket to another former client, Elmhurst Country Club, the GPS sends Dwight and Michael into a lake. *(Dunder Mifflin Infinity)*

- Dwight offers Mr. Galliado—a client lead he took from when he worked at Staples—10 percent off paper. *(Launch Party)*

the office book of lists

- When racing against the website's sales, Dwight sells ten reams to the US district court and forty reams to the battered women's shelter. *(Launch Party)*

- Dwight sells someone named Susan three reams of paper. *(Launch Party)*

- Michael, Jim, and Dwight pitch to Corcoran after they drop Staples. *(Branch Wars)*

- Jim and Andy play golf with Phil Maguire, who isn't looking to discuss changing paper suppliers. However, Jim is relentless and blocks his car for fifteen minutes to make the sale. *(Job Fair)*

- Mr. Prince gives Michael a list of his top clients as references. *(Prince Family Paper)*

- Andy looks in Julia's car to attempt to find out what music she likes and closes a sale. *(Lecture Circuit)*

- Blue Cross from Pennsylvania is Scranton's largest client. *(Golden Ticket)*

- Pam makes her first sale when Russell from the pancake luncheon calls and orders twenty-three boxes at $43 a box. *(The Michael Scott Paper Company)*

- Dwight feeds Michael's new company some potential clients like Ed's Tires. *(Heavy Competition)*

- Dwight has a long-term relationship with Daniel Schofield at HarperCollins and Michael attempts to steal him. *(Heavy Competition)*

- Bans Pet Grooming switches from Dunder Mifflin to the Michael Scott Paper Company; it is one of ten major clients Dunder Mifflin loses in a month. *(Broke)*

- Michael calls his client Jerry and asks to be paid more for the delivery they made yesterday. *(Broke)*

- Mr. Bart makes his first complaint in ten years. As Dwight screams at Ryan to give him the phone, they lose his account. *(Casual Friday)*

- Jim tries to go to Raskin Design on his own, but they want Michael to come, too. *(Koi Pond)*

- Pam and Andy cold-call Dean Trophies, Sherman Blinds and Rugs, and Palpabon Drilling at the Wilkes-Barre industrial park. *(Koi Pond)*

- Andy and Pam cold-call Keena Gifford, who thinks they're a couple. *(Koi Pond)*

- Pam fakes a call from Swartz Lumber to get out of lunch with her mom and Michael. *(Double Date)*

- Jim tells David Wallace he's working on a pitch for a big supermarket chain during the potential bankruptcy. *(Murder)*

- To impress the investment banker, Andy claims Dunder Mifflin is now the official paper supplier of the NFL. *(The Banker)*

- Michael gets a new client, a "gentleman's club" called Curves, which is actually a women's gym. *(The Manager and the Salesman)*

- Pam and Jim's first joint pitch is to Donna Newton, the manager of Sid and Dexter's, whom Michael is dating. *(Body Language)*

- Luke neglects to send samples to Lehigh Motors, which Phyllis says will lose her their business. *(Nepotism)*

- Steve Nash, chief buyer for Frames Select, is a client the branch loses to Danny Cordray. *(The Sting)*

- After Michael gives Andy his top clients, Andy almost immediately loses Porter Hardware. *(Goodbye, Michael)*

- Andy hears Mercy Hospital is back on the market for a supplier, as is the Barnacle Project, a nonprofit based in Mystic, Connecticut. *(The Inner Circle)*

- The sales team works together when Andy incentivizes them, and Phyllis tells Jim to ask for Donald at Bracken Auto, as Karen is bananas. *(The Incentive)*

- Rigo Escrow needs its refund by the end of the day when Dwight's accountability program is running. *(Doomsday)*

- When the team is processing orders for accounts in Florida, Andy is asked about Thornwood Wholesalers and Val's boyfriend tells Darryl he read Darryl's texts to Val. *(After Hours)*

- David calls to tell Dwight and Jim that the Scranton White Pages account is available. Those in the paper industry call it "the white whale." *(The Whale)*

- Phyllis says Gina Rogers at Apex Technology complained that Dwight called her "Jyna" throughout their entire meeting. *(The Whale)*

the office book of lists

- Meredith gets a complaint from Eastern Pennsylvania Seminary for calling it a "sausage factory." *(The Target)*

- Pam wants to get her first complaint from a client. She calls Heymont Brake and Tire and tells them an insulting joke. She gets the complaint. *(The Target)*

- David Wallace sends an instant message to Dwight to get Stone and Son Suit Warehouse's business. Jim and Dwight, as Jim and Dwight Shrupert, had previously pretended to be family to get business at other family-owned places like a law firm, a construction company, and a motorcycle store. Jim can't do it this time, so Dwight and Clark pretend to be father and son. *(Suit Warehouse)*

- Dwight cleans out the file cabinets for dead accounts like Scranton Mimeograph Corp., as he doubts they'll be doing business with them any time soon. *(Customer Loyalty)*

- In an attempt to thwart Dwight, Andy angers Jan and ends up costing the company the Scranton White Pages account. *(Couples Discount)*

- Since a potential client for the entire Lackawanna School District is Stanley's sister's friend, Stanley has to take the meeting. *(Stairmageddon)*

## VENDORS

All offices get supplies and services from somewhere, and vendors are always ready to get their business. At Dunder Mifflin, sometimes vendor relationships last a long time—and get Meredith a number of free steak dinners—and sometimes vendors don't make it past Pam's desk, especially if they are selling new phone systems.

- Katy Moore sets up and sells handbags in the conference room. Michael is smitten with her, but she ends up dating Jim for a while. *(Hot Girl)*

- When Jan brings the corporate attorney in, Michael thinks he needs a lawyer and hires James P. Albini, who specializes in free speech issues—and motorcycle head injuries, workers' comp, and diet pill lawsuits. *(Sexual Harassment)*

- Creed shifts the blame for the obscene watermark onto a floor manager, Debbie Brown, at the paper mill. She wasn't even there when the incident happened, but she gets fired. *(Product Recall)*

- Michael thinks the delivery woman from Hawk Transport and Courier Service is his strippergram. *(Michael's Birthday)*

- Michael pays $20 each time for the ID photographer to do a group shot and he has to shoot eight takes. *(Conflict Resolution)*

- Michael makes a deal to sell Hammermill products, even though they're exclusive to Staples. *(The Convention)*

- Dwight orders Elizabeth the stripper to answer phones. They paid for three work hours and they're going to get it. *(Ben Franklin)*

- Chad Lite, from the *Scranton Times*, is granted level-three security clearance for Michael's press conference. He writes a column called "The Lighter Side of Life" and "Breaking Corporate News" as well as the obituaries. *(Product Recall)*

- To accept the giant check for $340, Elizabeth the stripper is hired to come to the fun run, dressed as a nurse. *(Fun Run)*

- For six years, Meredith has been sleeping with Bruce Meyers, the Hammermill rep, to get discounts on their supplies—and Outback Steakhouse gift certificates. *(Business Ethics)*

- Angelo Grotti is an insurance salesman from Mutual of Harrisburg, who Dwight and Andy think is a mafioso. *(Mafia)*

- The phone salesman from Tech Star keeps coming by and Pam keeps him from Michael, not wanting a new phone system to replace her. Jim pretends to be Michael and eventually the salesman leaves, confused by Michael, Jim, and Dwight all imitating Fonzie. *(Blood Drive)*

- Eric Ward, the investment banker, is sent to sign off on the Scranton branch. *(The Banker)*

- Reggie, Deangelo's shaver, is the number-one Yelp-reviewed shaver in Scranton. *(Training Day)*

- Alan Olsen from North Dakota is Dunder Mifflin's first real "like" on social media. He also likes Hammermill and Georgia Pacific. *(Customer Loyalty)*

- Robert is the rep from WeyerHammer Paper who brought the check for $2,000 for the winner of the paper airplane competition. *(Paper Airplane)*

## COMPETITORS

With the rise of the big-box office supply stores, smaller suppliers like Dunder Mifflin face real challenges in keeping clients.

- Jim and Pam put Dwight's résumé on various online job sites. He gets a hit from competitor Cumberland Mills. He blows the initial phone interview when he argues with them about how important martial arts is on his résumé. *(Halloween)*

- Staples is a huge competitor and Dwight actually works for them briefly as a retail salesman. He then steals some clients from them. *(multiple episodes)*

- Michael explains that Office Depot is "kind of running us out of business." *(Take Your Daughter to Work Day)*

- While in Canada, Michael attempts to sell to a potential client who has been talking to Catalyst, whose prices are better than Dunder Mifflin's. *(Business Trip)*

the office book of lists

- Prince Paper services the Carbondale to Marshbrook area. *(Prince Family Paper)* After Michael quits, he calls Prince Paper to see if he can get a job and finds out it has gone out of business. His list of other prospective employers besides Prince Paper says "other companies." *(Two Weeks)*

- Michael decides to start his own company, the Michael Scott Paper Company. *(Two Weeks)*

- Angry at the preferential treatment of Ryan and Pam, Dwight and the others threaten to quit and form the Schrute-Bernard-Lapin-Vance-Stanley Paper Company. *(Casual Friday)*

- Danny Cordray works for Osprey Paper in Throop. *(The Sting)*

- To steal Binghamton's biggest client before Scranton or Syracuse, Andy shows up as a representative of the Big Red Paper Company. *(Turf War)*

## MERGERS AND TAKEOVERS

The corporate world can get nasty. As Dunder Mifflin and the rest of the paper supply industry fight off big competitors, the Corporate office has to make some tough decisions. Luckily, it all seems to work out . . . for most people.

- Camden, Yonkers, and Pittsfield are all shut down. *(multiple episodes)*

- The Stamford branch is set to absorb the Scranton branch and become Dunder Mifflin Northeast, until Josh quits. *(Branch Closing)*

- The company finds out Buffalo is closing at the company picnic. *(Company Picnic)*

- After Michael's company makes a big dent in Dunder Mifflin's sales, David realizes the cheapest option is to try and buy Michael's new company out, which Dunder Mifflin does—a mere month before the Michael Scott Paper Company would have gone out of business. *(Broke)*

- During the Christmas party, David tells Michael the company has a buyer and the board has no choice but to approve it. They'll be cleaning house at Corporate. *(Secret Santa)*

- At the last minute, an electronics company named Sabre buys Dunder Mifflin and saves the company. *(Sabre)*

- After Robert is made regional manager, he convinces Jo to make him CEO of Sabre. *(The List)*

- After Andy convinces David Wallace to purchase Dunder Mifflin, Jo decides to liquidate the rest of the company. *(Free Family Portrait Studio)*

## OFFICE PARTIES

Despite Jan's insistence that Michael can't expense the parties he always wants to throw, the celebrations never stop, even if Michael has to pay for them himself or get the Party Planning Committee to come up with ideas and themes.

- Pam asks Jim if he's going to Angela's cat party on Saturday. *(Pilot)*

- Michael plans Operation: Morale Improvement and throws a birthday party for Meredith, even though her birthday isn't until the following month. *(The Alliance)*

- Michael mentions an amazing '80s party the Party Planning Committee threw. *(The Alliance)*

- Jan tells Michael there's a budget for only one office party per year. He's already had a 05/05/05 party, a luau, and a tsunami "fun" raiser. *(Dundies)*

- Jim hosts a barbecue at his place and invites everyone but Michael. It's nothing personal—he just doesn't think people would be able to relax. *(Email Surveillance)*

- For Michael's birthday, Dwight interrupts the Party Planning Committee and says Michael wants trick candles and a strippergram. *(Michael's Birthday)*

- To celebrate Michael's birth moment at 11:23 a.m., Dwight wants to hoist Michael up on a chair in the Hebrew tradition. *(Michael's Birthday)*

- The warehouse is converted into a full-blown gambling hall for Casino Night. *(Casino Night)*

- The staff goes to the Lackawanna County Hindu-American Association's Family Diwali Celebration at West Scranton High School. *(Diwali)*

- Michael holds an Integration Celebration when the Stamford staff is absorbed into the Scranton branch. *(The Merger)*

- Karen suggests several ideas from previous Stamford celebrations to the Party Planning Committee that Angela vetoes because they're all terrible and not aligned with the theme of a Nutcracker Christmas. *(A Benihana Christmas)*

- Pam and Karen form the Committee to Plan Parties and hold a Margarita-Karaoke Christmas that competes with Angela's party. *(A Benihana Christmas)*

- Since inventory was put off until Michael came back from vacation, he decides to bring a little slice of paradise to the chore. He instructs the Party Planning Committee to plan a Luau Inventory. *(Back from Vacation)*

- Dunder Mifflin had a Disco Audit '05 and Pam says compared to that, Luau Inventory '07 was a success. *(Back from Vacation)*

- Michael is determined to have a celebration of Oscar—an Oscar Night, something that celebrates his "Mexicanity," with firecrackers, a Chihuahua, and a Swanson frozen foods chimichanga. *(The Return)*

- The women hold a luncheon bridal shower for Phyllis. Since Phyllis's shower is only for the women, Michael holds a Guys' Afternoon In—or GAI—in the warehouse. *(Ben Franklin)*

- Pam suggests Michael not say good-bye until the official goodbye party. *(The Job)*

For the launch of Dunder Mifflin Infinity, the main party for VIPs is held in New York City and is streamed to all the branches, which simultaneously hold satellite parties. Michael thinks he was invited to the launch party in New York and that it is in a club called Chatroom and the address has "www" at the beginning. Angela's budget for the launch party is $65 for a celebration the whole country will see and she has four idiots who do nothing but weigh her down. And her cat is still dead. Andy steals an ice sculpture of two swans for the launch party. Michael gives Angela a list of things he wants her to add to the launch party to compete with the party in New York:

- Beer and lite beer
- Streamers
- Orchids
- Better lighting
- Something made of ice
- Pizza, pizza with mushrooms, pizza without mushrooms, white pizza, and steak

- Chocolates
- Someone famous
- Cool music
- Confetti
- Go-go dancers

*(Launch Party)*

- Pam suspects Michael has a theme for everyone to come in on Saturday to update the website sales, like Scrambled Egg Saturday. *(Night Out)*

- Michael wants to make Toby's going-away party like a New Orleans funeral. He also wants an antigravity machine. *(Goodbye, Toby)*

- Kelly has an *America's Got Talent* finale party over the summer and gives out mugs with everyone's faces on them. *(Customer Survey)*

- Phyllis's theme for her first Christmas party as head of the Party Planning Committee is Nights in Morocco. Phyllis tells Angela to move her nativity scene off her desk, as it's not on theme for the Moroccan Christmas party. Phyllis lets the camel, sheep, elephant, and North African king stay, while everything else goes in the drawer. *(Moroccan Christmas)*

- Michael thinks an intervention is like a surprise party for people who have addictions and you get in their face and scream at them and make them feel badly about themselves and then they stop having an addiction. *(Moroccan Christmas)*

- Kelly says "screw you" to Jim and Dwight because they, as the new heads of the Party Planning Committee, forget her birthday. As they try to make up for it, Dwight chooses brown and gray balloons and decorations, as they match the carpet. *(Lecture Circuit)*

- For Michael's fifteenth work anniversary, Dwight has Michael ask David Wallace if hiring Cirque du Soleil as salaried employees will help with year-end tax stuff. David hangs up. *(New Boss)*

- Gabe and Erin host a *Glee* viewing party. *(Viewing Party)*

- Dwight hosts a Hay Festival in the parking lot, complete with a petting zoo, a goat roast, a historical reenactment of the Dunmore farm slaughters, an onion boil, and the activity of finding a needle in a haystack. *(WUPHF.com)*

- Andy throws a garden party at Schrute Farms to impress Robert and his family. *(Garden Party)*

- Robert makes the staff throw a welcome party for Nellie. Pam questions why they have to throw a party for someone who is being horrible. Pam, Angela, and Phyllis discuss hiring a magician (as Nellie hates magicians), serving carrot cake with real carrots, and putting up flickering fluorescent lights. *(Welcome Party)*

- When Angela forgets to plan the Christmas party, Dwight suggests a Pennsylvania Dutch Christmas with glühwein, hasenpfeffer, and Saint Nicholas's rural German companion, Belsnickel. Breaking the ceremonial pig rib is part of the festivities. *(Dwight Christmas)*

the office book of lists

# OFFICE TOYS

Forget stress balls! The Scranton staff has plenty of toys in the office to amuse themselves with. Perhaps no one has a bigger collection than Michael, though Dwight has the most bobbleheads.

- A large stuffed Homer Simpson sits on top of Phyllis's files. *(Diversity Day)*

- Michael has a toy Dunder Mifflin truck on his desk. *(Health Care)*

- There's a spinner toy that plays music on Michael's desk. *(Basketball)*

- Dwight has bobbleheads of the Phillies baseball team. *(The Alliance)*

- Dwight keeps a ball of rubber bands on his desk. *(Hot Girl)*

- As Toby finishes his sexual harassment refresher course, Michael brings in a blow-up doll. *(Sexual Harassment)*

- Michael has a boxing cat puppet he uses on Ryan, Angela, and Kevin's jar of M&Ms. *(Email Surveillance)*

- Michael has a toy train that Toby's daughter plays with. *(Take Your Daughter to Work Day)*

- Michael has a wooden train whistle that has "All Aboard for Sales" etched on it. *(Take Your Daughter to Work Day)*

- Dwight has several expensive collector's item bobbleheads on his desk that look like aliens and superheroes. Angela also had one made in his likeness. He later adds a Cornell one to annoy Andy. *(Take Your Daughter to Work Day)*

- Dwight is going to teach the kids in the office how to make cornhusk dolls. *(Take Your Daughter to Work Day)*

- Michael plays with a set of windup teeth on his desk. *(Initiation)*

- There's a rubber duck with a Byrd baseball jersey on Michael's desk. *(Diwali)*

- Dwight has a lightsaber fight with a boy at the Diwali festival. *(Diwali)*

- Kevin plays with a miniature football. *(Branch Closing)*

- Each year, Dwight researches the hottest toy and buys out all the local stock to sell at an enormous profit to desperate and lazy parents. The year of the Moroccan Christmas party, the toy is Princess Unicorn, whose catchphrase is "My horn can pierce the sky." *(Moroccan Christmas)*

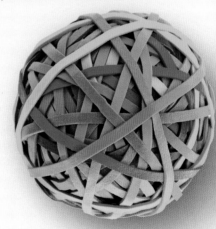

179

- Michael uses a sticky hand toy to grab a paper off Jim's desk. *(Two Weeks)*

- Michael gives Jim a "World's Best Boss" coffee mug with gin in it. *(The Promotion)*

- Dwight gives Jim a wooden mallard with a listening device in it. Jim gives it to Kelly, who names it Professor Damon D. Duck. *(The Lover)*

- Michael has a toy pool table on his desk. *(The Manager and the Salesman)*

- Holly places a toy Woody that A.J. gave her on her desk and Michael ruins it out of jealousy. *(Classy Christmas)*

- At the garage sale, Dwight trades up one thing after another from a thumbtack to a stuffed squid Erin has. *(Garage Sale)*

- Deangelo asks for Michael's favorite toy truck to make a stapler or pen holder out of. *(Goodbye, Michael)*

- Deangelo puts a kachina doll in place of the Dundie Award Michael has on his desk. *(The Inner Circle)*

- Erin pretends an evil witch named Angela turned her into a sock puppet when she went to drop off the FedEx forms. She needs a date with Andy to turn back into a real girl. *(Search Committee)*

- Jim and Dwight argue over whether Cece's brightly colored toy is a monkey or not. *(Turf War)*

- Toby wins a toy duck for Pam at Poor Richard's. *(Cocktails)*

- Erin spends a ton on tickets to win a large stuffed bear she dresses as Darryl and calls Bear-yl. *(Vandalism)*

- Creed flies a rainbow kite in the office above a fan. *(Vandalism)*

- Erin has a Dunder Mifflin Frisbee that she and Pete throw around in the parking lot. *(Couples Discount)*

- Dwight builds a *Battlestar Galactica* model in his office. *(A.A.R.M.)*

- Dwight has a summoning beanbag he throws at Jim when he wants his attention. *(A.A.R.M.)*

A balloon that was floating in the warehouse finally falls. It has been up there since:

- Oscar was still with Gil

- Kevin had hair like Rapunzel

- Dwight's Warcraft clan was still on speaking terms

- Meredith's kid didn't have a face tattoo

- Darryl was still thinking of going back to school

- Jim was still just a paper salesman

*(Get the Girl)*

# TYPES OF PAPER

There are hundreds, if not thousands, of varieties of paper, and the staff at Dunder Mifflin are experts on every tonnage and type.

- Jim knows the tonnage price of manila folders. *(Pilot)*

- Jim tries to push paper that will say "100 percent postconsumer content recycled paper" on the back to his biggest client. *(Diversity Day)*

- Jim tricks Dwight into hiding in a shipping box of toilet paper in the warehouse. *(The Alliance)*

- Jim asks Dwight what kind of discounts they give on the 20-pound white model. By the ream it's $9.78 with a 7 percent discount. *(The Fight)*

- Dwight tries to sabotage Jim's performance review by encouraging Jim to tell Michael to stock more double-tabbed manila file folders. *(Performance Review)*

- At Jim's barbecue, Stanley and Oscar talk about the sales of premium laser color copy batch. *(Email Surveillance)*

- Meredith once overordered fifty spiral pads. *(Take Your Daughter to Work Day)*

- Jim tells everyone they need to be pushing card stock while Michael is on vacation. *(Back from Vacation)*

- Roy shows Ryan how to "adjust" the Canariola copier paper that they appear to be short on—by scanning the same one multiple times. *(Back from Vacation)*

- Jim offers a potential client discounts on 30 percent recycled and ultra-premium laser, as well as discount prices on ink cartridges and any forms they need. *(Traveling Salesman)*

- A disgruntled employee at the paper mill puts an obscene watermark of two beloved cartoon characters performing unspeakable acts on four thousand reams of 24-pound cream letter stock paper. *(Product Recall)*

- At the job fair, all Pam can find to write on is a piece of Pendleton "crap." Michael tells her to go to the office and get the ultra-white card stock. *(Job Fair)*

- Michael asks if Prince Paper will put specialty paper, like a 94 brightness double bonded, on the same truck as conventional stock. *(Prince Family Paper)*

- Dwight listens to a recording of Jim discussing 28-pound bond, 38-pound bond, and 65-pound cover stock, which is the heaviest paper that will still feed smoothly through a desktop printer. *(The Lover)*

- To test the faulty printers, Andy uses a ream of 24-pound premium paper stock. *(The Cover-Up)*

- Gabe tries to get everyone to use Sticky Quips from Dunder Mifflin Sabre for the cartoon caption contest. *(The Search)*

- Jim says they need to load three hundred boxes of 20-pound white onto the truck. *(Lotto)*

- Order Reference number 00983-126 is for eight cases of bright white ink-jet. *(After Hours)*

- Nellie researches how to make child-proof paper that doesn't give someone paper cuts. *(Andy's Ancestry)*

- Dwight wants to go on the radio, because he knows he could sell ten reams of 40-pound bond easily if he was famous. *(The Boat)*

- Dwight gives Clark a theoretical sales problem involving having a ream of 16-bond paper. *(Junior Salesman)*

- WeyerHammer sponsors the paper airplane contest to promote its new Airstream Deluxe A4, which Dwight says is practically made of plastic. *(Paper Airplane)*

- Phillip tries to eat some of the 24-weight letter bond. Dwight says that's the most flavorful bond. *(A.A.R.M.)*

## MOONLIGHTING

Not every job pays enough to make ends meet. Over the years, some of the staff take part-time jobs or work on their own projects to get ahead. Only Stanley seems content to sit and wait for retirement.

- Dwight volunteers as a sheriff's deputy on the weekends. *(Pilot)*

- Dwight is proud of being a narc and says it's one of the hardest jobs you can have. *(Drug Testing)*

- Dwight resigns as a Lackawanna County volunteer sheriff's deputy when he gives Michael his urine for a drug test. *(Drug Testing)*

- Michael takes a job selling Lipophedrine diet pills and claims that because he loves sales so much, he took the job as kind of a hobby. Ryan forces him to quit when it interferes with his job at Dunder Mifflin. *(Money)*

- After Jan is fired, she tries to start a candle business called Serenity by Jan. *(Dinner Party)*

- After his trip to Thailand, Ryan works at Idle Hours Bowling Alley. *(Dream Team)*

- After David Wallace is let go, he works on an idea called Suck It, a vacuum for toys. He later sells it to the military and makes millions. *(Sabre)*

- A few years back, Dwight started an escort service that got a lot of responses—mostly creeps, but he made a few friends. *(The Delivery)*

the office book of lists

- Jim's friend starts a new sports marketing company in Philly based on an idea Jim has. **(New Guys)**

- After Kelly quits, Ryan also quits to move to southwestern Ohio, saying it's the next Silicon Valley—the Silicon Prairie. **(New Guys)**

- Jim asks Darryl if he wants to join his sports marketing company. **(Andy's Ancestry)**

- Jim's partners name the sports marketing company Athlead, which he doesn't like. **(The Target)**

- Darryl interviews with some of Athlead's employees. **(Suit Warehouse)**

- Pam interviews for a real estate company in Philly. She doesn't take the job. **(Moving On)**

- As Andy tries to become an actor, he buys a company printer that's better for headshots and asks David for money for cheek implants. **(Livin' the Dream)**

- Andy changes his mind about acting and David lets him stay on as a salesman. Andy then decides to quit after all and pretends Toby was groping him. **(Livin' the Dream)**

- Andy tries out for *America's Next A Capella Sensation*. **(A.A.R.M.)**

## STAFF MEETINGS AND TRAININGS

It seems like there are company-wide meetings almost every day—and for every reason—in the Scranton office, including some pretty memorable ones.

- Michael calls a meeting to tell the staff that either the Scranton or Stamford branch will be downsized. **(Pilot)**

- Mr. Brown holds a diversity training. Then Michael holds one. **(Diversity Day)**

To impress Jan with all the good ideas he and the branch have, Michael holds their "weekly" suggestion box meeting the day she arrives to do his performance review. Suggestions include:

- What should we do to prepare for Y2K?
- We need better outreach for employees fighting depression.
- You need to do something about your BO.
- You need to do something about your coffee breath.
- A piece of gum stuck to a piece of paper.
- Don't sleep with your boss.

**(Performance Review)**

- Michael gives a meeting on disabled icons with photos of Larry Flynt, Lyndon B. Johnson, and Tom Hanks—who played a mentally challenged person in *Forrest Gump* and a character battling AIDS in *Philadelphia*. *(The Injury)*

- Jan hosts a Women in the Workplace meeting that Michael is not allowed to attend—although he keeps trying. *(Boys and Girls)*

- For his branch's presentation to the CFO, Michael makes a video called *The Faces of Scranton* instead of presenting his branch's financial performance. *(Valentine's Day)*

- After Michael jokes about Dwight being a narc, Michael holds a meeting to reinforce how ridiculously antidrug he is. *(Drug Testing)*

- Michael calls a meeting for everyone—gay, straight, lesbian, or overweight—to discuss homosexuality and have Oscar officially come out. Michael forces Oscar to let him hug and kiss him. *(Gay Witch Hunt)*

- Michael holds a meeting to have everyone talk about someone special they know who died, and crying is encouraged. *(Grief Counseling)*

- Michael holds an Indian Culture Seminar before the Diwali party. *(Diwali)*

- Michael holds the official Merger Day All-Family Welcome Breakfast in the conference room, but all the good food is for the new staff. *(The Merger)*

- Michael hosts the Integration Celebration to let Scranton and Stamford come together as one. *(The Merger)*

- Michael tells Jim that as a person who has slept with more than one woman—definitely more than three—he is qualified to hold the Women's Appreciation meeting. *(Women's Appreciation)*

- Ryan holds a meeting to introduce the Dunder Mifflin Infinity business model. *(Dunder Mifflin Infinity)*

- Michael holds a meeting to talk about how the Discrimination and Employment Act of 1967 prohibited employment discrimination based on age. *(Dunder Mifflin Infinity)*

- Ryan comes to the branch to launch PowerPoint, and Michael forgets to prepare a presentation on how to give PowerPoint presentations. *(Money)*

- Michael holds a brainstorming meeting to discuss energizing the office. *(Did I Stutter?)*

- Holly holds her first ethics meeting and she and Michael come into the conference room singing "Let's Get Ethical" to the tune of "Physical." *(Business Ethics)*

- To recoup the losses of stolen items, Michael plans to hold Crime-Aid (Crime Reduces Innocence Makes Everyone Angry I Declare), a charity auction where people can bid on Dunder Mifflin's goods and services. *(Crime Aid)*

- After Stanley's heart attack, everyone has to get CPR training. *(Stress Relief)*

- Michael leads a meditation class in the conference room to help make the office as peaceful for Stanley as possible. *(Stress Relief)*

- Michael wants everyone to come up with ideas as good as his golden ticket promotion. *(Golden Ticket)*

- After Michael returns to Dunder Mifflin, he holds a meeting to have everyone look inward. *(Casual Friday)*

- Michael holds a meeting about introducing a line of toilet paper that then leads to a conversation about planets. *(The Promotion)*

- The staff holds a meeting to take Pam's mind off her impending labor. *(The Delivery)*

- Michael holds a meeting to get ideas for what he and Donna can do for the weekend. *(The Cover-Up)*

- Toby's meeting about the radon kits in the office devolves into a discussion on how one bullet can kill Hitler, bin Laden, and Toby at one time. *(The Chump)*

- Michael holds a brainstorming meeting for Quarterlies Crisis Mode! *(The Sting)*

- For Sabre Hygiene Day, Pam holds a meeting on staying healthy and demonstrates the "vampire cough." *(The Christening)*

- Gabe has to hold a meeting about PDA in the office when Michael and Holly can't keep their hands off each other. *(PDA)*

- Pam tricks Michael into having a meeting about how to propose to Holly so he won't write words in gas in the parking lot and light them on fire. *(Garage Sale)*

- Deangelo calls a mandatory meeting, then asks Michael if he usually starts the meetings with chitchat. *(Training Day)*

- Michael holds one last meeting to get an update on Pam's whereabouts and Phyllis's mittens status. He then has Ping say goodbye to everyone. *(Goodbye, Michael)*

- Dwight holds a Special Projects Orientation and replicates the Florida temperature of 85 degrees and 75 percent humidity in the conference room. He also releases three hundred mosquitoes. After the meeting, the frogs will take care of them. *(Special Project)*

- Nellie holds a meeting about impotence. *(Angry Andy)*

Andy has a meeting about everyone's ancestry based on Nellie's made-up research:

- Phyllis's great-great-grand-mother was responsible for spreading cholera to the US.

- Kevin is related to John Wayne Gacy and John Wayne Bobbitt.

- Jim Halpert is related to Richard Nixon.

- Dwight's grandfather was a member of the Bund and was a tax evader.

- Meredith is a blood relative of Lizzie Borden.

*(Andy's Ancestry)*

# OFFICE GAMES

A little friendly competition never hurt anyone. However, sometimes the staff takes it too far. From Flonkerton to bets on how many times Kelly will say "awesome," there is always something to break up the regular office routine.

- Pam plays FreeCell solitaire on her computer. *(Diversity Day)*

- The office staff plays basketball against the warehouse staff to see who has to work Saturday. *(Basketball)*

- Oscar and Kevin play paper football and call it "hate ball" because Angela hates it. *(Office Olympics)*

- Kevin often plays "Who Can Put the Most M&Ms in Their Mouth?" *(Office Olympics)*

- Toby bounces a ball off the wall and calls it "Dunderball." *(Office Olympics)*

- Stanley's game is called "Work Hard So My Kids Can Go to College." *(Office Olympics)*

- While Angela won't play games at work, at home she sings and dangles things in front of her cat. She calls this activity "cat dangling." *(Office Olympics)*

- Flonkerton is the national sport of Icelandic paper companies, in which players put boxes on their feet like snowshoes. *(Office Olympics)*

- Angela counts how many times Jim gets up from his desk to talk to Pam and calls the game "Pam-Pong." *(Office Olympics)*

- For the Office Olympics, the staff plays a paper basketball version of H-O-R-S-E. *(Office Olympics)*

- Everyone guesses which company the next employee out of the elevator works for. Ryan wins with Vance Refrigeration. *(Office Olympics)*

- Oscar and Toby race around the office without spilling coffee from their mugs. *(Office Olympics)*

- Michael gets a gold medal for closing on his condo. *(Office Olympics)*

**DID YOU KNOW?**

When the staff exits the building for a fire drill, Jim has the staff play three games: Desert Island, Who Would You Do?, and Would You Rather? *(The Fire)*

- Michael has Jan and his client play Truth or Dare at Chili's. *(The Client)*

- When Michael doesn't get the Secret Santa present he feels he deserves, he makes the staff play Yankee Swap so he can get a better one. *(Christmas Party)*

- The staff plays limbo on the booze cruise. *(Booze Cruise)*

- Pam plays a moderate-level game of sudoku in eighteen minutes. *(The Carpet)*

- Pam explains that Dwight is taking Ryan on a sales call. If they find Ryan's body in a heavily wooded area the next day, she owes Jim $30. It's an old bet, but a deal's a deal. *(Initiation)*

- Pam claims to be a roulette expert. *(Casino Night)*

- On Casino Night, Michael and Carol play no-limit Texas Hold'em and Toby wins. *(Casino Night)*

- Dwight plays craps on Casino Night. *(Casino Night)*

- Kevin claims to have won the 2002 $2,500 No-Limit, Deuce-to-Seven-Draw Tournament at the World Series of Poker in Las Vegas. *(Casino Night)*

- Almost everyone in the Stamford branch plays *Call of Duty* at work. *(The Coup)*

- Michael plays online Scrabble when no one will attend Movie Monday with him. *(The Coup)*

- At the Guys' Afternoon in the warehouse, Kevin deals no-limit deuce to seven lowball—"lines twenty-five fifty, nickels are worth ten, dimes twenty-five, and quarters fifty. Nothing wild." *(Ben Franklin)*

- The staff plays Up Jenkins at Poor Richard's. *(Cocktails)*

The staff begins betting on things:

- How many jellybeans are in the candy dish

- How many times Bob Vance calls Phyllis

- How long Kelly talks, how many times she says "awesome," and how many romantic comedies she mentions

- Whether Creed will notice a potato substituted for an apple (he doesn't)

- Whether Michael is serious about jumping off the roof

*(Safety Training)*

187

- Andy and Dwight have a stacking competition in the warehouse. *(Back from Vacation)*

- When Kevin bets his friend in Albany a month's salary that Karen will get the Corporate job, he wonders if he has a gambling problem. *(The Job)*

- The staff watches the DVD screen saver bounce around the screen and Pam claims to have seen it go into the corner. When Michael discusses the quarterly reports, it actually happens and everyone sees it. *(Launch Party)*

- Dwight plays *Second Life* in the office. In it, he's a paper salesman named Dwight, so it is absolutely the same as his real life. Except he can fly in the game. *(Local Ad)*

- Dwight's *Second Life* avatar creates a new world called Second Second Life, for those people who want to be removed even further from reality. *(Local Ad)*

- Jim's *Second Life* avatar is a sports-writer in Philadelphia who plays guitar. *(Local Ad)*

- Michael plays the Alphabet Game with Jim and Dwight in the car on the way to Utica. *(Branch Wars)*

- The warehouse staff gets a ping-pong table. Jim is no good and practices against Kevin, Meredith, and Dwight, who are excellent. *(The Deposition)*

- At Michael and Jan's dinner party, the group plays charades. Jim suggests Jan and Michael are also playing a game called "Let's See How Uncom-fortable We Can Make Our Guests." And they're both winning. *(Dinner Party)*

- When Toby gets locked out of the office, he offers to teach Pam to throw a football, but she already knows how. *(Night Out)*

- Andy and Angela play a tame game of Mad Libs. *(Did I Stutter?)*

- For Toby's going-away party, the office has a Ferris wheel and bouncy house in the parking lot. *(Goodbye, Toby)*

- Michael packs puzzles, strings for cat's cradles, puppets, and a road trip mix CD to move Holly back to Nashua. *(Employee Transfer)*

- Jim plays *Minesweeper* in the office, because "those mines aren't going to sweep themselves," when Phyllis invites him and Pam out for lunch with her and Bob. *(Blood Drive)*

- Bob Vance, Vance Refrigeration, has bowled a 280. *(Blood Drive)*

- Jim claims he plays soccer to impress Charles. *(Dream Team)*

- Creed and Jim play chess and Scrab-ble on casual Friday. *(Casual Friday)*

- Holly and Michael play Slumdunder Mifflinaire onstage at the company picnic. *(Company Picnic)*

- Michael was once picked for a team for a sport that doesn't exist—poop-ball. *(Gossip)*

- When Pam decides to punch Michael after work, Toby gives her pointers on the power of the punch coming from the back foot. *(Double Date)*

## DID YOU KNOW?

Michael keeps a lot of board games in his office, including Battleship (which helped him get through his parents' divorce), Operation (which helped him get through his vasectomy), Sorry, Connect 4, Trouble, Risk, and Toss Across (which helped him get over his breakup with Holly). *(Murder)*

Michael has the staff play Belles, Bourbon, and Bullets—a murder mystery dinner party game—to distract from the potential bankruptcy. Characters include:

Naughty Nellie Nutmeg: ERIN

Nathaniel Nutmeg: ANDY

Voodoo Mama Juju: ANGELA

Caleb Crawdad: MICHAEL

Deborah U. Tante: PAM

Miss Beatrix Bourbon: PHYLLIS

*(Murder)*

- Ryan and Kelly play a *Dance Dance Revolution*–type game. *(Happy Hour)*

- Dwight and Isabel play Whac-A-Mole. *(Happy Hour)*

- Jim and Pam play pool with Michael and Julie. *(Happy Hour)*

- The prize for the 2011 costume contest is the Scranton/Wilkes-Barre coupon book, worth over $15,000 in savings. *(Costume Contest)*

- Michael, Darryl, and Erin use a Ouija board at Halloween. *(Costume Contest)*

- Jim plays *Zombie Soccer* for two hours while Pam looks for new office space. *(China)*

- Pam's game of having Darryl's daughter find the star for the Christmas tree ends quickly when Andy does a magic trick and finds it in her ear. *(Classy Christmas)*

- The Knights of the Night play flashlight tag at their last meeting. *(Ultimatum)*

- Kevin, Andy, and Darryl play the *Dallas* TV board game. *(Garage Sale)*

- Erin puts a Pin the Wart on the Witch game on the wall at Halloween. *(Spooked)*

- Bert and Dwight play *StarCraft* and Bert uses Jim's computer. *(Spooked)*

- Erin brings out the game Pecker Poker—the game of cards that makes you hard. *(Spooked)*

- Jim attempts to play squash with Robert to distract him from the email Dwight's doomsday program is going to send. *(Doomsday)*

- Pam bets Dwight $5 to see if he can get Jim to admit he's lying about finding Cathy attractive. *(Pam's Replacement)*

The teams that play at Oscar's bar trivia contest are:

- Queerenstein Bears
- Joey Triviani
- Impish Impresarios
- Two Broke Dorks
- Late Onset Behar Fever
- Dunder Mifflin A-Team
- DM Backup Team
- Jason SoGay-Kiss
- Einsteins
- Ladies Gaga
- Aesop's Foibles
- Lawrence O'Trivier

*(Trivia)*

- Andy, Jessica, Dwight, Cathy, Kevin, and Erin all play chicken in Robert's pool. *(Pool Party)*

- Dwight suggests a drinking game where whoever has the most seeds in their pockets is the king and whoever has the least buttons is the hunchback. *(After Hours)*

- Before Stanley comes back from the hospital from his tonsillectomy, the staff can't remember whether Stanley has a mustache or not. They decide to vote. *(Welcome Party)*

- The final four in the paper airplane contest sponsored by WeyerHammer Paper are Dwight, Erin, Angela, and— God only knows how—Toby. The contest prize is $2,000, which Dwight wins when Angela throws the contest. *(Paper Airplane)*

the office book of lists

- In the A.A.R.M. Challenges, the challenges were Know Your Superior; Protocol; and Coffee Obstacle Course. *(A.A.R.M.)*

- For Darryl's goodbye, the staff agrees they want one dance with him. *(A.A.R.M.)*

- The staff does tai chi first thing in the morning after Dwight becomes regional manager. *(Finale)*

- When $3,000 is missing from petty cash, Kevin admits to taking $2,800 and betting it. He wins and returns it, but says it's unrelated to the other $3,000 that was missing. *(Webisode: The Accountants—Things Are Getting Tense)*

# INTEROFFICE COMMUNICATION

As Michael once said, "A company runs on efficiency of communication." Here are some of the more memorable memos, notes, and agendas that were written over the years.

- According to the kitchen regulations memo, any employee may dispose of a food item that risks contaminating other food items. *(Health Care)*

- Dwight's health care plan memo outlines that there is no dental or vision coverage and there's a $1,200 deductible. *(Health Care)*

- A week before the booze cruise, Michael sends out a mysterious memo: "It's time for our first-quarter camaraderie event, so pack a swimsuit, a toothbrush, rubber-soled shoes, and a ski mask." *(Booze Cruise)*

- Jan sends Michael a memo telling him that Jim is the number two after the merger, since he's the only one who has worked with both groups. *(The Merger)*

- After Phyllis is flashed, Dwight sends a memo explaining that women will be sent home if they are wearing makeup or heels exceeding one-quarter inch. Females are also not allowed to speak to strangers unless they are given written authorization by Dwight Schrute. They should wear clothes with sleeves that go down to the wrist, buttoned-up collars, and muted colors. *(Women's Appreciation)*

- After Pam copies Jim and Karen's documents for their interviews with Corporate, she leaves Jim a memo saying, "Don't forget us when you're famous," along with the yogurt lid "medal" he won in the Office Olympics. *(The Job)*

- Toby sends a memo reminding everyone of the policy about PDA in the office, because of Jim and Pam kissing in the break room. Michael thinks it's about him and Jan. *(Dunder Mifflin Infinity)*

- Ryan wants Michael to read the press release about the launch of Dunder Mifflin Infinity to everyone. *(Launch Party)*

- Jim sends a memo about holding shared birthday parties. *(Survivor Man)*

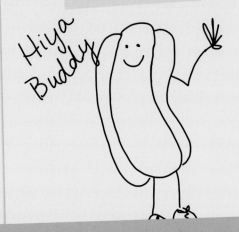

**DID YOU KNOW?**

Michael likes to have Pam come into meetings and bring in Post-it notes telling him who is on the phone, even though he doesn't get many calls. When Ryan is there, she draws on the note a hot dog doodle waving at Michael and saying "Hiya Buddy." Ryan forces Michael to take the nonexistent call. *(The Deposition)*

- Dwight has an org chart that tracks sales-related matters and menstrual cycles. It has an overlay chart for emergency disaster mode, where Dwight has full authority over everyone in the office. *(Did I Stutter?)*

- Pam posts a lengthy memo explaining how the microwave is a shared appliance and by not cleaning up, you are basically telling whoever follows that their time is less valuable, as they have to scrub out the disgusting splatter. She signs it "Disappointed." *(Frame Toby)*

- After Pam's first memo on the microwave, a second note appears calling the first writer an anonymous coward. *(Frame Toby)*

- When Michael wants to discuss his new business, he puts a note in Oscar's sandwich saying, "Meet me in the parking lot before lunch." *(Two Weeks)*

- The first mail Michael gets at his paper company is a letter from his condo board saying it's a violation of his condo agreement to conduct a business in his residence. *(Dream Team)*

- Michael wants to make eight hundred copies of a coupon for unparalleled customer service. *(The Michael Scott Paper Company)*

- When Dwight says he can't help Michael's new company by discussing the situation in code over the phone, Pam has to hold up a notepad to Michael saying, "He's talking about you!" Michael doesn't believe it. *(Heavy Competition)*

- When Dwight calls to tell Michael he's been sabotaged, Michael can't understand how Dwight knows. Pam holds up a notepad that says, "Dwight did it!!" *(Heavy Competition)*

the office book of lists

- Charles writes a memo to all departments that asks them to find ways to save money. *(Broke)*

- Dwight sends a memo called "New File System" with invisible ink to call the prior Dunder Mifflin salesmen to a secret meeting in the warehouse. He uses urine for the ink. *(Casual Friday)*

- David Wallace sends an email about the article in the *Wall Street Journal* on Dunder Mifflin's financial troubles as being conjecture. *(Murder)*

- Dwight leaves a copy of "My Diabolical Plan," his strategy to get rid of Jim, in the copier tray. Ryan reads it and joins his plan. *(Secret Santa)*

- Michael marks memos "Urgent A," "Urgent B," "Urgent C," and "Urgent D." A is most important; D you don't even really have to worry about. *(Training Day)*

Andy's agenda for his 9:30 casual chitchat with CEO Robert California includes the following items:

- Can he get everyone an extra-long Columbus Day weekend?

- Connect with the guy

- Time permitting, let him know they lost their biggest client

*(The List)*

- Kevin complains that Angela never lets him write the accounting memos. She lets him try, but they both get so frustrated, she ends up doing it. Kevin writes another memo that says, "To Whom It May Concern: Angela Stinks." *(Webisode: The Accountants— The Memo)*

## COMMITTEES AND TASK FORCES

Occasionally, an office staff needs to form a committee or task force to handle special initiatives. In the Scranton branch, the most powerful and long-standing committee has the most important focus of all—planning parties.

- Karen and Pam form the Committee to Plan Parties but dissolve it after their Christmas party. *(A Benihana Christmas)*

- Jim starts the Committee to Determine the Validity of the Two Committees and he's the sole member. He determines that the Committee to Plan Parties is valid. *(A Benihana Christmas)*

- Michael summons the Cri-Man-Squa (the Crisis Management Squad) when five hundred boxes of paper with an obscene watermark are delivered to clients. The squad includes everyone. *(Product Recall)*

- Oscar, Pam, and Toby form the Finer Things Club. Once a month they meet to discuss books and celebrate culture. There is no paper, plastic, or work talk allowed. *(Branch Wars)*

- After Toby's goodbye party, Phyllis takes over as head of the Party Planning Committee. *(Weight Loss)*

- After Phyllis blackmails Angela, Michael says the problem with having one head of the Party Planning Committee is that she would become too powerful, so he appoints Dwight and Jim as co-heads. *(Lecture Circuit)*

- After Phyllis is flashed, Dwight forms the Emergency Anti-Flashing Task Force. *(Women's Appreciation)*

- When the Party Planning Committee continues its meeting on Michael's anniversary party, Pam discusses the idea of smaller and smaller strippers popping out of cakes holding cakes. Jim brings up the two-way petting zoo, until Charles comes in and dissolves the Party Planning Committee. *(New Boss)*

- Once Pam becomes office administrator, she dissolves the Party Planning Committee since at its worst it was a toxic political club used to make others feel miserable and left out, and at its best it planned parties. *(Classy Christmas)*.

- For Michael's going-away party, all three of the former Party Planning Committee chairpeople—Angela, Phyllis, and Pam—work together to plan the party. *(Goodbye, Michael)*

- Jo puts Gabe, Jim, and Toby on the search committee to find a new manager. When Gabe is pulled off, Kelly is appointed. *(Search Committee)*

- Erin and Pete are the Youth Task Force. They create a fake profile for "Derek McBlack" and his "friends" and they all like Derek's likes for Dunder Mifflin. *(Customer Loyalty)*

the office book of lists

# DUNDIE AWARDS

Perhaps Michael's greatest contribution to office morale is the Dundies. Each year, he gives out awards to the entire staff. Though sometimes there are hiccups with engraving, or even hecklers at a Dundies venue, the Dundies are treasured by the staff. Well, maybe not Stanley. Or Jim. But most of the staff.

- Show Me the Money: Oscar *(The Dundies)*

- Longest Engagement: Pam *(The Dundies)*

- Busiest/Bushiest Beaver: Phyllis *(The Dundies)*

- Hottest in the Office: Ryan *(The Dundies)*

- Tight Ass: Angela *(The Dundies)*

- Spicy Curry: Kelly *(The Dundies)*

- Don't Go in There After Me: Kevin *(The Dundies)*

- Fine Work / Great Work (awarded the prior year): Stanley *(The Dundies)*

- Whitest Sneakers: Pam *(The Dundies)*

- Best Dad: Jim *(Michael's Last Dundies)*

- Best Mom: Meredith *(Michael's Last Dundies)*

- Hottest in the Office: Danny Cordray *(Michael's Last Dundies)*

- Diabetes Award: Stanley *(Michael's Last Dundies)*

- Promising Assistant Manager: Dwight *(Michael's Last Dundies)*

- Cutest Redhead in the Office: Erin *(Michael's Last Dundies)*

- Best Dundies Host: Deangelo Vickers *(Michael's Last Dundies)*

- Michael says Dwight should have gotten the Kind of a Bitch Award. *(Michael's Last Dundies)*

- Doobie Doobie Pothead Stoner of the Year: Andy *(Michael's Last Dundies)*

- Extreme Repulsiveness Award: Toby *(Michael's Last Dundies)*

- After Michael's last Dundies, the staff gives him the World's Best Boss Dundie. *(Goodbye, Michael)*

# OFFICE SIGNS, BANNERS, AND FLYERS

Often signs or flyers need to be printed up for meetings, holidays, or special occasions. Whether it is Angela trying to find a good home for Comstock or the staff leaving Sticky Quips on Gabe's back, there is never a shortage of signs, banners, and notes at Dunder Mifflin.

- Michael has a "Diversity Day Take 2!" sign printed out. *(Diversity Day)*

- Dwight puts up a sign saying "Dwight Schrute Workspace" on the conference room door. *(Health Care)*

- Stanley's file cabinet has a printed quote: "The difference between genius and stupidity is that genius has limits." —Unknown. *(Health Care)*

- Ryan holds up cue cards so Michael can rap at the Dundies. *(The Dundies)*

- Dwight makes a sign for his review presentation that spells out DWIGHT (Determined / Worker / Intense / Good Worker / Hard Worker / Terrific). *(Performance Review)*

- Pam shows Roy the flyer for the graphic design intern program. *(Boys and Girls)*

- Pam prints out a "Welcome Daughters!" sign above her desk on Take Your Daughter to Work Day. *(Take Your Daughter to Work Day)*

- No one but Dwight signs Michael's birthday poster. *(Michael's Birthday)*

- Michael thinks the poster of James Dean in his office on his birthday is Luke Perry. *(Michael's Birthday)*

- At the ice-skating rink, there's a sign saying "Happy Birthday Michael Scott!" *(Michael's Birthday)*

- At Casino Night, the sign for the prize reads: "Top Prize—The Most Chips Wins—$500 to the charity of your choice and a mini-fridge, courtesy of Bob Vance, Vance Refrigeration." *(Casino Night)*

- A sign in the warehouse reads: "This Department Has Worked ___ Days without a Lost Time Accident—Avoid Accidents." There was a "936" written in the blank space before Michael destroyed things with the lift and they had to change it to "0." *(Boys and Girls)*

- A "TOY DRIVE" sign is posted on the wall above the donation barrel at Christmastime. *(A Benihana Christmas)*

- Kevin has a sign saying "Don't eat the yellow snow" on his wall. *(Back from Vacation)*

- The warehouse staff prints the photo of Jan and Michael in Jamaica and puts it on the wall of the warehouse. *(Back from Vacation)*

- Pam puts a "Welcome Back Oscar" poster up for Oscar's party. *(The Return)*

- A "Congratulations Phyllis" sign is hung up in the conference room for her luncheon shower. *(Phyllis' Wedding)*

- Karen almost tears down the flyer for Pam's art show from the cabinet, but Oscar comes in. *(Business School)*

the office book of lists

DWIGHT SCHRUTE
WORKSPACE

DWIGHT SCHRUTE

DETERMINED
WORKER
INTENSE
GOOD WORKER
HARD WORKER
TERRIFIC

- There's a "Happenings" flyer on the refrigerator. *(Business School)*

- A flyer printed for Michael Scott's Dunder Mifflin Scranton Meredith Palmer Memorial Celebrity Rabies Awareness Pro-Am Fun Run Race for the Cure indicates Michael thinks a 5K is a 5,000-mile race. Free T-shirts are not guaranteed. *(Fun Run)*

- Near the copier there's an Outstanding Campaign Award from the United Way of Lackawanna County for Dunder Mifflin. *(The Deposition)*

- On the wall of the conference room, Holly puts up a "Body Image Celebration Day" sign. *(Weight Loss)*

- Phyllis hangs a baby shower sign in the conference room. She doesn't get storks, however, as Michael wants. *(Baby Shower)*

- A C.R.I.M.E.A.I.D. banner is hung in the warehouse. *(Crime Aid)*

- Michael once posted a photo of Meredith's bare boobs on the bulletin board with the caption reading "Gross." *(Stress Relief)*

- For Kelly's birthday, Dwight makes a sign that says "IT IS YOUR BIRTHDAY." *(Lecture Circuit)*

- Dwight makes what Jim calls a very effeminate sign to say Kelly's "Party Pushed to 3 PM," when he could have just made an announcement. *(Lecture Circuit)*

- A "Happy Valentine's Day" banner, cupids, and heart decorations are put up in the lobby and elevator of the building. *(Blood Drive)*

- Michael makes a Lonely Hearts Valentines Singles Mixer flyer for the office building. *(Blood Drive)*

- Michael doesn't put "Limit one per customer" on the golden tickets he inserts in random boxes. *(Golden Ticket)*

the office book of lists

- Jim holds up a sign saying "Dwight picked the wrong day to put a wooden mallard in my office." *(The Lover)*

- On the refrigerator, there's a sign that has a cartoon monster that says "Dunder Mifflin Keeping It Green." *(Counseling)*

- At Pam's office health meeting, there's a sign for Sabre Hygiene Day. *(The Christening)*

- Ryan prints a color sign about how WUPHF could triple their investment by January. *(WUPHF.com)*

- Dwight allows a giant A&J roach extermination business's billboard to cover the windows in the office. *(China)*

- The staff takes a photo for Christmas cards in front of a "Happy Holidays from Dunder Mifflin—a division of Sabre" banner. *(Classy Christmas)*

- For the seminar, there's a "Grow Your Small Business" banner in the conference room. *(The Seminar)*

- The staff leave Sticky Quips on Gabe's back saying "I'm a doosh" and "Do not climb." *(The Search)*

- Andy creates a sign-up sheet for "mods" (five-minute segments) in the conference room. *(Todd Packer)*

- After Michael has already left, there are two banners at his goodbye party in the conference room that read "Goodbye, Michael" and "Good luck in Colorado." *(Goodbye, Michael)*

- There's a sign that reads "Recycle Here" but no wastebasket. *(Dwight K. Schrute, (Acting) Manager)*

- Jim starts a social club and puts up flyers saying "Join the Fist," which is working on Operation: Overthrow when Dwight is acting manager. *(Dwight K. Schrute, (Acting) Manager)*

- Angela creates a lotto pool on whether Pam will have a fourteen-pound baby. *(Lotto)*

- Andy has three billboards made that get defaced with phallic symbols. *(Garden Party)*

- Andy pays $200 to commission a Dunder Mifflin flag. *(Gettysburg)*

- Jim shows the camera a note explaining, "We're on the longest silent streak in office history. Nobody has said anything in . . . 14 minutes." *(Trivia)*

Dwight puts posters of Florida challenges on the wall:

- CASEY ANTHONY
- ALLIGATORS
- OLD PEOPLE
- COCKROACHES
- HURRICANE(S)
- HURRICANE [again]
- HURRICANE
- SPRING BREAK
- KATHERINE HARRIS

*(Special Project)*

- A sign at the Sabre store for the Pyramid claims, "The eighth wonder of the world is in your hands." *(Test the Store)*

- Dwight and Nellie punish Jim by making him the sign spinner outside the Sabre store with a sign that says "Grand Opening." *(Test the Store)*

- The sign outside the Sabre retail says "Sabre Store Grand Opening—The infinite future is now." *(Test the Store)*

- In Dwight's free portrait studio, Ryan takes a photo alone with a sign that says, "Kelly, I know you are with someone but I love you. I will wait forever." Ryan also takes a photo with a sign that says, "Missed connection— Caffeine Corner—You were blonde w/a hat? I work at Dunder Mifflin. Hope to see you again." *(Free Family Portrait Studio)*

- Angela holds up a flyer saying that Comstock needs a good home. *(New Guys)*

- Erin puts a sign on Darryl's door claiming "Conference Call Do Not Disturb." *(Vandalism)*

- When Dwight tells the camera he and Jim run a no-nonsense office, Jim holds up a small chalk sign that says "5 days since our last nonsense." *(A.A.R.M.)*

## STAFF DÉCOR

Since an office (or cubicle) is a person's home eight hours a day, five days a week, it's no wonder employees like to personalize their workspaces. While much of the office décor consists of certificates and inspirational posters, there are a number of ways people bring their own personal touches to their workspaces.

- Michael bought his "World's Best Boss" mug from Spencer Gifts. *(Pilot)*

- Kevin has a sign on his bulletin board that reads, "People may doubt what you say but they will believe what you do." *(Pilot)*

- There is an Austin Lounge Lizards bumper sticker on the bulletin board. *(Health Care)*

- Angela has a cat calendar. *(Office Olympics)*

- A city map (presumably of Scranton) hangs in Michael's office. *(The Alliance)*

- A handheld vacuum cleaner hangs on the wall next to Creed's desk. *(Basketball)*

- Dwight keeps a Lackawanna volunteer sheriff's deputy mug on his desk. *(Office Olympics)*

- Someone puts out an inflatable pumpkin at Halloween. *(Halloween)*

- Dwight's file cabinet has a Froggy 101 bumper sticker on it. *(Performance Review)*

- Dwight's file cabinet also has a "Dunder Mifflin Tools of the Trade" postcard on it. *(Performance Review)*

- Angela has an American flag at her desk. *(Performance Review)*

- A "Commitment" poster hangs behind Ryan. *(Performance Review)*

- Michael keeps his "Seyko" watch's certificate of authenticity hanging in his office. *(Email Surveillance)*

- Michael hung a "Leadership" poster behind his door. *(The Secret)*

- Michael keeps a photo of Jan—cut from the staff newsletter—in his cabinet. *(Dwight's Speech)*

- Michael has a small British flag in a cup on his desk. *(Gay Witch Hunt)*

- Kelly has an "Attitude" poster on her wall. *(The Coup)*

- Kevin took the poster of Michael and Jan in Jamaica home since he doesn't have a lot of art. *(Back from Vacation)*

- Angela has small orange cat and frog figurines on her divider. *(Traveling Salesman)*

- Ryan hung a piñata up for Oscar's welcome-back party. *(The Return)*

- Elizabeth the stripper tells Angela she likes her poster of the babies playing saxophones. *(Ben Franklin)*

- Pam's honorable mention for the Dunder Mifflin Speed Dialing and Memo Sorting Competition is on her wall. *(Business School)*

- Michael buys Pam's watercolor of the office building and hangs it in the office. *(Business School)*

- Jim gets Dwight a "Certificate of Bravery" from the Scranton Police Department, but he throws it away. *(The Negotiation)*

- For his watermark apology video, Michael puts a printout of an American flag on the blinds behind him. *(Product Recall)*

- Michael frames and hangs the *Scranton Times* article about the recall near the watercooler. *(Product Recall)*

- Dwight paints Michael's office black when he becomes regional manager for one day. *(The Job)*

- A certificate for "The One Million Cut Trees Award to Dunder Mifflin Paper from the Rain Forest Harvester's Association" is on the wall near Oscar's desk. *(Dunder Mifflin Infinity)*

Michael needs the following in his office:

- SPACE HEATER
- HUMIDIFIER
- DEHUMIDIFIER
- FAN
- FOOT FAN
- FOOD DEHYDRATOR
- KEYBOARD

*(The Manager and the Salesman)*

- Darryl has a framed photo of a motorcycle in his office in the warehouse. *(Did I Stutter?)*

- David Wallace has an eagle statue behind his desk. *(The Duel)*

- There are "Lackawanna Wonderful" and "Rolling Into The Future—Steamtown" magnets on the refrigerator. *(Lecture Circuit)*

- On Valentine's Day, Kelly and Meredith tear heart decorations in two and rip the wings off cupids as they decorate the conference room for the Lonely Hearts Convention. *(Blood Drive)*

- A "Diversity" poster hangs in the Michael Scott Paper Company office. *(The Michael Scott Paper Company)*

- Kelly has a sign at her desk saying "Kelly's Nook." *(The Lover)*

- Darryl has a "Nobody Talks Everybody Walks" sign in his office. *(China)*

- Deangelo brought a painting of the American Southwest—his favorite region—to hang in his office. *(Training Day)*

- When he takes over as acting manager, Dwight puts in a marble desk that's a replica of Uday Hussein's, installs a fish tank with a rescue piranha in it, and adds a Beaumont-Adams gun in a glass case, which Jo happens to collect. *(Dwight K. Schrute, (Acting) Manager)*

- Andy has his diploma from Cornell and a Cornell pennant in his office. *(The List)*

- Andy has a sign saying "Friendship is the music of life" on the bulletin board in his office. *(The Incentive)*

- Nellie puts a couch in her office when she took Andy's job from him. *(Angry Andy)*

- Meredith has a 98.5 KRZ Listener Club flyer up on her bulletin board. *(Dwight Christmas)*

- When Dwight becomes manager, he hangs a painting of himself in the conference room that looks like a South Korean propaganda poster. *(A.A.R.M.)*

- Dwight has a hierarchy mobile hanging from a stand on the credenza with each person in the org chart hanging from strings. *(A.A.R.M.)*

## WASTING TIME AND RESOURCES

In a typical office there's arguably a certain amount of time and resources wasted—too many meetings, inflated expenses, and time theft. However, in the Scranton branch of Dunder Mifflin, it is sometimes hard to tell if *any* time or resources *aren't* being wasted.

- Michael buys a Starbucks digital barista as a sales incentive, then uses it to impress Katy. *(Hot Girl)*

- Michael stands in the pretzel line for two hours to make sure he gets his pretzel the way he wants it. *(Initiation)*

- Phyllis often knits at her desk. *(Branch Closing)*

- When Stanley tells Creed that Phyllis is out on her honeymoon for six weeks, Creed says he'll wait and sits down. *(Business School)*

- Holly explains that according to Corporate, spending a half hour at the watercooler is a form of stealing called time theft. She asks for other examples of time wasters and Stanley (ironically) says, "This meeting." *(Business Ethics)*

When Holly asks if anyone has faced ethical dilemmas at work, the following are brought up:

- Michael watched "Cookie Monster Sings Chocolate Rain" about a thousand times when he discovered YouTube.

- Oscar once in a while took a long lunch.

- Kelly sometimes downloaded pirated music onto her work computer.

- Angela once reported Oscar to INS.

- Meredith admits to sleeping with the Hammermill rep.

*(Business Ethics)*

- Jim clocks Dwight being away from his desk for nineteen minutes and forty-eight seconds, as Angela discreetly buttons up her blouse. *(Business Ethics)*

- When a $4,300 surplus in the budget is found, the staff fight over buying a new copier and chairs, getting air quality tests, or giving a 15 percent bonus to Michael. *(The Surplus)*

- Most of the staff go outside and run past the new radar gun to clock their running speeds. *(The Duel)*

- Stanley leads a discussion on whether Hilary Swank is hot or not. Jim puts it to a vote and it's five to five, with Angela abstaining. It turns into a full-on debate. Michael eventually comes in and offhandedly wins it for the hot side. *(Prince Family Paper)*

- Corporate has to pay $3,500 when Dwight cuts the face off the CPR dummy. *(Stress Relief)*

- Charles Miner tells the staff that there were 3 percent cuts across the board and discretionary spending cuts should be encouraged for areas like petty cash, supplies, and parties. *(New Boss)*

- Charles says the Party Planning Committee meeting isn't a good use of company time. *(New Boss)*

- Sabre puts site blockers on sites like Twitter and YouTube that are time wasters. *(Sabre)*

Erin lists the names of racehorses to distract Pam from her labor:

- Affirmed
- Seattle Slew
- Secretariat
- Citation
- Assault
- Count Fleet
- Whirlaway
- War Admiral
- Omaha
- Gallant Fox
- And one sired by Star Shoot

*(The Delivery)*

- Erin doesn't like Ryan using the color copier for his WUPHF business. Ryan also prints WUPHF T-shirts and condoms. *(WUPHF.com)*

- Meredith likes to play solitaire. *(WUPHF.com)*

- Creed asks Jim how long he can hold his breath. *(WUPHF.com)*

- Michael loses his corporate credit card temporarily after spending $80 at a magic shop buying tricks to impress clients. *(The Secret)*

- Jim and Pam spend the whole morning working on a response to Robert's text saying that Jim should pack his clubs for the trip to Florida. *(Special Project)*

- Michael spends a lot of money at Jack's Joke and Magic Shop. *(Webisode: The Accountants—Michael's Office)*

- It's the best day of Kevin's life when he discovers Angela logged the equipment depreciation twice and caused the $3,000 error they spent a lot of time questioning everyone about. *(Webisode: The Accountants—The Best Day of My Life)*

## SICK DAYS

While workplace safety is always important, accidents and injuries do occur. Toby apparently has forms and files for almost any incident, from abductions to accidents to drunk driving to lewd conduct. Of course, sometimes you just need a mental health day, so you might only have a case of Count Choculitis or a government-created killer nanorobot infection.

- While Michael wants to get the Gold health care plan, Jan explains even *she* doesn't have that and he has to pick a more inexpensive plan. *(Health Care)*

- Dwight gets sinus infections, which he cures by making tea from green tea leaf stems and pouring it into his nose. *(Christmas Party)*

the office book of lists

When Michael puts Dwight in charge of finding a health care plan, he gets the cheapest one, which covers virtually nothing. To address this, he has everyone write down the diseases they need covered. The staff claims to have some new ones, along with some real ones, including:

- COUNT CHOCULITIS (which Dwight suspects Jim made up because he knows Dwight loves the cereal)

- EBOLA

- MAD COW

- SPONTANEOUS DENTAL HYDROPLOSION

- LEPROSY

- FLESH-EATING BACTERIA

- HOT DOG FINGERS

- GOVERNMENT-CREATED KILLER NANOROBOT INFECTION

- INVERTED PENIS

- DERMATITIS

- ANAL FISSURES (which Dwight doesn't believe is real, but Kevin insists is)

*(Health Care)*

- Dwight has never missed a day of work, even when he had walking pneumonia. *(Performance Review)*

- Michael burns his foot very badly on his George Foreman grill. *(The Injury)*

- Oscar calls out sick on Spring Cleaning Day with chills, nausea, and a headache. He actually goes shopping. *(The Secret)*

- Michael gets suggestion box suggestions about his BO and coffee breath. *(Performance Review)*

- When Michael tries to prove he doesn't like Holly, he claims she smells like old tomatoes and dirt. *(Baby Shower)*

- Michael will not stop putting Q-tips in his ears, no matter how much it hurts. *(Frame Toby)*

- Michael tells Kevin laughter is the best medicine for his potential skin cancer, but Kevin says his doctor said the best medicine was a combination of interferon and dacarbazine. *(Michael's Birthday)*

- Dwight doesn't tip for things he can do himself, but he did tip his urologist, as he can't pulverize his own kidney stones. *(Michael's Birthday)*

- Dwight gets a concussion and vomits when he crashes his car into the pole in the parking lot. He also mistakes Creed for his dad. *(The Injury)*

- Dwight clips his fingernails at his desk and blows the clippings toward Ryan's desk. *(Gay Witch Hunt)*

- When Dwight goes to secretly meet Jan, he claims to have gone to his dentist, Dr. Crentist. *(The Coup)*

- When Pam says she might be too tired to go to the Diwali party, Dwight wonders if she has mono. *(Diwali)*

- Kevin has hyperhidrosis of the feet and Angela dislikes when he takes his shoes off. *(Grief Counseling)*

- Michael has a 2½-pound barbell in his trunk, as he's going for tone, not bulk. *(The Convict)*

- Dwight thinks the waitress at Benihana could have narcolepsy when she stands there with her eyes closed as Andy has her picture her dream house. *(A Benihana Christmas)*

- About forty times a year Michael gets really sick but has no symptoms, and Dwight is always gravely concerned. *(Beach Games)*

- Michael says sometimes all the body needs to heal itself is to be promoted. *(Beach Games)*

- Dwight's mom doesn't believe in vaccines. He got smallpox the old-fashioned way and survived. *(Dunder Mifflin Infinity)*

- When Michael hits Meredith with his car, she sustains a slight "pevical" fracture. *(Fun Run)*

- Michael thinks rabies causes a fear of water. *(Fun Run)*

- Michael ends up in the hospital for dehydration after the 5K. *(Fun Run)*

- Meredith asks Jim to sign her pelvic cast. *(Launch Party)*

- Alone in the wilderness, Michael yells that he has hemorrhoids. *(Survivor Man)*

- Michael claims his stomach hurts when Toby comes in his office. *(Did I Stutter?)*

- Stanley has a heart attack during Dwight's emergency preparedness test. *(Stress Relief)*

- Michael calls his doctor to ask if he can stick his mole with a pin. *(Lecture Circuit)*

- When dancing at Michael's Café Disco, Phyllis hurts her back. *(Café Disco)*

- Pam hurts her foot at the company picnic. While at the hospital, she and Jim discover she's pregnant. *(Company Picnic)*

- Michael asks Oscar for advice to make his colonoscopy more pleasurable for himself or the doctor. *(The Meeting)*

the office book of lists

- Andy tears his scrotum while trying to do a split while dancing before Pam's wedding. *(Niagara)*

- Dwight trains his major blood vessels to retract into his body on command. Also, he can retract his penis up into itself. *(Blood Drive)*

- Pam and Jim try to delay her labor until after midnight because the insurance company only covers a two-night stay at the hospital. *(The Delivery)*

- Phyllis is stung up her dress by a hornet. *(Sex Ed)*

- Michael has a cold sore and thinks he has herpes. It ultimately ends up being an ingrown hair. *(Sex Ed)*

- Gabe has powdered seahorse—one of the five Chinese virility herbs. *(Viewing Party)*

- Packer wants an office job after he gets "love bumps" on his "ding-dong." *(Todd Packer)*

- After Stanley wins a Dundie for diabetes, Phyllis says she has it, too, but you don't see her making a big deal about it. *(Michael's Last Dundies)*

- Andy's eardrum bursts after Dwight's gun goes off in the office. *(Dwight K. Schrute, (Acting) Manager)*

- Darryl develops a soy allergy at age thirty-five. *(Lotto)*

- Jim discovers he has high blood pressure when Dwight tries to use a drugstore monitor as a lie detector. *(Pam's Replacement)*

- Erin has scoliosis. *(Christmas Wishes)*

- Dwight claims he is a cholera survivor. *(Body Language)*

- Dwight has appendicitis the first day he's in Florida. He keeps his removed appendix as a souvenir for Phillip. *(Tallahassee)*

- Andy gets two black eyes—one from a little girl and one from breaking up a fight between Toby and Kelly. *(Test the Store)*

- When Ryan unravels before the presentation at the store, he calls his uncle Lucas to get a prescription for Ritalin. After all, he did it for his aunt Carol. *(Test the Store)*

- Stanley has a tonsillectomy. *(Welcome Party)*

- When Andy is impotent, Erin asks Dwight if he ever had "penial softiosis." *(Angry Andy)*

- Clark is good at balance and claims his doctor said he has gigantic inner ears. *(New Guys)*

- Dwight finds a Dumatril pill—used to treat anxiety symptoms such as panic attacks, excessive worrying, and fear. He thinks there's a madman in their midst. It's actually Nellie's. *(Here Comes Treble)*

- Toby has very fertile hair glands and grows a thick mustache for Movember. *(The Whale)*

- Cece gets lice and Pam brings it into the office. Meredith gets it and promptly shaves her head. *(Lice)*

- Erin had lice twenty-two times between the orphanage and foster homes. *(Lice)*

- Meredith once gave everyone pink eye. *(Lice)*

- Dwight bug bombs the office with piperonyl butoxide, which has hallucinogenic effects. *(Lice)*

- To try and catch Pete in a lie about Erin, Andy claims to have contracted "shla-mydia" from Erin. *(Moving On)*

- Gabe reveals he doesn't have the lung capacity to blow a whistle. *(Moving On)*

## WORK COMPUTERS

IT is always watching, but sometimes you just need to see how your cat is doing or work on your mystery novel. Here are some of the items found on the Scranton staff's work computers.

- Ryan installs File Share on all the computers in his first months in the office. *(Hot Girl)*

- While suffering from his head injury, Dwight names a file by typing "DWIGHT" over 135 times. *(The Injury)*

- Andy puts a screen saver of a cat in a cowboy hat on his computer. *(The Merger)*

- Creed places a screenshot of Hannah's left breast on his computer. *(The Merger)*

the office book of lists

- Michael has a photo of Jan—who he claims is a German woman named Urkel Grue—on his computer. It ends up circulating to the whole company. *(Back from Vacation)*

- Pam reminds everyone they don't give Kevin full internet access. *(Prince Family Paper)*

- Michael copies a document named "Dear Michael" from Holly's computer, which has an Ed Grimley screen saver. *(Lecture Circuit)*

- Andy has a soccer screen saver, which Charles notices. They bond over soccer, which Andy actually hates. *(Dream Team)*

- Ryan puts a photo of him and his friend Jasmine in Thailand on the shared laptop's desktop. *(The Michael Scott Paper Company)*

- Michael gets Frankie's "Dirty Joke of the Day" emails each day, as well as news alerts for "nip slips." *(Scott's Tots)*

- While looking for Michael's hotel reservation in his emails, Dwight discovers Michael has thousands of "affirmations" and he *did* get the Evite to Dwight's barbecue. *(The Manager and the Salesman)*

- Toby is writing a mystery novel on his office computer and Jo skims the first chapter of it. *(Whistleblower)*

- When trying to break his computer in order to force Pam to get him a new one, Andy allows all cookies, pop-ups, and streamed BitTorrent music from a Somalian music website. He also spits coffee on it and puts bologna in the CD drive. *(Todd Packer)*

- When Oscar tries to look on WebMD, he discovers that it's been blocked after Dwight became acting manager. *(Dwight K. Schrute, (Acting) Manager)*

- The Central Supply Index is open on Pam's computer when Dwight, Darryl, and Jim try to remove the planking Kevin from Dwight's desk. *(The List)*

- After discussing her fantasy of winning the lottery and buying a townhouse in SoHo, Pam has NYC loft listings open on her computer. *(Lotto)*

- Kelly gets viruses on her computer because she keeps clicking on Kardashian links. *(Christmas Wishes)*

- Robert catches Pam watching a music video of Drake featuring Swizz Beatz. *(Welcome Party)*

- Toby plays video games with Pete and Clark. *(New Guys)*

# MUSICAL PERFORMANCES

While Andy is perhaps the most musically talented employee, Dwight on the recorder is nothing to sneeze at. One of Kelly's many plans is to become a singer, and the staff often does karaoke and once did a lip dub of "Nobody but Me."

- At the Dundies, Michael sings song parodies of several classic songs, including "Tiny Dundie" (sung to the tune of "Tiny Dancer"). *(The Dundies)*

- During Jim's barbecue, several people perform karaoke. *(Email Surveillance)*

- Dwight sings "What Shall We Do with a Drunken Sailor?" while "steering" the ship. *(Booze Cruise)*

- Dwight plays "Greensleeves" on a green plastic recorder for the daughters at work. *(Take Your Daughter to Work Day)*

- Michael and Dwight sing "Teach Your Children" at the end of Take Your Daughter to Work Day. *(Take Your Daughter to Work Day)*

- Dwight plays "For the Longest Time" by "William Joel," Michael's favorite song, for Michael's birthday. *(Michael's Birthday)*

- Pam reviews wedding bands, like Till Death Do Us Rock; Kevin's band, Scrantonicity; and a Kiss cover band. *(Casino Night)*

- Andy sings "Closer to Fine" while working late and Jim joins in. *(Diwali)*

- Michael plays a steel drum and sings "Hot Hot Hot." *(Back from Vacation)*

- Kevin (and then everyone) sings Alanis Morissette's "You Oughta Know." *(A Benihana Christmas)*

- Andy and Michael sing "Your Body Is a Wonderland" to the Benihana waitresses. *(A Benihana Christmas)*

- Kelly sings "We Belong" to Ryan. *(A Benihana Christmas)*

- Creed sings "Spinnin' and Reelin'." *(A Benihana Christmas)*

- Dwight sings Styx's "Lady." *(A Benihana Christmas)*

- Angela sings "The Little Drummer Boy." *(A Benihana Christmas)*

- Phyllis's wedding is the third wedding Scrantonicity has played. *(Phyllis' Wedding)*

- Karen sings a song onstage with Scrantonicity at Phyllis's wedding. *(Phyllis' Wedding)*

- Kevin sings "The Gambler" on the bus ride to Beach Day and most everyone joins in. *(Beach Games)*

- Jim and Pam see Dwight sadly playing the recorder out by the dumpster as he pines for Angela. *(Money)*

the office book of lists

- Darryl plays keyboard and Creed, Andy, Kevin, and Kelly sing the jingle for Michael's proposed commercial for Dunder Mifflin Scranton, "the people person's paper people." However, Michael thought it was going to be a rap song. *(Local Ad)*

- Jan's old assistant Hunter records a CD called *The Hunter* and she plays one of his songs at the dinner party. The song tells the story of a woman making him into a man one night. *(Dinner Party)*

- Michael sings a goodbye song at the chair model's grave to the tune of "American Pie." *(Chair Model)*

- Dwight sings Ryan a German lullaby during their night in New York. *(Night Out)*

- Jan sings "Son of a Preacher Man" at her baby shower. *(Baby Shower)*

- Michael, Holly, and Darryl sing "Life Is a Highway" on the drive to Nashua. *(Employee Transfer)*

- After Holly and Michael break up, Michael and Darryl sing the blues on the drive back to Scranton. *(Employee Transfer)*

- Michael remembers the words to the Pledge of Allegiance by setting it to the tune of "Old MacDonald." *(Lecture Circuit)*

- Andy and Dwight try to outplay each other with "Take Me Home, Country Roads" in the break room to impress Erin. *(The Michael Scott Paper Company)*

- Andy says every song is better a capella. *(The Michael Scott Paper Company)*

- Andy and Erin sing a song about the Dunder Mifflin–Sabre merger to the tune of "Party in the USA." *(Sabre)*

- Gabe plays keyboards and likes to compose soundscapes. He plays "Earthrise on the Moon" for Andy. *(Viewing Party)*

- Curtis Dorough, Lisa, and the sportscaster from Channel 7 end up ousting Kevin, Darryl, and Andy from their own band. Val has to be the one to point out that they've been replaced. *(Pam's Replacement)*

- Dwight, Creed, Gabe, and Nate air guitar to the Trans-Siberian Orchestra's version of "Christmas Eve." *(Christmas Wishes)*

- Kevin sings a song about cookie season. *(Last Day in Florida)*

- Roy surprises Laura at their wedding by playing Billy Joel's "She's Got a Way" on the piano. He'd told her he was taking boxing lessons, but he was learning piano. *(Roy's Wedding)*

- Here Comes Treble sings "I'll Be," "Car," "Faith," and "Monster Mash." *(Here Comes Treble)*

- To make his siblings care about the farm, Dwight has them perform "Sons and Daughters" to make them nostalgic. *(The Farm)*

- For Darryl's last dance, the staff gets down to "Boogie Wonderland." *(A.A.R.M.)*

- Angela walks—on Phyllis's back—down the aisle to a violin arrangement of "Sweet Child o' Mine." *(Finale)*

# Chapter Five:
# Holidays

# NEW YEAR'S RESOLUTIONS

The staff at the Scranton branch of Dunder Mifflin sometimes has unique New Year's resolutions and doesn't always succeed in following them.

**Meredith:** Only drink during the week. *(Christmas Party)*

**Oscar:** Finish the living room. *(Ultimatum)*

**Gabe:** Be less squeamish around people's dogs and babies. *(Ultimatum)*

**Holly:** Cross-train. *(Ultimatum)*

**Kevin:** Eat more vegetables. *(Ultimatum)*

**Ryan:** Live life like it's an art project! *(Ultimatum)*

**Pam:** Drink less caffeine. *(Ultimatum)*

**Michael:** Floss—and never make Holly cry again. *(Ultimatum)*

**Angela:** Make time for romance—with the senator. *(Ultimatum)*

**Dwight:** Meet a loose woman. *(Ultimatum)*

**Erin:** Learn a new word every single day. *(Ultimatum)*

**Phyllis:** Yoga lessons with Bob. *(Ultimatum)*

**Meredith:** Two cigarettes a day. *(Ultimatum)*

**Creed:** Do a stunning, gorgeous cartwheel. (Michael helps him and Creed thinks he did one.) *(Ultimatum)*

**Kelly:** Get more attention by any means necessary. *(Ultimatum)*

**Darryl:** Read more. *(Ultimatum)*

**Andy:** Learn to cook for one—and meet a loose woman. *(Ultimatum)*

**Jim:** Bike more. *(Ultimatum)*

**Stanley:** Be a better husband and boyfriend. *(Ultimatum)*

ONLY DRINK DURING THE WEEK

## HALLOWEEN COSTUMES

For Michael and the staff of the Scranton branch, Halloween is one of the best holidays. Year after year, the whole office gets involved, though Jim's costumes tend to be low effort.

**Pam:** Cat costume *(Halloween)*

**Devon:** Hobo *(Halloween)*

**Phyllis:** Leopard *(Halloween)*

**Michael:** A second papier-mâché Michael Scott head on his shoulder. The year before Michael wore his double-headed outfit, he went as Janet Jackson's boob. The two previous years, he went as Monica Lewinsky, and before that, O. J. Simpson. *(Halloween)*

**Jim:** Three-Hole Punch Jim *(Halloween)*

**Dwight:** Sith lord *(Halloween)*

**Kevin:** Dunder Mifflin Man—a superhero like Mr. Incredible *(Halloween)*

**Angela:** Cat *(Halloween)*

**Kelly:** Dorothy *(Halloween)*

**Oscar:** A dress *(Halloween)*

**Creed:** Vampire *(Halloween)*

**Kelly:** Carrie Bradshaw from *Sex and the City (Employee Transfer)*

**Phyllis:** Raggedy Ann *(Employee Transfer)*

**Ryan:** Gordon Gekko *(Employee Transfer)*

**Creed:** The Joker *(Employee Transfer)*

**Kevin:** The Joker *(Employee Transfer)*

**Dwight:** The Joker (Dwight was not happy about the duplicated costumes) *(Employee Transfer)*

**Andy:** Kitten *(Employee Transfer)*

**Jim:** Dave *(Employee Transfer)*

**Pam:** Charlie Chaplin *(Employee Transfer)*

**Angela:** Same cat as before *(Employee Transfer)*

**Oscar:** Uncle Sam *(Employee Transfer)*

**Michael:** "Dick in a Box" character *(Koi Pond)*

**Jim:** Facebook, or "Book Face," depending on interpretation *(Koi Pond)*

**Dwight:** Puppet from the *Saw* films *(Koi Pond)*

**Darryl:** "Gangster Pumpkin" *(Koi Pond)*

**Angela:** Black Widow *(Koi Pond)*

**Erin:** Princess Fiona from *Shrek* *(Koi Pond)*

**Kevin:** Paul Blart, Mall Cop *(Koi Pond)*

**Kelly:** Leeloo from *The Fifth Element* *(Koi Pond)*

**Creed:** Vampire *(Koi Pond)*

**Ryan:** Goth dude / Edward Cullen *(Koi Pond)*

**Meredith:** Hobo *(Koi Pond)*

**Andy:** Michael Jackson *(Costume Contest)*

**Kevin:** Michael Moore *(Costume Contest)*

**Oscar:** Pimp / rational consumer (Oscar wins the contest) *(Costume Contest)*

**Angela:** Penguin/nurse *(Costume Contest)*

**Erin:** Monster mask *(Costume Contest)*

**Stanley:** Samurai *(Costume Contest)*

**Michael:** MacGruber *(Costume Contest)*

**Darryl:** Dracula *(Costume Contest)*

**Pam:** Olive Oyl *(Costume Contest)*

**Creed:** Mummy *(Costume Contest)*

**Dwight:** Scranton Strangler *(Costume Contest)*

**Gabe:** Lady Gaga *(Costume Contest)*

**Packer:** Pregnant nun *(Costume Contest)*

**Darryl:** Dracula *(Costume Contest)*

**Phyllis:** Judge *(Costume Contest)*

**Toby:** Hobo *(Costume Contest)*

**Kelly:** Katy Perry *(Costume Contest)*

**Ryan:** Justin Bieber *(Costume Contest)*

**Andy:** Bill Compton from *True Blood* *(Costume Contest)*

**Meredith:** Sookie Stackhouse from *True Blood* *(Costume Contest)*

**Jim:** Popeye *(Costume Contest)*

**Cece:** Swee'pea *(Costume Contest)*

the office book of lists

**Angela:** Sexy bunny *(Spooked)*

**Phyllis:** Sexy bunny *(Spooked)*

**Stanley:** Chef *(Spooked)*

**Kevin:** Michael vetoed his gorilla outfit *(Spooked)*

**Kelly:** Andy vetoed her Kate Middleton outfit *(Spooked)*

**Meredith:** Kate Middleton *(Spooked)*

**Andy:** Construction worker *(Spooked)*

**Erin:** Wendy's logo *(Spooked)*

**Darryl:** LeBron James *(Spooked)*

**Kevin:** Dwayne Wade *(Spooked)*

**Jim:** Chris Bosh *(Spooked)*

**Dwight:** Kerrigan, Queen of Blades, from *StarCraft*, with no weapons (in prior years, when he dressed as Pinhead and Freddy Krueger, Toby confiscated his weapons) *(Spooked)*

**Andy:** Construction worker *(Spooked)*

**Toby:** Glow-in-the-dark skeleton *(Spooked)*

**Pam:** Kangaroo *(Spooked)*

**Oscar:** Oscar Liar Wiener *(Spooked)*

**Kelly:** Glow-in-the-dark skeleton *(Spooked)*

**Gabe:** Glow-in-the-dark skeleton *(Spooked)*

**Creed:** Osama bin Laden *(Spooked)*

**Ryan:** Jesse Pinkman from *Breaking Bad (Spooked)*

**Dwight:** Pumpkin head / pig nose *(Here Comes Treble)*

**Pam:** Dr. Cinderella, a princess oncologist, to be a better role model for Cece *(Here Comes Treble)*

**Erin:** Puppy *(Here Comes Treble)*

**Jim:** Men in Black *(Here Comes Treble)*

**Andy:** George Michael *(Here Comes Treble)*

**Phyllis:** Cheerleader *(Here Comes Treble)*

**Kevin:** Charlie Brown *(Here Comes Treble)*

**Angela:** Nancy Reagan *(Here Comes Treble)*

**Oscar:** Dinosaur / electoral college *(Here Comes Treble)*

**Stanley:** Usain Bolt *(Here Comes Treble)*

**Meredith:** Black Widow *(Here Comes Treble)*

**Darryl:** Cowboy *(Here Comes Treble)*

**Nellie:** Sexy Toby *(Here Comes Treble)*

**Creed:** Has blood splattered on his shirt and appreciates the really, really good timing that it's Halloween *(Here Comes Treble)*

**Senator Lipton:** Ronald Reagan *(Here Comes Treble)*

# CHRISTMAS SECRET SANTA GIFTS

Exchanging Secret Santa gifts is a Dunder Mifflin tradition that most of the staff seem to like. However, when Michael doesn't get the gift he thinks he deserves, he makes sure to change the rules to get the gift he wants.

## DID YOU KNOW?

Jim gives Pam a teapot filled with inside jokes, including a cassette tape, his high school yearbook photo, a hot sauce packet, a miniature pencil, a Boggle timer, and a card. He originally includes a note telling Pam how he feels about her but takes it out. *(Christmas Party)*

- Oscar gives Creed a shamrock keychain. *(Christmas Party)*

- Kevin gives himself a footbath. *(Christmas Party)*

- Kelly gives Oscar a shower radio. *(Christmas Party)*

- Creed gives Jim an old shirt, whose sleeves are too short. *(Christmas Party)*

- Michael gives Ryan a video iPod—which was over the $20 limit. *(Christmas Party)*

- Stanley gives Kelly a personalized nameplate. *(Christmas Party)*

- Phyllis knits Michael an oven mitt. *(Christmas Party)*

- Stanley gives Kelly a nameplate. *(Christmas Party)*

- Dwight gives his Secret Santa paintball lessons with him, which Michael ends up with. *(Christmas Party)*

- Andy gives Erin the first five days of Christmas before she asks him to stop. How was he supposed to know the first five days are basically thirty birds? *(Secret Santa)*

- Stanley receives scented candles. *(Secret Santa)*

- Angela receives fabric. *(Secret Santa)*

- Kelly receives a *Twilight: New Moon* poster. *(Secret Santa)*

- Toby receives a kite and a *Kite Runner* book. *(Secret Santa)*

- Jim receives a vasectomy pamphlet from Meredith. *(Christmas Wishes)*

- The pregnant Angela gets a shirt that says "Ask then touch" from Kelly and Ryan. *(Christmas Wishes)*

- Kevin receives a sexy cookie jar from Oscar. *(Christmas Wishes)*

- Phyllis receives a set of rubber gaskets for canning jars on Pennsylvania Dutch Christmas. *(Dwight Christmas)*

- Pam receives a mousetrap from Belsnickel. *(Dwight Christmas)*

- Angela receives canning jars from Belsnickel. *(Dwight Christmas)*

the office book of lists

RECEPTION

- Stanley receives a slingshot. *(Dwight Christmas)*

- Pam makes Jim a comic book, "The Adventures of Jimmy Halpert." *(Classy Christmas)*

- Kevin gives Oscar Uggs. *(Classy Christmas)*

- Ryan gets a knitted iPad case from Phyllis. *(Classy Christmas)*

- Angela gives Creed deodorant. *(Classy Christmas)*

- Jim gives Pam a diamond bracelet. *(Classy Christmas)*

- Erin gives Andy a book on how to stop biting his nails. *(Classy Christmas)*

Stanley says he's suffered through a number of themed Christmas parties over the years working at Dunder Mifflin, including:

1) Honolulu Christmas
*(prior to the documentary filming)*

2) Pulp Fiction Christmas
*(prior to the documentary filming)*

3) Muslim Christmas
*(prior to the documentary filming)*

4) A Benihana Christmas (more of a lunch than a Christmas)
*(Season 3)*

5) Moroccan Christmas *(Season 5)*

6) Mo Rocca Christmas
*(prior to the documentary filming)*

7) Classy Christmas *(Season 7)*

8) Pennsylvania Dutch Christmas *(Season 9)*

## ST. PATRICK'S DAY

St. Patrick's Day is one of the biggest holidays in Scranton. The staff take celebrating St. Patrick's Day *very* seriously, which often includes wearing green, and some, like Andy, wear a kilt.

**Green ties:** Michael, Oscar, Ryan, Dwight, Jim *(St. Patrick's Day)*

**Green sweaters:** Erin, Phyllis *(St. Patrick's Day)*

**Green hat, suit, and shoes:** Kevin *(St. Patrick's Day)*

**Kilt:** Andy *(St. Patrick's Day)*

**St. Patrick's Day baby outfit:** Cece *(St. Patrick's Day)*

**Green coat and tie:** Todd Packer *(St. Patrick's Day)*

The EXIT sign is green instead of red. *(St. Patrick's Day)*

The watercooler has green water in it. *(St. Patrick's Day)*

# VALENTINE'S DAY

Valentine's Day is a time of love—and in the Scranton office, you never know how that is going to be expressed.

- Jim once gave Pam a card with Dwight's head on it. *(Valentine's Day)*

- Phyllis gets three bouquets of flowers and a huge stuffed bear from Bob Vance. *(Valentine's Day)*

- Jim planned a card game at home with friends for Valentine's Day before he was with Pam. *(Valentine's Day)*

- Angela gives Dwight a Dwight bobblehead. *(Valentine's Day)*

- Dwight thinks giving a ham is a good gesture on Valentine's Day. *(Valentine's Day)*

- Before he comes out to the staff, Oscar receives flowers he claims are from his mom. *(Valentine's Day)*

- Dwight gives Angela a key, apparently to his house. *(Valentine's Day)*

- Roy promises he will give Pam the best sex of her life as a Valentine's Day present. *(Valentine's Day)*

- Erin asks Andy for help with the clues Gabe is giving her for her Valentine's Day present. *(PDA)*

- Dwight's perfect Valentine's Day would be at home, three cell phones in front of him, fielding the desperate calls from people who want to buy one of the fifty restaurant reservations he made over six months ago. *(PDA)*

- Ryan thinks anyone can be a Prince Charming one day a year. What impresses him is when a guy can do that no days a year. *(PDA)*

- Kelly wants flowers, diamonds, a three-course meal, and a violinist who comes to the table to serenade her. *(PDA)*

- Kevin wants pizza, a soda, the moon, and someone to share it with. *(PDA)*

## OTHER HOLIDAYS

While the staff members go all out to celebrate the big holidays, they also take time to celebrate other holidays and cultures as a group.

- Michael says Diwali is essentially a Hindu Halloween. *(Diwali)*

- While Kelly is unfamiliar with the origins of Diwali, Dwight explains it's the celebration of the coronation of the god-king Rama, after his epic battle with Ravana, the demon king of Lanka. *(Diwali)*

- Michael shows slides of famous Indians to prepare the office team for Diwali, including Subrahmanyan Chandrasekhar, Apu from *The Simpsons*, M. Night Shyamalan, and Sir Ben Kingsley, whom he confuses with Gandhi. *(Diwali)*

- Stanley tells Michael he doesn't celebrate Kwanzaa. *(Diwali)*

- Michael likes to celebrate Groundhog's Day privately. *(Moroccan Christmas)*

- Michael takes Erin out to lunch for Secretary's Day but has to be prodded to do it. *(Secretary's Day)*

- Andy tries to get everyone a half day off for Columbus Day, even though they already had it. *(The List)*

- On Earth Day each year, Dwight dresses up as Recyclops to teach everyone about conservation. Recyclops starts out as a peaceful character with recycling tips, but eventually he becomes angry and wants to destroy the Earth. *(Shareholder Meeting)*

# Chapter Six:
# Locations

## SCHRUTE FARMS

Schrute Farms is an agritourism destination in Pennsylvania, owned by Dwight Schrute. Easy to find in the middle of the Root District, the sixty-acre working farm was passed down from Dwight's grandfather, and Dwight and Mose lived in the nine-bedroom, one-bathroom farmhouse.

- The closest size to a traditional-sized mattress the farm offers is a twin. *(Money)*

- There are three themed rooms at Schrute Farms: American, Irrigation, and Nighttime. *(Money)*

Activities on the farm include:

- Making wine from beets

- Spreading manure in the fields

- Dwight reading *Harry Potter* as a bedtime story

- Taking a dawn goose walk that "will tug at your heartstrings"

*(Money)*

- One of the farm's biggest attractions is its two-hundred-year-old mattresses, so Dwight is terrified of bringing bedbugs back from Florida. *(After Hours)*

- The farm is completely wireless once Mose hides all the wires on the morning Jim and Pam arrive. *(Money)*

- The farm has a number of birthday packages. The Pewter Package has the fewest goats; the Goat Package has the most goats. While Dwight claims he can get exotic meats, like hippo steaks and giraffe burgers, the meat will actually be goat. *(Garden Party)*

- In New York, Ryan asks about the farm and Dwight explains it is weevil season, when weevils lay their eggs in the unripe beet root, and then in spring the babies eat their way out. *(Night Out)*

the office book of lists

- Dwight offers Andy and Angela the Excalibur Wedding Package at the farm, in which he would work tirelessly over the coming months and be at Angela's constant disposal. *(Customer Survey)*

- Since there is only one bathroom on the farm, Dwight offers to dig a trench for Andy and Angela's wedding. *(The Surplus)*

- As the receiving line for Andy and Angela's wedding will be in the barn, Angela insists the manure be removed. However, the manure is covering up the smell of the slaughterhouse. *(The Surplus)*

- Dwight offers Angela a choice of a cow, goat, or sheep butter sculpture for her wedding. She wants a cat. *(The Surplus)*

- Dwight's directions to the farm for Andy are "156 paces from the light red mailbox, make a left. Walk until you hear the beehive." *(The Surplus)*

- Mose apparently has trouble staying out of the well, so Dwight has to rope it off. *(Heavy Competition)*

- When rumors of Dunder Mifflin's bankruptcy are in the *Wall Street Journal*, Dwight offers everyone jobs at the farm as human scarecrows, but the work won't pay much and they can't unionize. *(Murder)*

- Dwight creates a delicious beet vodka. *(The Manager and the Salesman)*

- To break into the high-end event-hosting industry, Dwight reads the only copy in the world of *The Ultimate Guide to Throwing a Garden Party* by "James Trickington." Coincidentally, Jim Halpert is disappointed that his book sells so poorly—only one copy. *(Garden Party)*

- The newest addition to Dwight's house was built by Erasmus Schrute in 1808 and doubled as a tuberculosis recovery room until 2009. *(Doomsday)*

- Dwight discovers there was a Battle of Schrute Farms during the Civil War. But it was not what he thought. The farm was a refuge for poets, artists, dancers, dandies, and dreamers—and an underground railroad for the "fabulous." *(Gettysburg)*

- Dwight invents a new power drink made from beet runoff. *(New Guys)*

- Dwight has an idea for beet salt de-icing. *(Vandalism)*

## RESTAURANTS AND BARS

While Scranton is not necessarily known for haute cuisine, the staff definitely has some favorite places to eat, drink, and socialize. Just make sure you get pizza from the correct Alfredo.

- Farley's *(Basketball)*

- Poor Richard's *(The Dundies / Christmas Party)*

- Chili's—"It's the new golf course, according to *Small Businessman* magazine." *(The Client / The Dundies)*

- A menu for City Slice is taped to a kitchen cabinet. *(The Client)*

- The Antler Lodge serves deer, a reputed aphrodisiac. *(Performance Review)*

- Members of Michael's improv class go to Bernie's Tavern but ask him not to come. *(Email Surveillance)*

- Michael claims to be sick of Chuck E. Cheese. *(The Injury)*

- Michael makes Jim go to Hooters for lunch. *(The Secret)*

- Jim is the ninth-place Salesmen of the Year and wins a pizza from Cugino's. *(Dwight's Speech)*

- Stanley's daughter tells Ryan about a cool coffee place called Jitters at the Steamtown Mall. *(Take Your Daughter to Work Day)*

- Ryan picks up pizza from Brunetti's. *(Take Your Daughter to Work Day)*

- When the Scranton employees plan a group lunch since they may not see one another again, Dee Jay's, Cugino's, Cooper's, and Hooters are all suggested. *(Branch Closing)*

- After Carol breaks up with Michael, Andy takes him to Benihana. Michael calls it Asian Hooters. *(A Benihana Christmas)*

- Jim takes Karen to Anna Maria's for their six-month anniversary. *(Women's Appreciation)*

- Toby wins a week of free pizzas from Alfredo's. *(Fun Run)*

the office book of lists

- For the launch party, Michael orders pizza from Alfredo's and thinks Alfredo's Pizza Café and Pizza by Alfredo are the same thing. Kevin claims Pizza by Alfredo is like eating a hot circle of garbage. It ends up costing $63.50, not including tip. *(Launch Party)*

- Kevin gives Michael the name of a potential date—"Wendy, hot and juicy redhead"—and the phone number for the local Wendy's restaurant. *(Chair Model)*

- Kevin and Holly go to the Glider Diner after Toby's goodbye party. *(Goodbye, Toby)*

- Darryl has menus for Terry's Diner and Miss Ellie's Cakes in his office. *(Did I Stutter?)*

- To discuss Meredith, Michael takes Holly to Cooper's Seafood House. *(Business Ethics)*

- In Winnipeg, the concierge suggests Matuski is a nice sushi place. *(Business Trip)*

- Meredith wonders what bar Michael is taking her to when they drive past Poor Richard's—the Bog, Cooper's, Kelly's, Brixx's, Carmen's, the Fort, or Andy Gavin's. He actually drives her to Sunrise Rehab. *(Moroccan Christmas)*

- Dwight and Michael argue about eating at Denny's or IHOP after meeting with Prince Paper. *(Prince Family Paper)*

- The summer interns go on a group date to Tink's. *(Gossip)*

- Michael has Erin go to Stop and Shop to get him coffee. *(Mafia)*

- Michael and Helene have reservations at Botticelli's. *(The Lover)*

- TCBY has a booth at the Garlic Festival. *(Koi Pond)*

- Jim and Pam double-date with Michael and Helene at Paparazzo's Italian Cuisine. *(Double Date)*

- Dwight has a client meeting at Shanny O'Gannigan's on St. Patrick's Day. *(St. Patrick's Day)*

- For happy hour, the staff goes to Sid and Dexter's, where Michael meets Donna. *(Happy Hour)*

- Michael doesn't like Hayworth's, as it's business casual and they always screw up your order. *(Secretary's Day)*

- The Great Wall is a Chinese food place Kelly likes. *(The Cover-Up)*

- Ryan would take Kelly to the Starlight Diner so his other girlfriend wouldn't see them. *(The Cover-Up)*

- When wandering around the sketchy part of Scranton, Michael goes to Mr. Choo's Chinese food, where "one egg roll could feed all of China." *(The Search)*

- Michael's last Dundie Awards is held at Louie Volpe's. *(Michael's Last Dundies)*

- The Banshee Pub is on the Scranton Haunted Walking Tour. *(Spooked)*

- The Liberty Well is the gay bar the staff travels to in Philadelphia to participate in a trivia contest. *(Trivia)*

- While on jury duty, Toby's jury reenacted the various stranglings using empanadas from Ernesto's, a food truck. *(Jury Duty)*

- Pam makes reservations at State Street Grill for lunch on Valentine's Day for her, Jim, Brian, and Alyssa. *(Couples Discount)*

## SCRANTON LANDMARKS

Founded in 1866, Scranton quickly became one of Pennsylvania's largest anthracite-mining communities. The office staff mention a number of real and fictional locations they frequent in the "Electric City."

- Dwight, who has access to computerized medical records, wonders if there are so many yeast infections in the county because it is downriver from the old bread factory. *(Email Surveillance)*

- The elevator in the Lackawanna Coal Mine goes down three hundred feet, but very slowly. *(Health Care)*

- Michael's mom lives in Dixon City. *(Take Your Daughter to Work Day)*

- Dwight wonders if Jan is staying at the Radisson, Super 8, Motel 6, Best Western, Holiday Inn, the Hyatt in Wilkes-Barre, or Michael's when she comes to Casino Night. *(Casino Night)*

- Michael films part of his *Lazy Scranton* video in front of the Anthracite Museum. *(The Merger)*

- Michael takes the women of the office to the Mall at Steamtown, which everyone refers to as the Steamtown Mall. *(Women's Appreciation)*

- To make others believe they aren't dating, Jim tells Pam he's going mountain biking on Montage Mountain over the weekend. Pam tells Jim she's going to the flea market at the drive-in. *(Fun Run)*

- Valley View High School holds a job fair that Michael goes to in order to find new interns. *(Job Fair)*

- Kevin goes to Gerrity's supermarket to get barbecue sauce and runs into a pregnant Jan. *(Goodbye, Toby)*

- While Michael thinks the Scranton Radisson gives off a "snooty vibe," Charles stays there for a month. *(The Client / Broke)*

- Jan uses the sperm bank next to the IHOP to get pregnant. *(Goodbye, Toby)*

- When Dwight and Michael discuss how to get to the hospital from Quincy Avenue to Gibson, Dwight says Gibson is covered in potholes. *(Baby Shower)*

- Jim bought his parent's house on Linden Avenue near the quarry. Creed says he lives by the quarry and suggests they hang out and throw things down there. *(Frame Toby)*

- There's a flea market near Dunmore High School. *(Prince Family Paper)*

the office book of lists

- The Michael Scott Paper Company is initially located at 126 Kellum Court, Scranton PA, 18510—Michael's condo. *(Dream Team)*

- The second location of the Michael Scott Paper Company is in the Scranton Business Park on the same floor as Dunder Mifflin. *(The Michael Scott Paper Company)*

- Jim and Pam interview at the Sandbox daycare for their future child. *(Sabre)*

- Dwight works out at the Flexopolis Gym to spy on Donna. *(The Cover-Up)*

- Donna wants to go to Vero Beach with Michael. *(The Cover-Up)*

- Michael is interviewed by WBRE-TV News. *(Whistleblower)*

- Jo's plane is at Castles and Cooke aviation airfield. *(Whistleblower)*

- After being refused service at Precious Heirlooms at the Steamtown Mall, Dwight wants everyone to boycott the entire mall for being "appearancist." *(Counseling)*

- The Loose Screw Playhouse hosts *Sweeney Todd: The Demon Barber of Fleet Street.* *(Andy's Play)*

- Dwight claims to have taken someone to the Penis Museum. *(The Sting)*

- Danny owns the bar, Public School, at Exit 11. *(Costume Contest)*

- Dwight wants to go to the Temptation strip club to fulfill his resolution of meeting loose women. Andy suggests they go across the street to Skateland roller rink. *(Ultimatum)*

- When Helene calls Jim to say that Cece is locked in the car, he leaves Michael in the bathroom at the gas station on Bennett. *(The Search)*

- Holly intuitively guesses Michael has gone to the top of a building to find his way back to Dunder Mifflin. *(The Search)*

## DID YOU KNOW?

Michael and Deangelo go to each staff member's house at 6 a.m. to present Dundie nominations. Stanley yells at them and Michael eggs Toby's house. Meredith, whose door is open while she does a walk of shame home, invites them in, but they run. *(Michael's Last Dundies)*

- Deangelo and Andy stop at Griffin Pond Animal Shelter before a sales call to adopt a dog. *(Goodbye, Michael)*

- Dwight considers a job at the Scranton Breadworks. *(Search Committee)*

- The senator asks Angela to have lunch with him at the Botanical Gardens, Scranton's hidden gem, where he proposes to her. *(Search Committee)*

- Pam thinks there's a gay bathhouse in the windowless building next to the Baskin-Robbins. *(Search Committee)*

- Andy gets a 'Nard dog tattooed on his butt at Madison Tattoo. *(The Incentive)*

- Robert mentions two clubs that may be erotic asphyxiation sex clubs off I-84—the Red Room and Dominick's. *(Fundraiser)*

- The senator hosts a fundraiser for the Scranton Animal Welfare Society. *(Fundraiser)*

- Angela gets her pedicure at Nail Luxury. *(Couples Discount)*

- Toby visits the Pennsylvania State Correctional Facility at Hunlock Creek and meets with the Scranton Strangler. *(Moving On)*

- Dwight says there's a shady grove out by Willard's Pond where the sun doesn't shine. *(Promos)*

- The address of Kevin's bar—the last place Dwight will visit—is 3030 Adams. *(Finale)*

- The reunion panel for the documentary is held at the Scranton Cultural Center. *(Finale)*

## BUSINESS TRIPS

For Michael and the staff of Dunder Mifflin Scranton, the term "business trip" can mean almost anything.

- Michael takes the office on a harbor cruise on Lake Wallenpaupack for the first-quarter camaraderie event. *(Booze Cruise)*

- The year prior to the harbor cruise, Michael took the staff to a bowling alley for a Bowl Over the Competition retreat. *(The Injury)*

- Michael and Dwight go to the Northeastern Sales Association Convention, where Dwight—as Dunder Mifflin Salesman of the Year—has to give a speech. *(Dwight's Speech)*

- Michael, Dwight, Jim, Josh, and Jan all attend the Northeastern Mid-Market Office Supply Convention in Philadelphia. *(The Convention— deleted scene)*

- The office goes to Lake Scranton, America's eighth-largest indigenous body of water, for Beach Day. *(Beach Games)*

- Jim and Karen go into New York City the night before their job interviews with Corporate and eat at the Spotted Pig, sneak into the second act of *Spamalot*, and go to a bar that used to be a church. *(The Job)*

- Michael has a trip to Cancún planned and wants to learn Spanish. He uses Post-it notes with genitalia drawn on them to remember if objects are masculine or feminine. *(Body Language)*

- Michael, Oscar, and Andy fly to Winnipeg, Canada, in mid-November to do a presentation. *(Business Trip)*

the office book of lists

- Michael, Andy, and Oscar fly Butte Airlines to Canada. *(Business Trip)*

- Michael and Pam go on a lecture circuit to all the branches (except Nashua) to tell them his secret recipe for success. *(Lecture Circuit)*

- Michael plans a ski trip for a WUPHF investors' trip. *(WUPHF.com)*

- Michael isn't sure where Holly's parents live. He thinks it might be "Mountainton." *(Goodbye, Michael)*

- Pam goes to Carbondale on Michael's last day to price shredders. She almost doesn't make it back in time to say goodbye. *(Goodbye, Michael)*

- Dwight, Jim, Stanley, Cathy, Ryan, and Erin all go to Tallahassee, Florida, to pilot the opening of the Sabre retail store. *(Tallahassee)*

- Andy takes half the office to visit Gettysburg for inspiration. *(Gettysburg)*

- Andy overshoots Tallahassee by two hundred miles and ends up at the ocean when he drives to Florida to get Erin. *(Get the Girl)*

- The staff heads to the lake on Dunder Mifflin Road Trip 2012 in the work bus. It goes as far as Laverne's Pies / Tires Fixed. *(Work Bus)*

- Clark goes to Italy as Jan's assistant and it sounds like more work than pleasure. *(Suit Warehouse)*

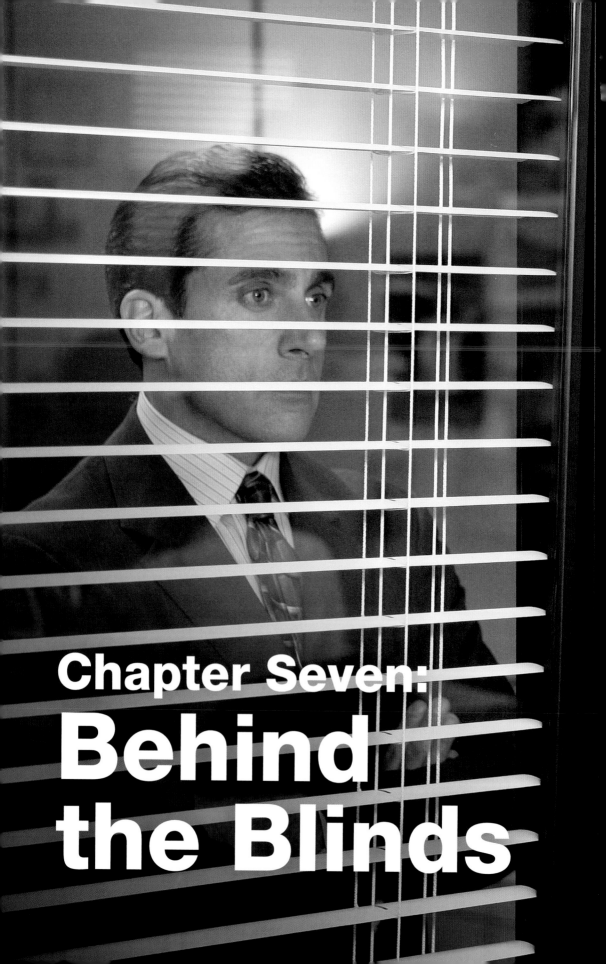

# Chapter Seven:
# Behind
# the Blinds

# DOCUMENTARY FILMING

*The Office: An American Workplace* is a PBS documentary that is filmed over the ten-year period from Michael Scott's fourth year as regional manager to a little before Dwight becomes manager of the Scranton branch. The crew is not supposed to get involved with the day-to-day activities, but occasionally the office staff and the crew can't help but interact.

- Michael asks if he needs to speak up and grabs the boom mic. *(Pilot)*

- Dwight argues with the camera crew when the boom mic is placed too close to him. It's in his blind spot, and since he is trained in several martial arts, he responds negatively to things right above his head. *(Pilot)*

- Michael tells the crew to get a shot of Meredith. *(The Alliance)*

- Michael tells Jim to show off his Dundies to the camera. Jim claims he hid them, as he doesn't want to get cocky. *(The Dundies)*

- Michael tells the crew to leave his office when he has to have a tough conversation with Jan about who is paying for the Dundies. *(The Dundies)*

- Pam is about to ask Jim something serious, then she looks at the camera and just says "thanks." *(The Dundies)*

- Jim pretends the blow-up doll is his "European" girlfriend and that she should have put on clothes, as he told her she was going to be on camera. *(Sexual Harassment)*

- The camera crew tells Pam that Michael said he might want to take a bath with her. *(Sexual Harassment)*

- Michael mouths "wow" to the camera when he finds out Jan got a divorce. *(The Client)*

- On a call with Jan after they spend the night together, Michael claims it was not caught on camera. *(The Client)*

- Jan asks Michael if the cameras are on him, as he tries to talk about their night together on the phone. *(Performance Review)*

- Jan won't discuss what happened between her and Michael on camera. Then she asks the crew, "Do you have a light?" *(Performance Review)*

- Pam, wondering about what "sensitive" emails Angela might erase on her computer, asks the camera crew if they saw anything. They later show her that Dwight was eating the second Baby Ruth that Angela got from the vending machine. *(Email Surveillance)*

- The camera crew points out to Michael that he missed seeing Conan O'Brien in New York. *(Valentine's Day)*

- The camera crew catches Dwight cussing. *(The Merger—deleted scene)*

the office book of lists

- Karen says she thinks it's going well with Jim, then asks the crew what Jim said about it. *(The Convict)*

- Jim asks the cameramen if "bold" is the right word to use to describe Michael. *(A Benihana Christmas)*

- Jim apologizes for interrupting Pam's interview when he returns from his Corporate interview, then asks her out on a date. *(The Job)*

- Pam says that when she falls in love, the last people she will talk about it with are a camera crew. Or her coworkers. *(Fun Run)*

- Angela thanks the crew for asking how Sprinkles is doing. No one else has asked about Sprinkles. *(Fun Run)*

- The crew shows Jim and Pam footage of them kissing in Pam's car and Jim jokingly asks them to edit it out. *(Fun Run)*

- Pam asks the crew if Jim plans to propose the night of Toby's goodbye party. *(Goodbye, Toby)*

- When Jim visits Pam at art school, he tells the crew to look at Pam's new art so they can have privacy and he shuts her door. There is nothing on the wall. *(Weight Loss)*

- Phyllis points out to Dwight that he knows the camera crew knows he has been sleeping with—and is still in love with—Angela. *(Crime Aid)*

- Pam points out the unclean microwave to the camera crew. *(Frame Toby)*

- Creed asks the crew to pretend like they are having a conversation while the police come into the office. *(Frame Toby)*

- When Pam offers to read the letter that Michael copied from Holly's computer, Pam looks at the crew and says, "What? I'm not in love with her." *(Lecture Circuit)*

- When Kelly races to find Charles Miner, she pushes the cameraman out of the way. *(New Boss)*

- Jim asks the crew if Pam is still upset about the plan for performance-based pay raises. *(The Promotion)*

- Ryan gives the crew a couple of catchphrases and tells them to use whichever one works. *(Counseling)*

- Angela gets offended at the crew's tone when she switches to the sexy nurse outfit for the costume contest. *(Costume Contest)*

- After Jim leaves him at the gas station, Michael goes for a walk and tells the crew not to follow him. *(The Search)*

- Jim asks if the crew is filming people in the bathroom now. *(Goodbye, Michael)*

- Michael asks the crew to let him know if the documentary ever airs. *(Goodbye, Michael)*

- Ryan says Michael has a way with words and then says the crew could play clips of him messing up words. Or whatever. He's not trying to tell them how to do their jobs. *(Goodbye, Michael)*

- The camera crew tells Jim and Pam that the crew is more following them than the paper company to see how they turn out. *(New Guys)*

- Darryl tries to knock out more sound bites to be efficient. It comes in handy minutes later. *(Andy's Ancestry)*

- When Pam breaks down, she addresses Brian, the sound guy, and he tells the crew to turn the camera off. *(Customer Loyalty)*

- Brian gets in trouble for talking to and for being sympathetic to Pam when she's crying. *(Junior Salesman)*

- Brian taps Pam's head with the boom mic to remind her she isn't alone. *(Vandalism)*

- When Frank looks like he's going to attack Pam, Brian clocks him with the boom mic. He then gets fired. *(Vandalism)*

- While Oscar is stuck upside down with his ab boots, an ad plays on his computer for *The Office: An American Workplace* on WVIA. *(Moving On)*

- Kevin doesn't realize the employees are being filmed for a documentary. He thinks they are specimens in a human zoo. *(Promos)*

- Pam asks Brian how much of the stuff the crew filmed and heard. He lets her know they have parabolic mics and can hear from one hundred yards away. She also asks if he thinks her and Jim's relationship has changed over the ten years. *(Promos)*

The ScrantonTimesTribune.com reviews the documentary prior to its release:

- Kevin is the Falstaffian accountant.

- Dwight Schrute is the head salesman, forever chasing a manager position he will never get.

- Andy Bernard is the rudderless trust fund child / middle manager, whose incompetence is emblematic of a declining American economy.

- The senator is in a lurid subplot that reveals his hypocrisy of having a gay affair while preaching family values.

*(Stairmageddon)*

- When Pam thinks she forced Jim into staying in Scranton, Jim asks the camera crew to make him a DVD of all their moments. *(A.A.R.M.)*

- Jim chokes up telling the doc crew they gave him a way to look back at his life. *(Finale)*

## ONE YEAR LATER

After the documentary, *The Office: An American Workplace*, airs, a lot of things change. One year later, the camera crew reassembles to get footage for a DVD extra. The filming coincides with both the cast reunion panel at the community center and Dwight and Angela's wedding.

- The staff does tai chi in the parking lot each morning.

- Kevin got fired (via cake) and was replaced by Dakota. He now runs a bar.

- Toby was also fired by cake.

- Oscar is running for state senate.

- Stanley retired to Florida and carves birds.

- Jim started biking to work.

- Dwight rehired Devon.

- Creed faked his own death again and sold drugs, according to his wanted poster.

- Nellie lives in Poland, which she calls "the Scranton of the European Union."

- Toby moved to New York to write the great American novel and he has six roommates.

- Andy works in the admissions office at Cornell.

- Dakota is the new accountant. She meets Creed, who says his name is Jeff Bomondo and he sells tile out of Newark.

- Most people brought cats as presents to Dwight and Angela's wedding.

- Kelly and Ravi show up at Dwight and Angela's wedding, but Kelly ends up running off with Ryan, who leaves his baby behind. Ryan's baby is eventually adopted by Nellie.

- Creed is still living in the office and plays guitar for everyone before the cops arrest him.

- Pam sold their house so she and Jim could move to Austin.

*(Finale)*

# CELEBRITY CAMEOS

As the popularity of *The Office* soared, celebrity fans often guest-starred. Some appeared as themselves, some were brief characters, and some, like James Spader and Kathy Bates, stayed on for a season or more.

**Amy Adams:** Played Katy the purse salesperson, who dated Jim briefly. *(Hot Girl)*

**Ken Jeong:** A fellow student in Michael's improv class. *(Email Surveillance)*

**Rob Riggle:** Steve Carell's fellow *Daily Show* alum played Captain Jack. *(Booze Cruise)*

**Conan O'Brien:** Michael ignored Conan walking in front of him on Valentine's Day when he thought he saw Tina Fey. *(Valentine's Day)*

**Jerome Bettis:** The NFL running back played himself signing autographs at the convention. *(The Convention)*

**Yvette Nicole Brown:** Played Dwight's coworker at Staples and she didn't like him, his giant head, or his beady little eyes. *(The Return)*

**Jeff Garlin:** Played a Corporate employee who knew Jim from Stamford and thought he went to school with Karen. *(The Job)*

**Jessica Alba**, **Jack Black**, and **Cloris Leachman:** "Starred" in the film Andy illegally downloaded, *Mrs. Albert Hannaday*. *(Stress Relief)*

**Idris Elba:** Played VP Charles Miner. *(New Boss)*

**Christian Slater:** Narrated the Sabre merger video. *(Sabre)*

**Kathy Bates:** Played Jo Bennett, the CEO of Sabre. *(Sabre)*

**Evan Peters:** Played Michael's nephew, Luke Cooper. *(Nepotism)*

**Timothy Olyphant:** Played rival salesman Danny Cordray. *(The Sting)*

**Ricky Gervais:** *The Office* series creator played his UK *Office* character, David Brent, then later appeared as a candidate for Michael's job. *(The Seminar / Search Committee)*

**Will Ferrell:** Played Deangelo Vickers. *(Training Day)*

**Will Arnett:** Cameoed as Fred Henry, an interviewee for the regional manager position. He said he had a three-part plan to double the company's profits but wouldn't reveal the plan. *(Search Committee)*

**Warren Buffett:** The billionaire cameoed as a candidate for Michael's job. He was extremely cost-conscious. *(Search Committee)*

**James Spader:** Played Robert California, who became regional manager, then CEO for a short time. *(Search Committee)*

the office book of lists

**Ray Romano:** Cameoed as Merv Bronte, a candidate for Michael's job. *(Search Committee)*

**Catherine Tate:** Played Nellie Bertram, a candidate for Michael's job. She doesn't get it, but later she's hired as the president of Sabre's special projects. *(Search Committee)*

**Jim Carrey:** Cameoed as a candidate for Michael's job who had to travel to the Finger Lakes often. *(Search Committee)*

**Josh Groban:** Played Andy's brother, Walter Jr. *(Garden Party / The Boat)*

**Wally Amos:** Of Famous Amos cookies. Cameoed as himself at Nellie's presentation. *(Tallahassee)*

**Tig Notaro:** Cameoed as the mom of the girl who punched Andy. *(Test the Store)*

**Georgia Engel:** Played Irene, who hired Erin as a live-in helper. *(Test the Store)*

**Dan Castellaneta:** The voice of Homer Simpson. Played Mr. Ramish, the CEO of Prestige Direct Mail Solutions. *(Turf War)*

**Randall Park:** Guest-starred as "Jim" during a prank on Dwight. *(Andy's Ancestry)*

**Stephen Colbert:** Cameoed as Broccoli Rob. *(Here Comes Treble)*

**Julius "Dr. J." Erving:** Cameoed as himself. *(Lice)*

**Bob Odenkirk:** Played Mark at Simon Realty, where Pam interviewed in Philly. He was a lot like Michael Scott. *(Moving On)*

**Roseanne Barr:** Played Andy's talent agent, Carla Fern. *(Stairmageddon)*

**Ryan Howard:** The Phillies player cameoed as himself and had a lot of ideas on marketing himself with Jim's company. *(Promos)*

**Mark McGrath:** Cameoed as himself and told the contestants on *America's Next A Capella Sensation* that there was a mole in line. *(A.A.R.M.)*

**Clay Aiken**, **Santigold**, and **Aaron Rodgers:** Cameoed as themselves as judges on *America's Next A Capella Sensation*. *(A.A.R.M.)*

**Bill Hader and Seth Meyers:** Parodied Andy as Baby Wawa on *SNL*'s Weekend Update. *(Finale)*

**Joan Cusack and Ed Begley Jr.:** Cameoed as Erin's birth parents. *(Finale)*

## WEBISODES

Over the years, the production staff made a number of webisodes featuring the supporting cast.

- The accountants try to solve the mystery of the missing $3,000. *(The Accountants)* (10 episodes)

- A frustrated Ryan tries to make a low-budget horror film like *Paranormal Activity*. *(The Third Floor)* (3 episodes)

- Kelly and Erin start a band—Subtle Sexuality—and film a music video. *(Subtle Sexuality)* (3 episodes)

- Kevin tries to get a loan to pay off his gambling debts. *(Kevin's Loan)* (4 episodes)

- Creed tries to blackmail his coworkers with their embarrassing secrets. *(Blackmail)* (4 episodes)

- Erin wants to try accounting and Angela mentors her. *(The Mentor)* (5 episodes)

- Oscar mystifies the office when he yells at someone over the phone. *(The Outburst)* (4 episodes)

- Gabe tries to record a podcast. *(The Podcast)* (3 episodes)